75-83
142-153

0000
7777
9229
2468
5936

9432

7179

4284
8415

1-7
9-29

6529
1530
5901
8514

Speech/
Communication

SECOND EDITION

Speech/ Communication

SECOND EDITION

Saundra Hybels

LOCK HAVEN STATE COLLEGE

Richard L. Weaver, II

BOWLING GREEN STATE UNIVERSITY

D. VAN NOSTRAND COMPANY

New York   Cincinnati   Toronto   London   Melbourne

D. Van Nostrand Company Regional Offices:
New York   Cincinnati

D. Van Nostrand Company International Offices:
London   Toronto   Melbourne

Copyright © 1979 by Litton Educational Publishing, Inc.

Library of Congress Catalog Card Number: 78-52699
ISBN: 0-442-23621-2

Published by D. Van Nostrand Company
135 West 50th Street, New York, N. Y. 10020

10 9 8 7 6 5 4 3 2 1

Preface

When authors set out to write a second edition, their main problem is to retain what has worked and has been useful in the first edition and to eliminate or rewrite those portions that are unclear or dated. Their second task is to integrate the new research and thinking in the field and to organize the book in such a way that it will have maximum use in the classroom.

The first edition, published in 1974, was written during a time of conflict and confrontation. The models for rhetoric came from militant groups, protesters, and campus demonstrators. At the same time, interpersonal communication was emerging as a subject for serious study, and many people working in this area were influenced by the new sensitivity and encounter groups.

The Second Edition draws examples from a quieter period in history and reflects a more back-to-basics approach. Although we believe that a basic knowledge of intrapersonal and interpersonal communication is important, we also recognize the need for more information about public speaking. We have included an additional chapter on this subject.

Our book is designed for the introductory course in speech communication. Realizing that many students take only a single course in speech, we have written and organized this book so as to give an overview of the field and to give students the information needed to develop basic skills in communication.

We have tried to organize the book in the way that most communication courses are taught. The chapters are integrated so that they move from a focus on the individual, through interpersonal communication, and concluding with sections on small-group and public-speaking situations.

We believe that the study of communication and the practice of communication skills should be enjoyable and rewarding activities for the beginning student. We hope that our book will serve this end.

ACKNOWLEDGEMENTS

We would like to thank Dorothy Vaughn, of Lock Haven State College, for her many helpful suggestions for the Verbal Communication chapter. We are also grateful to the following reviewers for their constructive suggestions: Professor Judy Goldberg, Anapahoe Community College; Professor Linda Moore, Kent State University; Professor George Cavanagh, Broward Community College. Finally, we would like to thank Bill Stephens, the *Key* staff photographers, and the Bowling Green Photo Service for the photographs that illustrate the text.

Contents

⑧ **Persuasive Communication**   205

Speech/
Communication

SECOND EDITION

Introduction

The Need for Dialogue

The more you study communication, the more you are amazed that people communicate at all. Imagine, for example, a middle-aged insurance salesman who has always lived in Alabama trying to communicate his ideas and values to a young woman student who comes from Chicago. Both speak the same language and are citizens of the same country, but they probably differ in most of the following areas: ideas, experiences, attitudes, beliefs, knowledge, interests, group memberships, goals, needs, values, and communication abilities. Their only hope for communication is their strong desire to communicate with each other and a willingness to try to understand each other's point of view.

These two people will have difficulty communicating for the same reason that most of us have difficulty much of the time. Each of us is an individual with a particular frame of reference, a way of looking at things that has been developing since we were born and will continue to develop and grow until we die. Everyone has a special point of view, his or her individual way of seeing the world. You can never entirely comprehend another person's frame of reference, and he or she can never totally understand yours. In this sense, we are all alone. But all of us need to communicate with other people, to share our lives and our thoughts with

1

them. Understanding how communication works and becoming more aware of your own communication needs and skills can help you to share more of yourself with others and to understand more about your own life and that of others. In fact, communication is the only way we can understand other people.

Communication, then, is of central importance. It is also a subject of increasing interest to Americans. There are numerous communication courses in colleges and universities, but the study of communication is by no means limited to the academic world. A tough Army sergeant is advised not to yell at the new recruits but to communicate with them. Magazines run countless articles full of advice about improving communication between husbands and wives, parents and children. Ministers, priests, and rabbis no longer spend all their theological training learning how to prepare sermons and to explain the ideas of their faith—they are also taught to communicate with the congregation and to help members of the congregation communicate among themselves. The number of people learning how to communicate is endless; hardly a day goes by that we do not receive some sort of information or advice about communication.

COMMUNICATION: THE CHANGING EMPHASIS

So many Americans are engrossed and perhaps even obsessed with communication that one might ask why we, as a nation, are so interested in this subject. The question is so complex that it is impossible to give a complete and comprehensive answer. However, we can suggest some of the possible reasons.

The first is that in recent times American society has gone through great changes in its social structure. Look back at your grandparents. Chances are that they were born, lived, and died in the same community. Not only did they remain in the same place; they probably had the same job, went to the same church, and kept the same friends all their lives. In the next generation—your parents'—there was probably greater mobility and change. Their circle broadened; they changed jobs and living places more than your grandparents. In your generation, there is likely to be even greater change. You will probably change your job, your dwelling place, and even many of your close friends several times during different periods of your life. You also have a good statistical chance of changing your mate.

This increased mobility greatly affects our communication. We have been called a nation of strangers because we are often in the position of communicating more with strangers than with people we have known all, or even part, of our lives. When we meet and interact with new people all the time it is often too exhausting and time-consuming a process to make the effort of establishing lasting friendships. Relationships must be formed quickly—before we or our new friends move on to a new place. We can, of course, involve ourselves only in superficial relationships in which we exchange the information required in day-to-day situations. Most people, however, become increasingly lonely if they do not develop deeper, more personal relationships.

These relationships are even more important in the anonymity of a technological, industrial society. Many of us are best known to our school, our employer, and the government by our social security number. The academic progress of many future students will be determined by how well they do on examinations graded by computers. Using the city and state on the address of a letter is becoming superfluous; the zip code is much more important. Although the assignment of numbers to individuals, cities, and states makes our society run more efficiently, it also creates a greater need for us to hold onto our individual identity. If our communication with humans increases and is satisfying, we feel less helpless about being numbered by machines. Previous generations may have been able to take communication for granted; those of us who are depersonalized by institutions and organizations look to communication to express our individuality and humanity.

The social upheaval of the sixties influenced much of our thinking about communication. Roles were questioned: women, blacks, students, and many other groups began to demand that they be allowed to participate in new and different ways in American society. When their demands increased, it became clear that much more emphasis had to be put on interpersonal (one-to-one) communication and that more study should be devoted to conflict and the role it plays in communication.

This period was also a time of increased interest in the psychological implications of communication. Many people emphasized the importance of recognizing feelings and the importance of mutual trust in communication. Communication began to be seen as a dialogue, emphasizing sharing, spontaneity, and the responsibility that people have to each other.

In many ways, the seventies has become a period of assessing what happened in the tumultuous sixties. With the disbanding of many protest groups, the study of conflict and communication is no longer considered a priority. The idea that everyone should be completely honest in all their communications has also begun to be questioned in the wake of hurt feelings and broken relationships among various groups and between men and women. Nevertheless, it is clear that the emphasis placed on interpersonal communication in the sixties is still important, since this kind of communication affects everyone.

In this book we have tried to cover the types of communication that affect our lives the most. We will cover all the areas described in the chapters that follow:

Self and Communication is concerned with the idea that the messages you send are intricately tied in with the images you have of yourself and of others, and that a message cannot exist apart from the self.

Interpersonal Communication discusses how we communicate with one person or a small number of people on an informal, nonstructured level.

Verbal and *Nonverbal Communication* deal with how we use language and nonverbal communication (a gesture, a frown, a touch).

Small Group Communication deals with how we work and communicate in small groups to solve problems, to run organizations, to make decisions, to heighten sensitivity, to facilitate social give-and-take, and so on.

Public Speaking is concerned with how we communicate as speakers to an audience in a formal and structured setting.

Persuasive Communication discusses how we can use persuasion and suggestion effectively and how we are in turn influenced by them.

Each of these types of communication is different, and each requires various skills. The basic process of communication is the same, however, in that there are certain components that are always present when communication is taking place.

COMMUNICATION AS A PROCESS

When we speak of communication as a process, we mean that it is ongoing, that is, not confined to the actual time when people exchange words and ideas. Before we engage in any communication, we make *predictions* about what will occur. If we are getting ready to confront an instructor about a late paper, we might predict that the communication will be hostile; if we are looking forward to a date, we predict that the communication will be enjoyable.

Once the communication event is over, we engage in *assessment*—an evaluation of the communication event. We might come away exhilarated because we have learned something new; we might be irritated because another person did not agree with our ideas. Our assessment of what did occur may be different from our expectations. Our instructor, for example, may have been friendly and forgiving, and our date boring and depressing.

Our predictions and assessments are important parts of the communication process; in fact, they are often more important than the communication itself. Too often we believe our communication was unsuccessful only because of what we said. But when communication is seen as a process, we then realize it is just as likely to break down because of inaccurate predictions and assessments. Focusing on the communication process, then, will give us a much broader and more useful perspective about how communication works.

COMMUNICATION AS A TRANSACTION

When we speak of communication as a transaction, we mean that our idea of ourselves and of those with whom we are communicating is just as important as what we are communicating. We don't just talk to people; our communication is based on how we see the people we are talking to and how we think they see us. A person talks differently to a teacher than to a parent, a boyfriend, a stranger, or a friend. Therefore, transactional communication puts a major emphasis on relationships and the roles we play within these relationships.

Transactional communication also involves continuous exchanges between participants. In a typical communication transaction between two persons (or a small group), all or both are likely to ask questions, make comments, smile, and so forth. The communication will also probably involve interruptions, laughter, and gestures—many of these elements occurring simultaneously on both sides.

Figure 1 (see page 6) illustrates a transactional communication model involving two persons.

The communication transaction becomes more complicated as the number of participants increase. If four participants are involved, there will be more roles, more complex relationships, and many more verbal and nonverbal messages.

PUBLIC SPEAKING

The transactional model works well when small groups of people are involved in the communication process. When we talk about public speaking, however, the perspective changes. As can be seen in Figure 2, the most important roles and relationships in public speaking are those of speaker and audience.

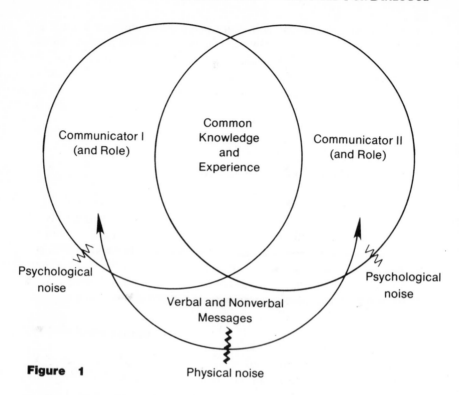

Figure 1

In a public-speaking situation, the audience is largely passive. Unlike interpersonal communication, the listeners are not likely to engage in verbal feedback and generally limit their responses to nonverbal signs such as applause or laughter. The speaker's feedback is also limited. Although he or she might try to restructure the message because of the interest or lack of interest shown by the audience, the speaker cannot make very drastic changes while he or she is delivering the speech.

In both the interpersonal and the public-speaking situation, messages might not get through because of distracting and unwanted stimuli. The most common distraction is called *noise,* and it can be either physical or psychological. Disturbing physical noise can occur when someone uses a power mower outside the classroom as you are trying to give a speech or when there is static on the radio and you can't hear your favorite station. Psychological noise occurs in the mind of the sender or receiver of communication and distracts him or her from the message. If you are hungry, angry, or upset, any of these factors might hamper your receiving a message or lead you to misunderstand what someone is saying.

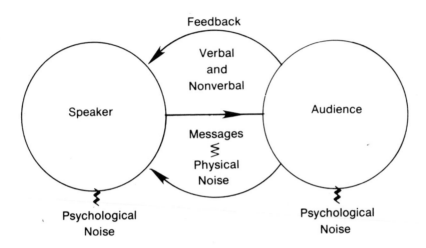

Feedback

Verbal and Nonverbal

Speaker

Audience

Messages

Physical Noise

Psychological Noise

Psychological Noise

Figure 2

All communication, whether it is one-to-one or public speaking, is influenced by the culture in which it occurs. The language we choose, the nonverbal signals we use, the roles we play, the responses we receive are all culturally determined. If we were moved to another culture, many of these communication elements would change.

This book is written on the assumption that all of us can improve our communication, both as those who send communication messages and as those who receive them. We hope to increase your understanding of the process of communication, why people communicate the way they do, and why some communications succeed and others fail. We will emphasize the development and improvement of your communication skills. We hope to help improve your communication so that it will be satisfying and rewarding to you and to those with whom you communicate.

chapter 1

Self and Communication

There is an exercise called "Who Are You?" that was developed by encounter and sensitivity groups. In the exercise the entire group is divided into pairs, and one person in a pair is instructed to ask his or her partner, "Who are you?" After the questioner listens to the response, he or she repeats the question again. The process may go on for ten or twenty minutes. Although the question is always the same, the response becomes more varied and complex as the exercise continues. The person responding typically begins with basic information such as name, profession, relationships to others (mother, wife, brother), or perhaps the groups he or she belongs to (church, lodge, school). As the exercise continues, however, the respondent runs out of vital statistics and often begins responding with emotional information: "I am unhappy. I am hostile. I am a loving mother." Sometimes the respondent gets exasperated with the repetition of the question and begins to respond angrily or aggressively to the questioner. At other times, respondents reveal more and more of themselves as the repeated question causes deeper and deeper probing.

9

WHO ARE YOU?

This exercise reveals how complex the self really is. Each of us is made up of a complicated web of experiences, knowledge, attitudes, and values, all of which help to define and explain who we are—both to ourselves and to others. *Self-identity* is the image we have of ourselves, or as R. D. Laing, a psychoanalyst and psychiatrist, puts it, "One's self-identity is the story one tells one's self of who one is."[1]

Some of us have considerable insight about ourselves. We know who we are, where we have been, and where we are going. Others may feel great doubt. Most of us combine certainty and uncertainty, depending on the circumstances. Our self-knowledge also changes over the years as we acquire understanding and experience. The way we see ourselves at twenty is probably different from the way we see ourselves at forty or at seventy.

A self-concept is never created in isolation; it depends on the response and reaction of other people. The impressions people have of us and the way they react to us are very much determined by the way we communicate with them. This feedback process can also work in the other direction; when we see how people react to us and the impression they have of us, we may attempt to change the way we communicate because other people's reaction to us is not compatible with the way we see ourselves. Thus, the image you have of yourself and the image that others have of you are all intertwined in communication.

YOU ARE WHO YOU ARE TOLD YOU ARE

Our earliest identity is not our own; it is conferred on us by someone else. Our parents, or the first person who takes care of us, tell us through their words and actions that we are good, bad, stupid, intelligent, lovable, or unlovable. They are also likely to teach us our first words, and so, in many ways, we are their creation. From this early experience, according to R. D. Laing, "We learn to be who we are told we are."[2]

As we continue to grow, we receive many messages from those who surround us about who we are and whom we are expected to become. These messages are so concrete and specific that some people have labeled them as *scripts*.[3]

Scripts are given to us by our parents, and they contain directions that are just as explicit as any script intended for the stage. We are given our lines ("Say thank you to the nice lady"), our gestures ("Don't touch yourself"), and our characterization ("You're a good boy"). The scripts tell us how to play future scenes ("Everyone in our family has gone to college"), and what is expected of us ("I will be so happy when you make us grandparents").

People outside our family also contribute to our scripts. Teachers, coaches, ministers, friends, and even media, all tell us what they expect from us and how we should play our roles. By the time we are adults we find it difficult to separate who we are from what others say we are, and our self-concept is intricately tied to how others define us.

Many of us, throughout our lives, find it rewarding and necessary to examine and reexamine our self-concept. Many of the scripts that we follow are, by their very nature, designed to keep us from reaching our full potential. Often, the greatest growth and development of a self-concept that is uniquely ours begins when we go against the script, or venture into unscripted areas. This venture, however, often involves considerable risk.

For many people, psychological *safety*—the approval and support that we get from people we love, admire, and respect—is an important need. Our safety needs prompt us to seek out and to get approval from people who love and respect us and to avoid people we see as hostile and threatening. For example, many people face great anxiety when they are going to give a speech. Although they feel safe talking to friends and colleagues, the thought of facing an audience is very threatening because there is no assurance of getting the kind of psychological support they need. A person's needs for safety may determine an entire life style. Do you go away to college or do you stay at home and go to a college in your own hometown? Do you make an attempt to meet new people with new ideas, or do you prefer to stay with old friends? The answer to these questions, and many others, may be determined by your safety needs.

Humans also have a need to grow. A child continues to try to walk even though she falls countless times. Her need to grow is far greater than her need to feel safe. If we were afraid of growth, we would never travel to new places or meet new people; in fact we would probably never leave our homes.

Abraham Maslow, the late psychologist who emphasized human self-fulfillment, put the human needs for safety and growth in the following diagram.[4] Maslow said that the more a person needs to feel safe, the less likely it is that the person will be able to grow. Conversely, the individual is able to grow to the degree that he or she does not have a

Figure 1-1

constant need for psychological safety. However, moving toward growth rather than toward safety can be very risky.

Margaret Mead, the anthropologist, describes such a risk in her autobiography, *Blackberry Winter*. She speaks about leaving the familiar safety of her home in the East to go to college at DePauw in rural Indiana:

> I arrived with books of poetry, portraits of great personalities to hang on the walls, and the snobberies of the East, such as the expectation that one dressed in the evening for members of one's own family. And I was confronted by the snobbery and cruelty of the sorority system at its worst. . . .
>
> When the invitations came out, I was invited to the Kappa rushing party. But when I arrived wearing my unusual and unfashionable dress that was designed to look like a wheat field with poppies blooming in it, my correspondent turned her back on me and never spoke to me again. I found the whole evening strangely confusing. I could not know, of course, that everyone had been given a signal that inviting me had been a mistake. Afterward, my roommates got the bids they expected, but I did not get a bid.[5]

Mead describes a situation that you may have experienced in fantasy, if not in reality. There are few things as uncomfortable as being in a room where you are not only ignored but are labeled as an unsuitable outsider. Thus, you may seek situations where you know this cannot happen—where you are assured of safety.

All our communication behavior is closely tied to our need for psychological safety. We play roles that are expected of us by our peers and family; we communicate in a way that will make people like us; we often avoid communicating our most important feelings because we are afraid of rejection. When we communicate only what people want to hear, or what we think they want to hear, we can get into serious trouble. Our communication and our identity are so intertwined that it is impossible to separate them. If we get into a pattern of never communicating our self, we no longer have a self that is uniquely ours; we are only a reflection of how others see us. In the pages that follow, we will discuss how and why we communicate for safety and for growth and consider the implication this kind of communication has for our lives.

ROLES

One of the most fascinating stories of childhood is "The Emperor's New Clothes." As you may remember, two unscrupulous tailors tell the emperor that they can make him a suit of clothes that can be seen only by those fit to hold office. The emperor agrees to have the clothes made. When they are "completed," they are admired by the emperor, his ministers, and all his subjects. The hoax is not revealed until one small child, who does not know any better, says, "But—the King has no clothes on at all."

The tailors were shrewd psychologists. They knew that no person would admit that he or she was incompetent. They could count on the emperor to play the role of the qualified ruler and knew that the others would play admiring subjects, even if it meant admiring something that was not there. The child was so young that he did not know about the role he was expected to play in the kingdom. The storyteller does not tell us what happened after the child uttered his fatal words, but we can assume that the social structure of the kingdom was badly shaken and that the role of the emperor and the relationship of his subjects to him were changed forever.

In its broadest sense, the term *role* refers to how you behave at a particular point in time. When the emperor in the story was holding court, he was playing the role of the emperor by behaving the way an emperor is supposed to behave—wearing a crown, giving orders, and so on. After the hoax was revealed, the emperor may have gone into his private chambers to talk to his wife about the crisis; in that situation he would play the role of a husband in trouble. These two roles represent an entirely different set of behaviors. In each case, the role that the emperor was playing was partly determined by what he had learned from his culture about how emperors and husbands in trouble, respectively, are supposed to behave.

Like the emperor, we all play many roles. But it is important to emphasize that roles are not necessarily false or phony. With friends and family the roles we play might be consistent with the way we see ourselves. In social settings, which are outside intimate relationships, our roles are often more structured and predictable. We might, for example, go to a dull party and tell our host that we had a marvelous time. When we get home, however, we are free to tell a good friend how dull the party really was. Although it is important to be involved with people with whom our role is consistent with our self-concept, it is equally important that we learn to play what society defines as an appropriate role in a particular social setting. Although these roles may not be consistent with our sense of self, they are important in protecting the feelings of individuals and the rituals and conventions of society.

We begin to learn our sociocultural roles as small children. We are taught that it is impolite to spit in public, that children must behave in certain ways when adults are present, and that it is selfish not to share toys with a brother, sister, or visitor. By the time we are young adults, we know how to dress and behave at parties, at funerals, at work, and at school. We tell our aunt that we like her new dress even when we privately feel that it that blacks first reject all the white definitions of black people and then

is not very flattering. We do *not* tell our boss that he would do a better job as a janitor or our teacher that the assignment was useless busywork. These social behaviors are determined by our culture's definitions of roles such as child, guest, student, and so on; they may vary greatly from one culture to another.

Many of our roles are conferred on us as permanent members of certain groups. We are all members of general groups such as women, men, blacks, and whites. As members of these groups, we are expected by our society and culture to play certain roles. Even though roles are changing, there are many men who try to live out the traditional role of being strong, achievement-oriented, and unsentimental. If a male does not play this role, those who have traditional role expectations may consider him to be inferior to other males.

The question raised by societal roles is what good and what damage can they do to the individuals and groups who play them? Roles, at their best, provide some psychological safety and a sense of identity. If you know the role you are playing, you can conform to the rules of society and be accepted. In a traditional role, for example, a teacher can go into a classroom and feel confident that, by virtue of his position, he will be paid a certain amount of attention and respect (or that students will play the role of giving attention and respect). He can ask for a term paper, give an examination, and fail those who do not play the role of the conscientious student. Although his traditional role may not stimulate motivation and intellectual excitement, it is safe.

Violating role expectations can be a threatening experience. Let's assume that the same teacher decides to abolish his traditional role. He enters the classroom and says, "Call me Bob. There will be no papers, and you will all grade yourselves." Now the students are in uncharted territory; they don't know what is expected of them or how to respond to this teacher who has changed both his role and the role of his students. Unless the teacher imposes another structure, clearly understood by the students, the abandonment of the traditional teacher role may prove to be very threatening to the teacher, the students, and even the school.

Role expectations can be damaging both to individuals and to society. Every role that you play defines you. If that definition is congruent with some essential part of you, then the role is comfortable and you can play it well. For example, there are some women who are happy with the role of homemaker. They enjoy taking care of their home and children and have no desire to pursue a career or to find fulfillment outside the home. Other women, however, are angry when they are expected to play this role; they insist on more flexible roles for women. In the black movement, Stokely Carmichael's most revolutionary and far-reaching demand was to insist define themselves. The new black definitions would, in turn, determine the role that blacks were to play in society.

If our societal role is incompatible with the way we define ourselves, we have only a few options: we can redefine ourselves to fit in with society's definition; we can refuse to play the societal role and thus become the exception to it; or we can try to change the overall societal concept of the role. Unfortunately, for those of us who want change, none of these options is easy.

Playing Someone Else

What happens if the role or roles you play are not congruent with your self-image? Sidney Jourard writes:

> But what we forget is the fact that it is a *person* who is playing a role. The person has a self, or should I say he *is* a self. All too often the roles that a person plays do not do justice to all of his self. In fact, there may be nowhere that he may just be himself. Even more, the person may not *know* his self. He may be alienated. His real self becomes a feared and distrusted stranger.[6]

Carl Rogers, a psychologist with a special interest in communication, also writes of the role player:

> He discovers how much of his life is guided by what he *thinks* he should be, not by what he is. Often he discovers that he exists only in response to the demands of others, that he has no self of his own, that he is only trying to think, feel and behave in the way that others believe he *ought* to think, feel and behave.[7]

Ultimately, then, the question is to what extent our roles fit our own self-image. This question can be answered only in very individual terms, for we all play roles according to our own needs. However, when roles become damaging to our sense of identity, they must be dropped or modified if we are to continue to grow. When the feminist movement gained momentum, for example, many women started to look at their homemaker/mother roles and found them unsatisfying. Some dropped the role completely by getting a divorce and giving their husbands custody of the children. Others changed their role: they split up the housework with their husbands, put their children in child-care centers, and began to pursue their own professional interests. These role changes were not easy and were accomplished over long periods of time.

Most of us are not able to completely drop or change the roles we do not like. Our deepest and most vital roles are ingrained in us from our earliest childhood. Even though we might want to change them, we cling to them with great tenacity. If we are able to change, it is a slow ongoing process.

When we are given the chance to change our roles, we often do not find the new role any more satisfying. People who break away from unhappy marriages, for example, often find that instead of playing the role of a happy, carefree single, they are lonely and still unhappy. Although a new school or a new job may at first lead to a sense of optimism or renewed expectations, the same old problems and disappointments often occur in the new situation.

Unless we are willing to make drastic changes in our lives, we usually must find a way to live with the roles that have been conferred on us by society. Although we may choose or accept the role of dutiful child, responsible employee, or tactful neighbor, we still have some role choices left to us. Because we are forced to play a number of roles, it is important to find people with whom we can play a role that is close to our own self-concept. We can seek out situations and circumstances where we can be ourselves. These situations are most likely to occur in close personal relationships. Some of us will best be able to be ourselves among family; others will find mates or friends to be the most receptive to who we are.

It doesn't matter whom we find; the important thing is that we find people who will accept us in the way we see ourselves—people with whom we share the same language of feelings and beliefs. With these people we have the best chance of developing a real sense of self.

TRUST, DISCLOSURE, AND NONDISCLOSURE

We can be ourselves with people we trust. In some relationships, trust automatically exists. Few families would betray the trust of a family member, and few spouses or lovers would betray the trust of a mate. In the area of friendship, however, the issue of trust becomes more complex. Friends have no legal or blood ties to each other. They enter our lives at all stages and in many cases have little idea of our past, our motives, or the rituals we consider important. Yet friends fulfill an important function and often provide the primary emotional relationships in our highly mobile lives. If we go away to college or move to a new area, for example, we must depend on friends, most of them new, to share our secrets, hopes, and problems.

The most important ingredient of friendship is trust. In order for trust to exist there must be the possibility of a continuing relationship. Few people would reveal personal information to persons whom they meet on only a casual basis. Even when we meet a person we like very much, we are likely to divulge little more than superficial information about important areas of our lives if we think that person will not be accessible to us.

We also choose to trust those people who we predict will react to us in the way we want them to. In order to predict reactions from others, we must be around them for some time. When we discover that they share our attitudes and values and that they react to situations and events the way we do, then we can predict that these are people whom we can trust.

Once an atmosphere of trust is present, we may decide to disclose something about ourselves to another person. *Disclosure* is revealing your self to another person. It also involves revealing information about yourself that the other person would not ordinarily know—revealing your "private" self rather than revealing only your "public" self.

We all make choices about what to disclose and what to keep to ourselves. Our areas of choice in a typical communication situation can be seen in the Johari Window (see Figure 1–2).[8]

The Areas of the Self

	Known to Self	Unknown to Self
Known to Others	1. Free to self and others	2. Blind to self, seen by others
Unknown to Others	3. Hidden area: Self hidden from others	4. Unknown self

Figure 1-2

The "free to self and others" area is the greatest disclosure area; it involves information about ourselves that we are willing to communicate as well as information we are unable to hide. A group of students, for example, meet for the first time in a classroom and, following the instructor's suggestion, introduce themselves. Most of them will stick to vital statistics: their name, where they come from, and their major. Although some students do not reveal much more than superficial descriptive information, other students will make judgments about them based on their speech and style of clothing. When people do not know each other very well, the "free to self and others" area is smaller than when people get to know each other better.

The area labeled "blind to self, seen by others" is a kind of accidental disclosure area; there are certain things we do not know about ourselves that others know about us. This information often becomes known when others are able to recognize our roles. For example, we may see that the man who must always have the latest model of an expensive car is really trying to hide his own sense of inadequacy and insecurity. Some people who see themselves as sympathetic and helpful are seen as bossy and manipulative by others. Advertisers like to play with our blind areas. They suggest, for instance, that you do not know that you have bad breath, but everyone else knows.

The hidden area, where the self is hidden from others, is a deliberate nondisclosure area; there are certain things that you know about yourself that you do not want known, so you deliberately conceal them from others. Most people hide those things that might evoke disapproval from those they love and admire. Some of us have hidden areas that are not revealed to anyone. Others keep certain areas hidden from one person but open to another. For example, a woman is more likely to tell her best friend than her mother that she is no longer a virgin.

The unknown area is also a nondisclosure area; it provides no possibility of disclosure because it is not known to the self or to others. This is not to say, however, that unknown areas can never be known. Psychologists commonly help patients to discover these areas. Experience can also lead us into the unknown area.

The disclosure and nondisclosure areas are not static and unchanging. Figure 1-3 shows how the disclosure areas might look in a close relationship. The area "free to self and others" becomes much larger because, in close relationships, a person is likely to disclose more. When disclosure increases, people not only reveal more information about themselves but are also likely to discover things about themselves that they had not previously known. If we adapted these figures to all our relationships, the four areas would probably change with each relationship.

The Areas of Self in a Close Relationship

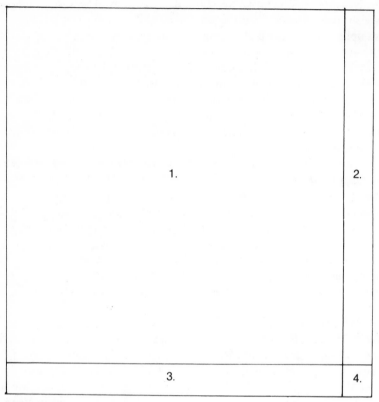

Figure 1-3

All of us can make a choice about what areas of our lives we want to reveal to others and what areas we want to keep hidden. If we decide in favor of disclosure, we face a certain amount of risk. Some of us are afraid of the self-knowledge that disclosure might bring. We may suspect certain things about ourselves, but we prefer that they remain in our hidden area. Some of us are afraid of intimacy. Disclosure may cause us to feel responsible for the personal information we receive. For example, if a friend tells us that she is unhappy, we may feel a certain sense of responsibility for helping her to feel happier. Some of us fear that if we tell another person too much about ourselves, he or she might try to control us. If we tell a lover of our great need for affection, he or she could withhold affection in order to manipulate us. Disclosure means that we must drop many of our roles. Perhaps the greatest individual fear in disclosure is negative feedback; we are afraid disclosure will mean that the other person will no longer love, accept, or want us.

Because our culture has traditionally permitted women to show their feelings and has required men to hide theirs, disclosure has been more likely to occur among women than among men. In a relationship in which a woman discloses and a man does not, the woman loses power and becomes more vulnerable; her secrets are known and his are not. Disclosure demands reciprocity; it is a process of sharing. If both parties are not willing to share, disclosure becomes very risky.

Another risk in self-disclosure is that although you might discover that honesty and openness are very good for you, too much openness might be harmful to other people. If we all went through life being completely honest, so many hurt feelings might result that communication would cease altogether. We can all think of times when it was better to be less honest in order to avoid hurting another person, for instance, when we said how nice the party was despite the fact that everyone had to struggle to keep awake.

Self-disclosure can occur only in an atmosphere of trust and goodwill. There are people who can harm us or who would like to harm us; with these people we are better off playing the roles that they expect of us. There are also people who will not understand our feelings even though they may feel favorably toward us. These people are generally not self-disclosers themselves, and they keep a great deal of their lives in the hidden area.

If disclosure is so filled with risks, why disclose anything about ourselves at all? We believe that disclosure is an important part of our self-concept and of our sense of self-esteem. In situations where we are able to disclose, we can play the role that comes closest to how we see ourselves; we are able to *be* ourselves.

Disclosure also permits us to *see* ourselves. By discussing aspects of ourselves with other people, we can check the accuracy of our perceptions, our thoughts, and our feelings. Other people, in turn, give us a chance to challenge or reinforce our perceptions.

For example, several students were discussing their fears and discovered that they were all apprehensive about going into the dining hall alone. All of them felt relieved to discover that others felt the same way; each had thought that he or she was alone in perceiving the dining hall as a fearful place.

Self-disclosure also creates a bond with other people. If we are willing to disclose, the person with whom we share our disclosure may be able to reciprocate. Thus, rather than merely projecting a variety of roles, people learn to share the feelings, thoughts, and hopes that are vital to their lives. Unless we disclose our needs, we have no chance of their ever being met. Some people, for example, never show their anger. They appear calm and peaceful to their closest friends and associates, even though they may be in inner turmoil. Because they cannot disclose their anger, they have no way of stopping the behavior that makes them angry. Other people are able to disclose anger at appropriate moments and in the right circumstances. They are able to distinguish between irritation and anger and to channel their anger in the right direction. Still others may overdisclose anger in inappropriate circumstances. We are all familiar with the man who kicks his dog and yells at his secretary when he is really angry with his wife or boss. There is a wide range in the degrees of self-disclosure. All of us learn through experience which reactions are appropriate.

One of the great excitements of self-disclosure is that it gives us a chance to experience the fact that no human emotion is unique. Perhaps this can best be illustrated through an example of a group experience. An individual within a group was going through a very anxious period in her life. To cope with her feelings, she had developed a fantasy, which she described to the group. It involved being committed to a rest home for six months. While she was there, all her food would be prepared and brought to her, everyone would greet her with warm and friendly smiles and, most important, for the entire time she was there, she would not have to make a single decision or to think about the things that were making her anxious. At the end of the six-month period, she would be able to resume her previous life with calmness and stability. After she told her fantasy to the group, every single member of the group admitted to having had a similar fantasy at one time or another. The knowledge that others share your emotions is a great help to self-disclosure.

Some of us disclose very little information about ourselves. If we decide that we want to increase our disclosure, how do we go about it? First, we must find someone who shares our basic view of the world, a person who is likely to have attitudes and values similar to our own. We must also be confident that this person likes us and that he or she is trustworthy. In choosing what to disclose, it is probably wise to reveal something that you do not consider to be too private. According to research about self-disclosure, information that presents us positively is more likely to be regarded favorably than information that presents us negatively.[9] You would probably get more favorable feedback, for example, if you told someone about a great party rather than disclose that you feel lonely all the time. Once you try disclosure and the other person accepts what you have said and reciprocates, the foundation for meaningful communication with that person has been created.

Occasionally, people will not respond in the way we assumed they would. If we get a negative response, for example, we must assess where we went wrong. As we stated in the introduction to this book, much of effective communication is prediction and assessment. Once we assess what went wrong in our communication, we can more accurately predict what the reaction to our next communication will be. None of us is completely successful in disclosure. What is important, when we are not successful, is to be willing to analyze what happened and to try again.

COMMUNICATING THE SELF TO OTHERS

Even when we have many friends we trust and find many opportunities for disclosure, many of us still present ourselves in ways that hamper our communication efforts. This is due to the difference between the way we see ourselves and the way other people see us. For example, we are told by someone who has become a close friend that we give the impression at first of being aloof and forbidding. Although our self-perception is that we are kind and helpful, people tell us that they were afraid of us when they first met us. From these experiences, it is clear that even when we have a well-defined sense of who we are, we do not always accurately communicate this sense of self to others.

Although it is impossible to list all the barriers that prevent us from effective communication, we would like to discuss typical problems that often occur in communication situations.

Evaluative Judgments

Carl Rogers says that the single greatest cause of communication breakdown is the individual's tendency to judge—to approve, disapprove, or otherwise evaluate the communication of another person. Most of us grow up hearing a series of negative evaluative judgments. "You are sloppy," "You should study harder," and "You shouldn't feel that way" are all typical examples. Therefore, it is not surprising that we repeat these judgments without thinking about what we are saying or about the effect we might have. Yet you will probably also recall that as soon as someone makes an evaluative judgment about you, particularly if it is negative, you immediately feel the necessity to defend yourself. Also, if you have the choice, your reaction might be to avoid the person who made the judgment.

Although some situations call for negative judgments, they should be made with care and thought. Rogers suggests that when we have a negative reaction, we should make an attempt to identify with the other person and to feel what that person is feeling. As with dropping roles and disclosure, however, identification with another person's feelings can be risky. Roger says:

> If you really understand another person in this way, if you are willing to enter his private world and see the way life appears to him, without any attempt to make evaluative judgments, you run the risk of being changed yourself. You might see it his way, you might find yourself influenced in your attitudes or your personality. The risk of being changed is one of the most frightening prospects most of us can face.[10]

A typical evaluative statement that we often make, and one we seldom think about, is telling someone, "You shouldn't feel that way." When we think about this statement, it is clear that we can't tell people how to feel—we can tell then that we either like or don't like their feeling—but we can't tell them *how* to feel, for feelings are unique to the individual.

Many of us who are scripted to make negative judgments are not as quick to make positive ones. Yet we all know that positive reinforcement is important to all of us.

Avoidance

When a situation is filled with conflict and our feelings are involved, we often try to avoid any communication about the situation. Some of us will refuse to discuss it, some will find ways of changing the subject, while others will avoid situations and relationships in which conflict might appear.

When we are involved in an intimate relationship, avoidance is not the best tactic. If a husband and wife, for example, cannot agree on how to spend their money, they might face eventual bankruptcy if they never discuss their financial situation. Even in a less extreme situation, many of us could either resolve the conflict or reach a compromise by confronting the issue at hand. If you think that someone is angry with you, for example, it is probably better to ask the person if and why they are angry rather than avoiding him or her. If you feel that someone is manipulating you, you might be able to solve the problem by asking him or her about it. Many of us would not have to avoid unpleasant situations if we were able to confront them.

Not all conflict can be resolved by better communication strategies, however. Some people could talk for years and end up further apart. We often understand another person's position perfectly well but know that we will never agree with it. In these cases, we have no choice but to structure our communication situation so that we can avoid areas of conflict as much as possible.

Listening

We have been told all our lives to listen to others, that it is rude to monopolize a conversation. Yet some of us regard listening as taking turns: you speak, then it's my turn to speak, and so on. If you are conscious that your turn is coming up soon and are already planning in your mind what you are going to say, you are probably not listening very well.

Listening is sharing rather than taking turns. It often requires a response to what the other person has said rather than continuing with what interests you. Good listening is active in the sense that it requires the listener to reflect about what the speaker has said. Active listening also asks us to evaluate what is really being said. Many people are giving us a series of messages—some of them hidden. A mother, for example, who says that she does not permit her in-laws to give her child candy because sugar is bad for teeth, might also be telling us that she doesn't like her in-laws very much. Not all messages, of course, have hidden meanings. Still, we should be aware of the possibility of hidden meanings and respond to them when they occur.

Listening is part of the process of self-growth. If we listen only to ourselves, we don't learn very much. The sharing that takes place in listening helps us to understand how other people perceive the world and helps us to understand how other people view us.

Criticism

Although few human beings would say that they are perfect, even fewer are willing to have their imperfections pointed out by others. In some cases, criticism does not serve a very worthwhile purpose. It doesn't do us any good, for example, to be told that we are too short, too fat, or that our hairline is receding—we are well aware of these "imperfections" and would do something to correct them if we could.

In other areas, criticism can be more useful. If we are told that we are making grammatical errors in our writing, we can go about learning the correct way. if we know that our speech or paper is not very clear, we can seek help about how to make it clearer.

The ability to evaluate criticism means that we are willing to choose between psychological safety and risk. For example, if our instructor says that a paper is badly written, it is much safer to take the paper to our best friend and have him or her say that the instructor doesn't know what she is talking about. It is much more risky to ask ourselves whether the instructor might be right in her assessment. The ability to evaluate and to look at criticism objectively is often a means to psychological growth.

In our relationships with others it is important to recognize how threatening criticism can be and to criticize in ways that are not harmful to other people. Telling a roommate that he or she is a slob, for example, will probably not lead to productive communication or behavior. Telling him or her that such untidiness is very discomforting might lead him or her to clean up the room.

Evaluative judgments, avoidance, listening, and criticism are all areas that are intricately tied to how we see ourselves and how we perceive our place in relation to others. When we have insight into these areas, we often discover how we have hampered our own self-growth and communication with others.

If we are going to go about communication in a positive way, it might be useful to look at the precepts that Carl Rogers set for himself. Several years ago, he was asked to talk to a university audience about his life, his work, and what he had learned. In reply, he said:

1) In my relationships with persons I have found that it does not help, in the long run, to act as if I were someone I am not.

2) I find I am more effective when I can listen acceptantly to myself, and can be myself.

3) I have found it of enormous value when I can permit myself to understand another person.

4) I have found it enriching to open channels whereby others can communicate their feelings, their private perceptual worlds, to me.

5) I have found it highly rewarding when I can accept another person.[11]

We believe that Rogers' discoveries about himself apply to all of us. His insights can lead us to fuller communication with ourselves and with others.

SUMMARY

The way we communicate reflects our sense of self, a self that is a complex mixture of experience, knowledge, attitudes, and values. These factors, combined with the perceptions and reactions of others to us, all combine to create the impression of who we are.

We all use communication to present our selves to others. Although we may attempt to communicate our true selves, we may also use communication to hide the self. The greater our need for psychological safety, the more we will try to communicate in ways that are safe—ways that will obtain approval and respect from others. If we can escape from our safety needs and communicate our true feelings, however, we find that both our communication and our life can become more satisfying.

We all play a series of roles in our transactions with others. These roles help to preserve the structure and rituals of society, but if we play only the roles that are expected of us, we are in danger of forgetting who we really are.

In order to be ourselves, we must find people with whom we can play a role close to our own self-concept. When we find people whom we can trust and who are able to accept important disclosures, we are best able to be ourselves.

Many of us do not reach our full potential because we engage in evaluative judgments, avoid unpleasant topics, do not listen well, and are unable to accept and deal with valid criticism. Once we are aware of these barriers and can work to overcome them, we will be better able to get "what we say" and "who we are" together.

FURTHER READING

Maya Angelou. *I Know Why the Caged Bird Sings*. New York: Random House, 1969; *Gather Together in My Name*. New York: Random House, 1974; *Singin' and Swingin' and Getting Merry Like Christmas*. New York: Random House, 1976.
> These lively autobiographical accounts begin with the story of growing up black and female in the rural South and continue with the author's later experiences in the entertainment world of the North. The author describes her struggles with identity, love, and the oppression of self in such a realistic way that the reader feels a strong identification with her.

Sidney M. Jourard. *The Transparent Self*, rev. ed. New York: D. Van Nostrand, 1971.
> The importance of self-disclosure to psychological well-being is stressed in this informal and readable discussion. The book is greatly enhanced by the author's willingness to disclose his own life and feelings.

Mike McGrady. *The Kitchen Sink Papers*. New York: New American Library, 1976.
> An amusing and insightful book about what it's like to change your

role in life. In this true account, the wife goes out to work and the husband stays behind to run the household.

R. D. Rosen. *Psychobabble.* New York: Atheneum, 1977.
The author examines several of the popular psychological movements that offer instant cures to their clients. He concludes that although these crash courses have great appeal to Americans, they have little to offer in resolving psychological problems.

Liv Ullman. *Changing.* New York: Alfred A. Knopf, 1977.
A well-known actress writes about her problems of insecurity and the difficulty of defining herself. Although she moves in the world of fame and glamour, it is clear that she shares with us the universal problems of self-discovery and self-esteem.

Richard Wright. *American Hunger.* New York: Harper & Row, 1977.
This great American novelist writes about his life and how he was unable to find his place or reach his potential in American society. Although the book is written from the perspective of an American black man, it speaks to everyone who is faced with the problem of not fitting into a role that society has assigned.

NOTES

[1]R. D. Laing, *Self and Others* (New York: Pantheon Books, 1969), p. 77.

[2]Laing, p. 78.

[3]Muriel James and Dorothy Jongeward, *Born to Win* (Reading, Mass.; Addison-Wesley, 1976), pp. 68–100.

[4]Abraham H. Maslow, *Toward a Psychology of Being*, 2d. ed. (New York: D. Van Nostrand, 1968), p. 46.

[5]Margaret Mead, *Blackberry Winter* (New York: William Morrow, 1972), pp. 92, 94–95.

[6]Sidney M. Jourard, *The Transparent Self*, rev. ed. (New York: D. Van Nostrand, 1971), p. 30.

[7]Carl Rogers, *On Becoming a Person* (Boston: Houghton Mifflin, 1961), p. 110.

[8]Joseph Luft, *Group Process: An Introduction to Group Dynamics*, 2d. ed. (Palo Alto: National Press, 1970), pp. 11–12.

[9]S. J. Gilbert, "Empirical and Theoretical Extensions in Self Disclosure," in G. R. Miller (Ed.), *Explorations in Interpersonal Communication* (Beverly Hills: Sage, 1976), pp. 197–215.

[10]Rogers, p. 333.

[11]Rogers, p. 3.

chapter 2

Interpersonal
Communication

The most common communication in our lives occurs in situations so ordinary that often we do not think of them as involving communication skills at all. We talk to an instructor about our grade, we discuss our plans for the holidays with our parents, or we argue about which movie to see with a group of friends. In all these communication situations we are sending and receiving a variety of verbal and nonverbal messages. This type of communication, which involves one other person or a few persons, is called *interpersonal communication.*

Interpersonal communication most commonly occurs in face-to-face situations, where we can see, hear, and even touch the other person or persons. It also offers the opportunity for immediate feedback, with the result that we have a chance to structure and restructure communication based on the response of the persons we are talking to.

Interpersonal communication is crucial to our lives because it affects nearly every aspect of our existence. We could go through life without ever having to write a paper, give a speech, or prepare a television broadcast. If we went through life without any interpersonal communication, however, we would be living in complete isolation.

Although most of our communication is interpersonal, analysis of all

31

types of this communication is not possible because there are so many of them. There are also many variables in interpersonal communication; we find ourselves in different situations, and our relationships in these situations differ according to the people we talk to. Even our mood on a particular day may affect all our communication transactions.

There are, however, certain skills that can be developed to improve interpersonal communication. Simply becoming aware of what is involved in this kind of communication can make you more effective in interpersonal relationships. To help you understand some of the relevant factors, we will first discuss channels, feedback, and noise—all essential elements in the interpersonal process.

INTERPERSONAL PROCESS: THREE ESSENTIAL ELEMENTS

Communicating with another person is an ongoing, changing, continually developing process. Effective interpersonal communication is organic rather than mechanical and generates new ways of behaving and new possibilities for growth in the participants. This growth is dependent upon the availability of channels, the amount of feedback, and the level of noise present when communication takes place.

Channels

We tend to remember another person better if we can touch, hear, and see that person than if we can do only one of these—hearing the person's voice on the telephone, for example. When you increase the number of channels you use to communicate with others, you not only heighten the interest that others have in your communication, but you also increase the support for your message, the potential level of understanding on the part of your listener, and your own image or credibility. If you are talking to another person about the damage done to your car in an accident, you are using one channel—sound, or hearing. If you show the person a picture, you double the channels—using both sight and sound. You can triple the channels by taking the other person to see the car so that he or she can touch it, see it, and hear you talk about it. If the other person were at the scene of the accident, he or she could also smell the burning rubber, the spilled gasoline, and the escaping radiator steam. The last image would be experienced, understood, and retained the best, whereas the first description would soon fade from memory. When more channels are used, more of the receiver's senses come into play and, thus, the likelihood that the receiver will become more emotionally involved is increased. With emotional involvement—that is, when a person's feelings are affected—greater concern for the message, that is, the ideas being conveyed, will occur. The more channels you use, then, the more effective your communication will be.

Because of the intimacy involved in interpersonal communication, it is easier for us to use all the channels. A handshake or an embrace, the strong scent of perfume or after-shave lotion, conversation that is reinforced by one person reaching into his wallet or her purse for pictures of the kids indicate some of the many characteristic ways in which channels are used in an interpersonal transaction between two old friends who have not seen each other for awhile.

Feedback

When, instead of writing a person a letter, you decide that it would be better to see him or her in person, part of your decision may reflect a desire to see how the other person will respond to your message, what his or her feedback will be. Just as the source has more success in communicating through a number of channels, so too can the receiver increase feedback if it is communicated through a variety of channels. In interpersonal settings, facial expressions indicate responses from our listener as well as vocal and verbal responses. Body movements, too, are sometimes used. You might question the truth of another person's generalization by raising an eyebrow. You might show that you are interested by looking the person directly in the eye. You acknowledge receipt of messages with vocal responses such as "yeah . . . yeah," "uh-huh," or "mmmm." You use verbal feedback such as "I know," "I see what you mean," and "right!" A slouched posture may reveal apathy while slightly turning away from the other person may indicate lack of.interest. Because interpersonal communication is two-way, extensive feedback through a variety of channels is possible.

Feedback goes on all the time between people engaged in interpersonal communication. It is not confined to speaker or listener alone but flows from both throughout a transaction. Just as nobody can avoid communicating, nobody can avoid providing feedback. It is an important ingredient in increasing the accuracy of communication and removing barriers to understanding.

Noise

You have undoubtedly had the experience of talking to someone about something you consider important and being interrupted. A husband and wife are discussing their plans when suddenly the baby cries; you and a friend are driving along the expressway discussing whether to pull off the highway for lunch and your communication is drowned out by a noisy trailer truck. Such interruptions cause frustration, especially if they are repeated. The term we have used in our communications model for such interference is *noise*.

Noise affects the message by causing a discrepancy between the message transmitted and the message received. *Physical noise* is technical interference. It may be caused by disturbance in the channel—a bad telephone connection, for example—or by a speech disorder in the source or deafness in the receiver. *Psychological noise* occurs within the communicator or within the listener. When a speaker uses incorrect words to express an idea and causes misunderstanding in the listener, the speaker creates this kind of noise. Psychological noise could also be caused by distortion in feedback. Whenever the distortion occurs in the mind of the communicator or listener, the interference can be labeled psychological.

The best way to reduce the influence of noise is to eliminate the cause. The couple in the first example can first feed the baby and then go on with their planning. In the second example, you can slow down so as not to miss the exit while the trailer truck passes. People dial a phone number a second time to get a better connection. Handling psychological noise can be more difficult since it may be more elusive and more difficult to perceive. When we realize that people are distracted and unable to concentrate, it is probably wise to try communicating at a later date. Sometimes, when one is aware of psychological noise, it can be helpful to ask the listener why he or she is unable to listen or to understand what is being said. We are all familiar with the situation when the person says, "I'm so upset about what happened this morning that I just can't concentrate." If there always seems to be psychological noise present with some people, it is probably caused by a difference in attitudes and values. A born-again Christian and a Jew, for example, might have to decide that the subject of religion causes so much psychological noise that their conversations will have to be limited to different subjects.

THE COMMUNICATION ENVIRONMENT

Interpersonal communication is influenced by the environment in which it occurs. How we react to this environment is determined by our culture, our sociological roles, and our psychological makeup. Although these elements are present in every communication situation, one may be more dominant than another—depending upon the relationship between the communicators.

Cultural Rules

Every culture has rules that its members are expected to follow. In our culture, small children are trained to say thank you, people are expected to wait patiently in line rather than shove their way to the front, and shoppers with carts filled with groceries are not supposed to go through the express line at the supermarket. When we meet people on a one-time or superficial basis, we follow the rules of our culture—rules that are so well established we are scarcely aware of them unless they are violated.

Cultural rules help a society to function smoothly. We don't have to worry about what we will wear to a wedding or a funeral—this is determined by our culture. We know how to deal with clerks in stores, how to order in restaurants, and how to greet people whom we meet on the street. Cultural rules are useful guides in our day-to-day casual relationships.

Sociological Rules

In addition to cultural guides, every society has well-established sociological roles. When we are in situations where roles are well defined, we structure our communication accordingly, and the roles dictate our behavior. No student, for example, would go to a classroom and initiate discussion in the class; that is the role of the teacher. When students go to see instructors in their offices, they often wait to be invited to sit down and let the instructor set the tone for the conversation that will follow.

Every society has a set of identifiable roles. Parent/child, teacher/student, boss/employee are just a few of the roles that we have played or will play, and most of us have an idea of how we should communicate within these roles.

Communication based on sociological roles is often more complex and intense than communication based on cultural rules because many sociological roles occur in intimate as well as in impersonal relationships. Sociological roles pose limitations on interpersonal communication because we often cannot escape our consciousness of the role. Even when we talk to a teacher as a friend, there is always the awareness that he or she will eventually have to give us a grade. This awareness is likely to make our communication less free and open.

Psychological Rules

Unlike cultural and sociological rules imposed on us from the world around us, psychological rules are internal. Psychological rules are based on the attitudes, values, and beliefs that we have acquired throughout our lives.

In some cases, our psychological rules may be in conflict with our cultural or sociological rules. Our culture may say, for example, that it is inappropriate for a man to be a nurse. Yet a man who knows that nursing would be an interesting and fulfilling career might be able to ignore societal rules and follow his own psychological needs.

The most satisfying interpersonal communication occurs in relationships where we can follow our psychological needs rather than cultural and sociological rules. When we have relationships in which our psychological inclinations are allowed to flourish, communication becomes more satisfying and fulfilling; in such cases we are not bound by rules that dictate how to believe, act, and feel.

Although cultural, sociological, and psychological rules have been discussed separately, it is important to remember that they can and usually do overlap. It is probable, for example, that we will have a close psychological relationship with someone who comes from a similar cultural or sociological background. On the other hand, roles that seem inflexible at first do not always remain that way. There are many examples of students and teachers and bosses and employees who have become close friends and who meet each other's psychological needs. When we are able to distinguish among cultural, sociological, and psychological needs and rules, we are more likely to make accurate predictions and respond accordingly. Understanding these rules also permits us to face new situations and experiences with greater confidence.

INTERPERSONAL NEEDS

In interpersonal communication there are basic psychological needs. William Schutz identifies these needs as inclusion, control, and affection.[1] *Inclusion* is our need to be accepted by some individuals and groups who will give us a sense of belonging. We feel anxiety about inclusion (or exclusion) throughout our lives. Not being chosen for a team, going alone to a restaurant, or being snubbed by an acquaintance are examples of experiences that show the need for inclusion.

In all our relationships and experiences it is necessary to have some feeling of *control*. People are afraid of giving speeches because they fear that they might lose control by forgetting what they have to say or revealing to the audience how nervous they are. Control is a power word that implies dominance and authority. In an interpersonal sense it also means having options and choices in life rather than always being manipulated by and submitting to people and circumstances.

Affection is the feeling of warm, emotional attachments to other people. Affection typically occurs in relationships such as friendship, dating, marriage, and parenting. Affection is a one-to-one emotion. Unlike inclusion and control, which can occur in situations where several people are present, affection is a matter of singling out a particular person.[2]

Understanding the importance of inclusion, control, and affection is vital to the way we conduct our interpersonal relationships. It is necessary to realize that we are not the only ones with these needs—they exist in all of us. These needs also give us an indication of the intensity of an interpersonal relationship. Inclusion exists in many relationships. It commonly exists, for example, in our associations with schools, clubs, and organizations. As relationships become closer, control, or the balance of control, also becomes an important issue, since not many of us would continue relationships in which we had no control. Finally, the relationship becomes most intense when affection is involved. Although inclusion and control are part of many interpersonal relationships, affection characterizes those that are the closest and the most intimate.

COMMUNICATION RELATIONSHIPS

Interpersonal communication is based on relationships. You can't communicate as a wife unless you have a husband, you can't be a teacher unless you have a student, and you can't be a parent without a child. Even within relationships, communication can take place on different levels. For example, a boss and employee who become friends communicate both as boss/employee and as friend/friend. A husband and wife who work together on the same job have a husband-wife relationship as well as the relationship of professional colleagues.

Because relations are so complicated, we should like to discuss two kinds of relationships commonly found in interpersonal communication: complementary and symmetrical, and competitive and cooperative.

Complementary and Symmetrical

Think about the last time you talked face-to-face with either or both of your parents. The way in which you spoke with each other and the information you conveyed revealed a definite relationship between you. You are probably aware, for instance, that the relationship between you and your parents is not based on equality. Your parents were brought up differently from you, in a different period, with emphasis on different values. They may think they know what is "right" or "best" for you and as

a result, try to influence your life. In attempting to influence you, they maintain a somewhat "superior" position. All relationships are influenced by the degree of equality that exists between the participants.

Paul Watzlawick, Janet Beavin, and Don Jackson have written about interactional patterns in *Pragmatics of Human Communication.* They label relationships as either complementary or symmetrical.[3] A communication relationship based on equality is called a *symmetrical* relationship and involves participants who treat each other as equals and mirror each other's behavior. Such relationships sometimes occur between peers—people of the same rank with respect to mental and/or physical endowments, status, or other qualifications. In a *complementary* relationship—based on differences—one communicator is superior to the other. The instructor talking to the student, the doctor to the patient, or the boss to the employee represent the complementary situation. Fewer relationships are based on equality than on differences; interpersonal situations are often based on a certain amount of both. Equality is likely to be a characteristic that is easily eroded, depending on the subject, the mood, or the situation. When you no longer have equality in a relationship, you either have no relationship at all or you have a difference. The difference might be as simple as one person knowing more about a topic than another person, one person expressing an "I'll take care of you" or "I'd like to help you" feeling, or a situation in which one person has been asked to take charge or be responsible for the other. Whether a relationship is equal or different will affect the kind of communication that occurs. It may affect the amount of threat that permeates the situation, the courtesy and respect one person shows for another, or even the degree of openness and honesty that is permitted.

Competitive and Cooperative

A great deal of interpersonal communication is characterized by either competitive or cooperative behavior. When the communicators are rivals, communication is competitive, with the participants trying to out-maneuver each other. When communicators are friends, or acting in a noncompetitive situation, communication is more likely to be cooperative.

Competition and competitive strategies are important pursuits in our society. Best-selling books, such as *Winning Through Intimidation* and *Looking Out for Number One,* concentrate on power strategies for people in competitive situations. In these books, advice is given on how to command, manipulate, dazzle, and deceive one's opponents.

In attempting to understand interpersonal communication, it is important to distinguish between cooperation and competition. In cooperative communication, people try to work together—the emphasis is on teamwork—and the end result is a group rather than an individual effort.

If, on the other hand, you believe that a problem should be solved through cooperation, but other participants have competition in mind, solving the problem becomes difficult. Competitive situations do not lend themselves to close friendships and self-disclosure, because the other persons are seen as opponents. Competition is likely to be guided by cultural rules and sociological roles, while cooperation is influenced by psychological needs.

Both competition and cooperation have their place in our society. When people are trying to get promoted, win a game, or sell a product, they will probably be successful if they are competitive. But for those who are trying to solve a problem or form close personal relationships, cooperation is a better way of achieving these goals. What is important is that we recognize the difference between competition and cooperation and realize that we communicate differently in each situation.

COMMUNICATION PERCEPTIONS

If you see me as I see me and if I see you as you see you, we would probably have great success in communicating. Unfortunately, our perception of ourself and another person's perception of us can be very different.

Whenever we communicate with another person, six different levels of perception are involved:

1. *How I see myself*
2. *How I see you*
3. *How I think you see me*
4. *How you see yourself*
5. *How you see me*
6. *How you think I see you*

These different perceptual levels help to explain why communication can break down; they don't, however, give us many hints about improving our communication. Even if we were to do a better job of projecting who we are, there would be no guarantee that our communication partners would like us or understand us any better. Their perceptions are influenced by their own values and attitudes, which may be very different from our own.

These six perceptual levels are useful in explaining why we do or do not get along with certain people. Friends, for example, are likely to be people with whom we share accurate self-concepts; our image of them is similar to how they see themselves, and they are likely to see us as we see ourselves. In each case, both parties largely approve of what they see. Even though we might like or admire another person, we don't have a very good chance for a close friendship if we don't share similar perceptual levels.

The way in which you perceive yourself bears directly on your success in interpersonal relationships. If you perceive yourself as being liked, wanted, acceptable to others, capable, and worthy, it is probable that other people will see you this way too. Communication in such relationships will undoubtly be easy, open, honest, and satisfying for you. On the other hand, if you are anxious, insecure, cynical, or depressed, you are more likely to perceive communication situations as threatening. For example, if you are unsure of yourself in a new job, and you receive some negative feedback from your boss on several tasks, you may begin to think that your boss "has it in for you"—that he or she does not like you or your attitude. Within the framework of such negative responses, you might begin to interpret other signs as negative, although ordinarily they might not be considered negative at all. You begin to perceive that the boss is "picking on you" by walking by you without speaking or watching you while you work. If he or she asks for a progress report—an otherwise normal procedure—you may respond with "Why me?" Because you hold a negative attitude about yourself, it is likely that others will hold a negative attitude toward you. The expectations you have about how others react to you often determine the reactions you receive. A person who is confident will appear capable and worthy and will, very likely, engage in less defensive behavior and communication than someone who lacks confidence. Thus, others tend to see that person as confident.

The way you perceive yourself and others, and the way that others perceive you, are at the heart of interpersonal communication. If you feel anxious or that a particular situation involves a great deal of risk, these feelings may become a barrier to effective communication. Sometimes, the most helpful thing to do in a situation that feels risky to you is simply to acknowledge—to yourself and, if you can, to the other person—that you are feeling vulnerable. Disclosing your true feelings in this manner can help build trust and focus on the difficulty in the communication rather than avoiding it. Sometimes, anxiety is inevitable, and the best you can do is to be aware of its effect on the situation. It is rare for communication barriers in interpersonal transactions to be created by only one person. If you recognize your own contribution to the barrier, you will be on your way to learning how to overcome such communication difficulties.

IMPROVING INTERPERSONAL COMMUNICATION

We have all had experience with communication in which we could have handled ourselves better. Therefore, the more we learn about why we have succeeded or failed in our communication efforts the more likely we are to be successful in our future communication attempts. With this in mind, we shall discuss some of the areas that can improve interpersonal communication.

Adaptation and Credibility

Becoming an effective communicator in interpersonal relationships involves a broad range of skills. Most of the skills require *adaptation*—altering our communication behavior to fit the circumstances. Most of them, too, are perfected over time, because experience provides more information on which to operate. Through experience we learn what is appropriate and inappropriate for certain situations, people, and messages. We learn that certain circumstances call for cooperation rather than conflict or competition, and that certain relationships will be ongoing and long-range rather than temporary and short-lived. In an interview situation, for example, where you have a strong desire to gain employment, you will very likely assume a cooperative attitude or position. If you are involved in a debate with an instructor or an administrator over a procedure or policy that you dislike, the appropriate attitude would be one of conflict or opposition. You would use a different approach in talking with a visitor to your school or campus whom you knew you would never see again than in a conversation with the person with whom you shared a loving relationship. Adaptive behavior is normal and necessary, as we have seen in our previous discussions of role-playing. In addition to the context in which communication takes place, there are some factors that the responsible communicator should consider as far as adaptive behavior is concerned.

The first factor is that interpersonal communication is a simultaneous process involving sharing. All persons engaged in the process send messages and receive messages at the same time. Each is constantly sharing information, whether it be verbal or nonverbal, and is, thus, affecting other people in the communication. Perception of the process in this way involves or implies an important skill. The process is dynamic; since you are a communicator as well as a receiver in face-to-face interpersonal communication, you must be more alert to the signals you are sending and receiving. Increased awareness is a skill that you can develop—a skill partially dependent upon recognition of the communication factors involved.

The second factor is your *credibility*—the extent to which you are worthy of another's beliefs or confidence. If your best friend tells you that your lover is seeing someone else on the sly, you will be much more willing to accept that information as true than if one of your "enemies" told you the same thing. In much the same manner, we would be more willing to accept as true the information that one of our local legislators cheated on his income tax if that information came from the governor or another legislator than if it came from someone we distrusted or someone who did not seem to be in a position to know. Your credibility as a source for information depends upon how much trust another person has in you, how reliable you are, and the dynamism with which you present your ideas. A person who does not know what he is talking about or whose trustworthiness is in doubt, can sometimes generate credibility, at least temporarily, by stating ideas forcefully—with dynamism.

Credibility depends, in part, upon personal integrity. To be trusted by others, we must be seen by others as trustworthy. To be treated as loyal to the cause—any cause—we must be perceived by others as a loyal person. For our responses toward others to be taken as amicable, we must be perceived as a friendly, kind, and perhaps, helpful person. A person who is considered bitter or cynical could make friendly comments and be perceived as sarcastic rather than friendly.

Credibility is subject to reevaluation as circumstances alter. The setting and the time may change as well as the receiver and the subject. A professor of economics might be considered especially credible in speaking out on problems about the handling of the economy but no more credible than others in speaking out against problems in criminal justice. Credibility is also a characteristic that is determined or created over a period of time. A reputation for honesty is developed by a person who gives honest responses in a variety of situations.

A person's race, word choice, group affiliation, and social status affect the way that person's message is viewed, because these factors also affect that person's credibility. For example, an American Indian who uses revolutionary language might be considered a threat, no matter what the situation. It would be a hopeful sign if we had moved beyond such evaluation in our society. A person's race (black, white, yellow, or red), group affiliation (Bircher, Ku Klux Klan member, or liberal), or social status (blue collar, businessman, or industrialist) can have much more influence on how that person's message is received than what that person stands for. But since we *do* make evaluations on the basis of such factors, they should be considered when estimating probable effects. We usually respond more to who a person is than to what he or she says.

Exchanging Information

At its simplest level, the exchange of information in interpersonal communication leads to greater clarity and precision. Often, it is helpful in gaining a clearer definition of a problem. Such a response may be appropriate when an instructor tries to find out why a student has performed poorly in a class or when there is a misunderstanding between two people about the definition of a concept or term used in a discussion. In such a case, one needs to question the other person in order to establish a common base for further discussion.

Questions also help people gain insight or increase the intensity of an interpersonal relationship. A variety of questions can be used. Those that begin with "What do you think about . . . ?" "How do you feel about . . . ?" often lead to thoughtful and reflective answers. Questions such as "If you were the student government president, how would you . . . ?" are often stimulating and provide insight into how other people solve problems and view the world. Often, the most interesting questions are personal ones. Few people can resist such queries as: "What are your motivations and drives?" "What objectives do you want to accomplish?" When people answer this type of question, their answers often reveal their values and attitudes as well as their individual qualities.

Asking questions may be the most important element of interpersonal communication. Most people feel a great sense of self-esteem when interest is expressed in how they think and feel; they are usually willing, and even eager, to answer questions. People who seldom ask questions are often perceived as lacking interest in others or, even worse, as being interested only in themselves.

As we mentioned in Chapter 1, self-disclosure is an important part of communication. Few interpersonal relationships can become personal and fulfilling unless people engage in self-disclosure. Few people, however, would engage in self-disclosure unless they felt that others were interested in what they had to say. Thus, the right kind of questions often prompt self-disclosure. There are certain people who are frequently told "I have never said this to anyone before." People who invite such confidences are facilitators; they ask the right questions and create an atmosphere of self-disclosure. This ability is necessary in order to develop intimate relationships.

Listening and Responding

In communicating with other people, speakers need to know whether they are having an impact. They need to know, for example, if the listener is really listening—if he or she understands the message and responds to the emotions being conveyed. Listeners, thus, serve as a necessary component in interpersonal communication because of the reassurance and support they can provide the speaker. Such support is readily noticeable when the listener's side of a telephone conversation is observed. The "uhh-huh," "um-m-m," and "yeah's" that are heard are reassurances to the speaker that someone is listening. These responses do not necessarily mean that the message is getting through. Many people learn to provide reassurance to the speaker even though they are not fully listening. This often pacifies those who "bend your ear" at the slightest opportunity. When such reassurances are not received, the speaker stops and says, "Do you know what I mean?" "Do you understand?" "Do you see how I feel?" or "Are you listening to me?"

Effective listener responses often need to be more elaborate than a simple reassurance that someone is listening. The strongest style of listener response, the one that provides the greatest amount of feedback, is an *understanding response*. This response leads to greater fidelity and clarity of communication between individuals because by using it the listener indicates a desire to find out whether he or she has understood the sender correctly. The basis of an understanding response is the ability to *paraphrase*— to restate an idea in a new way or in other words. The receiver paraphrases the sender's message in the receiver's own words, using his or her own expressions. Merely repeating an idea in the sender's words does not really reveal understanding.

An understanding response requires the listener to see the speaker's message from the speaker's point of view. Further elaboration of a position clarifies it and avoids controversy so that a solid base or common frame of reference can be established. Many conversations are best begun, then, by using the understanding response. We do this by completing a sentence or thought of the sender, by providing further illustrations to support those provided by the sender, or by commenting upon the significance of the ideas. By doing this in simple, clear language, we can better ensure accurate communication and, thus, fidelity.

The problem with much interpersonal communication is that we carry with us a need or desire to judge, evaluate, approve, or disapprove of certain situations, participants, and messages. We become involved in communication with preestablished barriers to mutual understanding. *Evaluative responses*—indications that the listener has made a personal judgment about the relative goodness, rightness, effectiveness, or appropriateness of the sender's message—are especially harmful in the early stages of a relationship or communication; once a value statement is conveyed, it is likely to generate another one. When a wife says to her husband, "You've been mean for the past three days," the husband's tendency is to respond with a comment like "You've been mean since I married you!" We have a need to show our superiority to another person by using a technique commonly referred to as "one-upsmanship."

Evaluative responses are also harmful because, once stated, they become public commitments to certain stands or positions and often force the one who makes the statement to defend it with further evaluative responses. Backed into a corner, a person becomes defensive and communication becomes emotional. Evaluative responses and judgments are appropriate, however, when you are specifically asked to make a value judgment or when you wish to convey your own attitudes.

Listening with Empathy   When you respond to another's joy with joy, to another's apathy with the same indifference, and to another's sadness with equal sorrow, you are showing *empathy.* You are identifying with the feeling or spirit of the other person. The extent to which you are able to do this will often determine how well you can respond. Total empathy is not possible, for we cannot know exactly what the other person is feeling or the extent or degree of that feeling. Also, it is difficult to understand another person's feelings if we have never experienced similar feelings ourselves. Can you know the emotion a person experiences when someone who is extremely close to him or her dies? Or the hate a person feels because his or her race has been put down and persecuted throughout history? Or the overwhelming exhilaration of a person who has just achieved the ultimate desire of his or her life? One of the tips given to aspiring actors and actresses is to get out into the world and experience—feel. The more experience an actor or actress has, the more likely it will be that he or she can re-create a feeling or experience on the stage.

We can practice increasing our sense of empathy by role-taking—assuming the role of someone else. Role-taking involves imitation—copying the behavior, mannerisms, and responses of others. For example, assume the role of a dean of students and have another person try to convince you that he or she deserves another chance at college after three failures. Assume the role of an ex-convict trying to persuade an employer that he or she badly needs the cashier's job that is open. Take the role of your parents as they try to persuade you to cut your hair and beard or change your manner of dress. Your ability to respond sensitively to another person may depend on your being able to feel what that person is feeling. We all have feelings that may be part of the message. To empathize is to listen for and respond to the feeling conveyed in the message. It is similar to reading between the lines. Knowing that empathic listening is important often enables us to foresee, and thus resolve, potential conflict.

Listening, according to Charles M. Kelley, a writer on the subject, must be empathic because "a person understands what he has heard, only to the extent that he can share in the meaning, spirit, or feeling of what the communicator has said."[4] To overcome the obvious problems of not

wanting to listen, or simply not having the ability to do so, Kelley suggests that you make a strong commitment to do so, that you prepare, that you focus on the sender as a communicator, and that you listen to him or her completely.

Assertiveness

Assertiveness is speaking and acting on the basis of our needs, speaking up when we have something to say, and committing ourselves to experiences and activities that have value for us. Our sense of self-esteem often determines how assertive we are. If we have a sense of self-worth and hold strong convictions and principles, we are likely to be assertive.

Everyone goes through periods when they don't feel very assertive. Faced with a new experience, for example, we are inclined not to call attention to ourselves. When we know that people have power over us, we usually defer to their authority. Some people, however, go through life without ever expressing their needs. They sit in the back row at meetings, let others make decisions for them, and find themselves doing things they don't like to do.

Many of us do not speak about or act on our needs because it is too risky and we are afraid of rejection and disapproval. On the other hand, unless we are assertive, we cannot take control of our lives. If we never make decisions for ourselves, we are likely to remain unhappy and even angry.

The question, then, is how can we be assertive in interpersonal relationships without putting ourselves in jeopardy? Perhaps the best guide is to understand the distinctions between aggression and assertion. Aggression is getting our own way regardless of the consequences; assertion is making our needs known in a way that is not deliberately harmful to others. It should be pointed out, however, that assertiveness can be harmful to some relationships—especially when assertion brings about a major change in who controls the relationship. For example, if a woman has done the household work by herself for ten years and then decides that her husband should share it, there will probably be a problem in working out this new relationship. In some cases, assertiveness can be risky and the cause of some relationships breaking up.

Whether our assertiveness is effective often depends on how we go about establishing it. One way is to express our needs when they occur. There is an old joke about a man who asks for a divorce after twenty years of marriage because he can no longer stand the way his wife squeezes the toothpaste tube. Many of us also make the mistake of assuming that, because others love or like us, they will know what we want. This assumption puts a burden on any relationship. If you want to be remembered on your birthday, it is a good idea to let people know that your birthday is coming up. If you want a green mohair sweater, it is better to ask for it rather than running the risk of getting an orange orlon shirt. This strategy applies to behavior as well as to objects. If you don't want people to ask why you aren't married, it is better to tell them as tactfully as possible that you don't like the question rather than being angry every time they ask you.

As with all communication, assertiveness is often a matter of how you say something as it is what you say. If you say, "I don't like your attitude," the probable reply will be, "I don't like yours either." Generally, assertive statements are much more acceptable when they are introduced with such phrases as "I might be wrong but I feel . . ." or "I feel uncomfortable when you . . ."

Although it has its risks and perils, assertiveness is important if we are going to be ourselves and speak about and act on our needs. It is the best way we have of gaining control over our lives.

Interpersonal Ethics

Because interpersonal communication deals with so much information that is personal and private, it poses particular ethical considerations. The most obvious ethical consideration is that of trust. Most of us would agree that we have an obligation not to reveal to others information we have received in confidence. Unfortunately, some of us are, by nature, indiscreet. If you fall into this category it seems only fair to warn other people that they should either not confide important personal information in you or that they should give you a special reminder that certain information is private and not to be shared with others.

Preserving social harmony is also an ethical consideration. During the 1960's there was a good deal of emphasis on communicating exactly what one was feeling and thinking. Carried to an extreme, much of this communication caused hurt feelings and distress. Although we believe that people should have relationships in which they can express their thoughts and feelings, we also believe that this is a limited freedom and should be used with care.

Certain types of communication are destructive. Manipulation, gossip, rumor, exploration are all typical examples. The destructive nature of these kinds of interpersonal communication can be circumvented by an awareness of other people's needs and feelings. If we respect the rights of others and work to participate in situations where others feel secure enough to express their own needs, feelings, and thoughts, we can create an ethical atmosphere that enhances communication. Such an atmosphere should be a goal for people who aspire to a high level of communication.

SUMMARY

Interpersonal communication is communicating with one person or several people. It is the most frequent form of communication, and it usually occurs in face-to-face situations that offer the opportunity for immediate feedback.

Interpersonal communication is affected by our cultural background, the sociological roles we play, and our psychological needs. The more we are involved in intimate relationships, the more our responses will be based on our psychological needs rather than on our sociocultural background. Interpersonal needs are for inclusion, control, and affection.

Much of interpersonal communication is determined by our relationships. Relational patterns are complementary (when people are different), and symmetrical (when people are equal). Communication behavior is also governed by whether relationships are cooperative or competitive.

All interpersonal communication involves a variety of perceptual levels that influence communication. How we see ourselves is probably the most important factor governing communication relationships.

There are many ways in which we can improve interpersonal communication. They include adaptation—altering our communication behavior to fit the circumstances—and credibility—the extent to which we are worthy of another person's confidence or trust. As speakers, we should be aware of the importance of asking questions and of self-disclosure. As listeners, we should understand the importance of avoiding evaluative judgments and of listening with empathy. All people interested in communication should be aware of assertiveness and use it when appropriate. Finally, communicators should also be aware of interpersonal ethics and work to create an atmosphere in which all participants can comfortably express their thoughts and feelings.

FURTHER READING

Anne Baxter, *Intermission*. New York: Ballantine Books, 1976.
    An autobiographical account by a Hollywood actress who left her career to marry a rancher in Australia. The book warns us that even though a relationship is based on love, problems that cannot be solved do occur.

Reuel L. Howe, *The Miracle of Dialogue.* New York: Seabury, 1963.
Expanding on the ideas of Martin Buber, the author provides a highly readable discussion of authenticity, openness, discipline, and responsibility as the characteristics of effective communication. Borrowing examples from his pastoral experience, he develops the concept of dialogue as central to communication between people as well as between individuals and God.

Rod McKuen, *Finding My Father.* Los Angeles: Cheval Books, 1977.
The author, a popular poet and musician, sets out to discover the facts of his illegitimacy and to find the father he never knew. His story reaffirms the necessity of being familiar with our personal history in order to achieve a sense of identity.

Mary Jane Moffat and Charlotte Painter (eds.), *Revelations: Diaries of Women.* New York: Vintage Books, 1974.
This book, a collection of excerpts from diaries by women, provides insight into how women have coped with their lives and problems from the nineteenth century to the present. The book shows us that human problems, regardless of time or place, remain the same.

Nena O'Neill and George O'Neill, *Open Marriage: A New Life Style for Couples.* New York: Avon Books, 1972.
On the premise that free-flowing communication is crucial to the building of an open marriage, the authors relate nonverbal communication, self-disclosure, feedback, and roles to the development of a mutual bond between independent partners in which there is maximum individual freedom and growth. This paperback is relevant for anyone involved in an intimate relationship, especially those who are married or contemplating marriage.

John Powell, S. J., *Why Am I Afraid to Tell You Who I Am?* (*Insights on Self-Awareness, Personal Growth and Interpersonal Communication*). Niles, Illinois: Argus Communications, 1969.
In this clear and succinct paperback filled with pop art and witty sayings, the author provides insights into self-awareness, growth, and communication. The material is presented in an enjoyable manner that involves the reader in ideas relating to his or her growth, emotions, and ego defenses.

Gail Sheehy, *Passages: Predictable Crises of Adult Life.* New York: E. P. Dutton & Co., 1976.
This book, probably more relevant to readers who are thirty and over, documents the crises that people encounter once they reach middle age. The book also provides insights into the goals and stresses of our society.

NOTES

[1]William Schutz, "The Postulate of Interpersonal Needs," in *Messages: A Reader in Human Communication,* 2nd ed., ed. Jean M. Civikly (New York: Random House, 1977), pp. 174–184.

[2]*Ibid.,* p. 179.

[3]Paul Watzlawick, Janet Helmick Beavin, and Don D. Jackson, *Pragmatics of Human Communication: A Study of Interactional Patterns, Pathologies, and Paradoxes* (New York: W. W. Norton, 1967).

[4]Charles M. Kelley, "Empathic Listening," in Robert S. Cathcart and Larry A. Samovar, *Small Group Communication: A Reader* (Dubuque, Iowa: William C. Brown, 1974), pp. 340–347.

chapter 3

Nonverbal
Communication

An interesting event which involved communication occurred in
Germany at the turn of the century. A schoolteacher owned a horse who
became known as Clever Hans. After the teacher retired, he devoted his
attention to teaching Hans arithmetic, to tell time, to recognize photographs, and so forth. Clever Hans learned his lessons well and responded to all the teacher's questions by tapping his hoof. Not only could
he tap out numbers, he could tap out the alphabet: one tap for "A," two
taps for "B," and so on. Even though the horse could not speak, he seemed
to understand and conceptualize in a language.

The news of Clever Hans's feat spread throughout Germany. Many
famous professors came great distances to study and marvel at the knowledgeable horse. Hans became the subject of so much research and writing
that his accomplishments began to prompt scientists to revise their views
of animal behavior.

Then the bubble burst. One researcher decided to test Clever Hans by
putting him in a position where he could not see his trainer. All the horse's
language skill disappeared, and he could no longer answer a single
question. He had been relying on his teacher's facial and body cues for the
answers—cues the teacher was not even aware of. Although Hans was

undoubtedly clever, it was clear that he had no verbal skills. He did, however, demonstrate the importance of nonverbal communication.

Albert Mehrabian, a contemporary writer on nonverbal communication, has determined from his research that as much as 93 percent of the impact of a message depends upon the nonverbal.[2] *Nonverbal elements* include anything communicated that is not specifically verbal (expressed in words). Thus the way a person uses time, space, body movements (eye contact, facial expression, gesture, posture, and motion), voice, and objects is an essential part of every message that a person sends. The cultural background of the sender greatly affects his or her use of nonverbal elements, and the list of elements could be expanded to include time of day, weather conditions, and any other variable that is not transmitted by the spoken or written word but might affect communication. However, only those elements over which we have some control or some awareness will be discussed here.

The first day you walk into a class, even before you say a single word, you are communicating. You are sending messages to everyone in sight. The way you present yourself, including how you dress and how you act, often says more about you and your feelings than anything you could say in words.

At the same time you are sending nonverbal messages, you are also, of course, receiving them. You make *observations* about the instructor and the other students in the class, just as they make observations about you. These observations are based on *cues*—specific indicators that are used to determine how another person is feeling. (A slump in posture, for example, might be a cue that a person is tired or depressed.) The cues you send provide the first impression your instructor and your classmates have of you. Later communications may change that impression, but many judgments are based on first communications. In male-female relationships, for example, the initial attraction between two people is generated by their mutual first impressions—and often the nonverbal messages are more important than the verbal ones.

The people you meet are greatly influenced by nonverbal cues. Some cues—such as space, time, body movements, voice, and objects—can be controlled by the communicator to produce the desired effect on the listener. But the communicator can exert little or no control over other cues—such as sex, race, body size, age, region of origin, social status, and, to a certain degree, the communicator's emotional state. Whether control is exerted or not, all these elements are part of any face-to-face communication situation, although, even as listeners, we are not always consciously aware of them. Much nonverbal communication exists at a low level of awareness. Although it can be significant, it is difficult to define. We often send and receive nonverbal cues unconsciously.

Most nonverbal communication involves several related messages. Posture alone is no proof that a person is sad or depressed. A number of other elements would affect our judgment—downcast eyes, an absence of gestures, and a lack of vitality in the voice. As we get to know people better, we become more familiar with their mannerisms and the way they express themselves. Cues become personalized. Some of the cues we observe in close friends are different from those we observe in strangers. With experience, we become aware of more cues, and nonverbal communication becomes even more diffuse. Think about how you indicate nonverbally to someone that you are frustrated, angry, lonely, or indifferent. Then ask someone else to demonstrate those same feelings without using words, and you will see how many different cues can be used to reveal the same emotion—an indication of the variety of nonverbal communication. Some nonverbal cues go unnoticed; others become extremely important. A nonverbal cue, just like a verbal cue, takes on meaning in the interpretation of another person.

In the models presented in the introduction to this book (see Figures 1 and 2), nonverbal communication is included as an integral part of the message. A message contains verbal stimuli (see Chapter 3) and many nonverbal stimuli. Nonverbal stimuli include space, time, body movement, objects, and vocal stimuli. In discussing the nonverbal stimuli, we will ask questions such as these: What cues is your instructor observing as he first takes notice of you? What cues are you reacting to as you begin to "psyche out" your instructor? What cues influence you to decide to go out with a member of the opposite sex? Many cues have universal application, even though the control and interpretation of cues vary from individual to individual and from society to society.

SPACE

The moment you enter a classroom you are faced with a decision that relates to how you use space. You have to decide where to sit. You may choose to sit in the back because you do not want to be noticed, because you feel that it is a "safer" distance from the teacher, because you do not want people behind you staring at you, or because it will give you an opportunity to see other students' reactions and, thus, give you confidence. You may select a front-row seat because you have a great deal of confidence and security or because you want to be noticed. Where you choose to sit is an indication of how you use space.

An instructor might interpret where you choose to sit on the first day of class as an indication of your feeling about the course. Your choosing a seat in the back row might be seen as a sign of coldness or lack of concern;

your choice of a front-row seat might be read as a sign of warmth or desire for intimacy. Of course, the instructor might not react to this particular decision at all. Your classmates may interpret the front-seat choice as "getting brownie points," "apple polishing," or trying to get a good mark. They would probably not react to the choice of a back-row seat because that is the place most often chosen by students. Students who seek to call little attention to themselves usually find seats in the middle or near the back as the most comfortable and least conspicuous.

Often we do not realize how important space is until our space is violated. A patient confined in a hospital loses space—the world shrinks from houses, fields, streets, and open spaces to an area sometimes less than ten feet by ten feet. The patient's space is violated by nurses, interns, doctors, and others who come right up and sometimes even touch. There is nothing the patient can do about it. Less dramatic examples can be found in everyday situations in which the violation of space causes tension. Conflicts often develop between roommates over the control of their dormitory space. The head of a household sometimes has a special chair, and visiting friends can inadvertently cause discomfort by sitting in the "wrong" place.

Body space—a term used to describe the personal distance we use when we communicate with others or closely associate with others —operates in much the same way. We do not realize its importance until it is violated, and then we become nervous, uncomfortable, defensive and, sometimes, even unwilling to communicate. We make judgments about how others think and how they feel toward us and toward the ideas they are communicating from the way they use their body space. Edward T. Hall, author of *The Silent Language* and *The Hidden Dimension*, two popular books on nonverbal communicationn has labeled the study of space and distance *proxemics.*[3] In our approach to proxemics—a broad concept that includes body space as well as the other uses of space—we will discuss the variables of warmth and coldness, formality and informality, and relationships and status. Following the consideration of these variables, we will discuss some of the important choices speakers can make regarding space.

Warmth and Coldness

How close you stand when you are talking to another person often reflects how you feel about that person at a particular time. Closeness generally reflects warmth. Think of yourself having an intimate conversation with a close friend; the image of physical closeness comes to mind. Think of yourself taking a seat in a doctor's waiting room full of people; you picture yourself trying to find a seat that is separate or apart from the rest of the patients. It is more comfortable to sit on a couch with two close friends than it is to sit on a couch with two strangers. A gathering of friends is more relaxing than a party with strangers because it is more enjoyable to share space with people you know.

In intimate situations such as petting or making love, the nonverbal cues used to reflect warmth are intensified. Physical closeness multiplies the channels of communication. In expressing intimacy, you not only hear and see the other person; you also touch, smell, and taste. You become enveloped in the stimuli emanating from the other person. The lover's skin and hair, body heat and fragrance, breathing and movements intensify the intimacy—feelings of warmth seldom demonstrated in public. In accidental or forced situations like riding elevators and crowded subways, the same stimuli cause uneasiness.

To compensate for accidentally being placed in close physical proximity to a stranger, we often demonstrate characteristics associated with coldness. We frown, show a lack of interest, or assume a "poker face." We often lean away from the other individual or become tense. We avoid looking in the other person's eyes, concentrating instead on the floor-indicator lights in the elevator or looking at the floor. If possible, we avoid touching the stranger. We close ourselves to the other person in every possible way—keeping him or her at some mental distance from us. Such nonverbal cues are often reinforced by the absence of any verbal communication.

To better understand the role of nonverbal cues in communicating warmth and coldness, try spending one hour responding to everything and everyone in the warmest possible way, and note the reactions you get. Do the same with coldness, and compare and contrast the results. Strive to use as many aspects of nonverbal communication as you can in your responses, and see which cues are most important in eliciting reactions from others.

Formality and Informality

Coldness and warmth are directly related to formality and informality. A formal situation tends to be colder than an informal one. Most business discourse is conducted in a formal way with participants standing from seven to twelve feet apart. Eye contact at this distance is of utmost importance because if it is not sustained, communication stops. As the distance increases, so does the formality of the situation. Interpersonal communication and most social discourse are informal and conducted at fairly close range—usually no more than a few feet apart—while public communication is more formal and conducted at quite a distance—from twelve to twenty-five feet. Speakers at public gatherings and classroom teachers are examples of those who often maintain the more formal distance.

As the distance between the source and the receiver is increased, the emphasis on nonverbal communication shifts to an emphasis on verbal communication. Words become more important because details of face and body are lost.

To show how space affects the informality or formality of a situation, consider the arrangement of an instructor's office as shown in Figure 4.1. The instructor has arranged the only other seat in the office directly across the desk from where he sits. The desk provides authority and status for the instructor as well as a barrier to communication. Conversation must occur across the desk. Formality is thus built into the situation.

Compare the above setting with that depicted in Figure 4.2. The instructor retains some of the formality by staying behind the desk but increases the informality by talking to the student directly—without speaking over the desk. This spatial arrangement is probably still not conducive to full and free conversation because it is still the instructor's office and he or she is still in control of the space. However, the informality of this arrangement is likely to increase the student's willingness to respond.

Spatial distance is also affected by the formality or informality of the message being transmitted. Chatting with a friend requires a comfortable but informal distance. Relating an experience to a stranger requires a different use of space. A serious message is often conveyed with some formality, whereas a humorous message requires informality. Think of the distance you would assume in reprimanding your roommate for putting things on your desk—your space. Now think of the distance you would use in telling him or her about something that happened on a recent date.

Spatial distance is also affected by the formality or informality of the situation. Chatting with a friend in the campus hangout often involves sitting close together. Talking with him or her in the classroom or while being watched by another person may require more distance. The arrangement of many physical spaces is determined by what happens in that space. Churches, schools, and offices seem to exude formality and distance, whereas bedrooms, some restaurants, and bars often display the opposite.

Relationship and Status

The relationship and status of those communicating also affects their use of space. When participants in a communication have an equal relat-

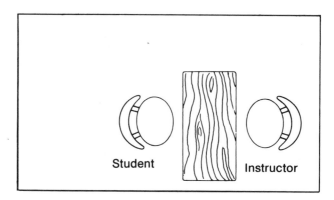

Figure 3.1

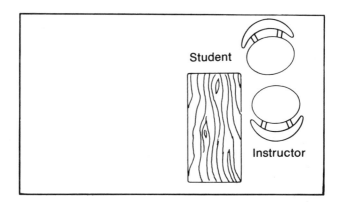

Figure 3.2

ionship, their dealings with each other are likely to be warm and in-formal. The greater the difference in status between people—such as some student-teacher, doctor-patient, and employer-employee relation-ships—the greater the spatial distance when these people are engaged in communication.

People with greater status control more space, and that space is usually more attractive. Executives, presidents of colleges, and high government officials all have large offices with windows and elaborate furnishings, while their secretaries and support staff are in smaller spaces—spaces that are often used by several people. In a household, children have the least amount of space. Even if they have their own private room, that space is often controlled by adults. It is planned and decorated by an adult, and the adult sets the rules for how the space will be used. Adults also punish children by depriving them of space. Commands

such as "Go to your room" or "Stay out of my room" limit children's access to space within the household.

When people have their own space, they can control those who enter it. One of the nonverbal factors affecting communication in the settings illustrated in Figure 3.1 and Figure 3.2 involves the relationship between the teacher and the student. If, instead of a teacher and student, the participants were doctor and patient, one would expect the furniture arrangement to be more like Figure 3.1 than 3.2. If two friends were talking, one would expect the arrangement to be more like Figure 3.2. If the student and the teacher "hit it off" well together, 3.2 would be preferred to 3.1.

As an exercise, think about the spatial arrangements you would expect to find in several settings and try to visualize the results. Imagine talking with the President of the United States and standing within an arm's length of him with nothing between you. Imagine talking with a good friend about a personal topic from a distance of twelve feet.

In many situations it is possible to change spatial relationships. For example, if you entered an office, you could change the chair from the position shown in Figure 3.1 to the position in 3.2. It is important to remember, however, that space is often deliberately planned and controlled to indicate status and power. If you initiate a change in someone else's space, you could jeopardize the relationship and the communication.

Choices about Space for Speakers

How close a speaker stands to his audience can reflect a range of qualities—from formality and coldness when the distance is great to informality and warmth when the distance between the speaker and the audience is small. A speaker's choices about space are likely to be dependent upon the topic, the audience, the occasion, and the location. These factors will not always be clear-cut distinctions; they are directly related to each other in every communication setting.

The Topic   If a speaker chooses to reminisce with an audience or to relate a series of anecdotes or stories, a close, informal, and warm distance would be appropriate. If, instead, the speaker chooses an issue that requires presentation of information or evidence, a more formal distance might be more appropriate. Generally, a topic that the audience might be hostile to—such as increasing taxes—is best given at a formal distance. When people are resistant to your ideas, it is better not to move too quickly into their space.

The Audience   The audience should figure prominently in any decision the speaker makes about space, for their expectations may affect the success of the speech. Do they expect a formal address? Do they expect a warm, personal message? Would they be offended if the speaker left the platform and moved among them? Would they feel dismay if, instead, the speaker spoke formally from the lectern and never approached them at all?

The influence of audience expectations can sometimes be seen when a political candidate is going to speak. When the audience knows that the candidate is planning to deliver a major-policy address, there seems to be less of a desire and opportunity to reach out and touch the candidate. If, on the other hand, the stop is just another in a whole list of stops, they demand that the candidate move among them, speak informally, and make specific references to the locale in a warm, personal manner. A major-policy speech usually occurs in a formal atmosphere, whereas town-to-town campaigning demands immediacy and contact.

The size and the age of the audience may also be governing factors. A large audience demands distance so that all can see; if the audience is composed of from three to fifteen people, sitting among them might be more effective. An elementary-school audience might prefer this arrangement as long as everyone can see and hear. An elderly audience might prefer to have the speaker stand before them. Such generalizations, however, should be considered in the context of the total situation. The topic, occasion, and location should be reviewed along with the expectations, size, and age of the audience.

The Occasion   Most Sunday sermons require some distance between the minister and the congregation. Most teachers lecture with some distance between themselves and the class. Formal occasions such as commencements, student-government meetings, and state-of-the-nation addresses require this same distance. In these cases, the occasion governs the decision about where the speaker will stand.

Other occasions are informal. A poetry reading, class discussion, or committee meeting are all occasions when communication will be more effective if the participants sit together. The informal setting gives the participants a chance to interact.

The Location   Choices about spatial distance may be governed by the physical setting in which the communication takes place. A campus assembly hall generally has a lectern located at the middle of the head table because speeches given there are often fairly formal. A campus organization holding its first mass meeting in such a hall may wish to convey informality by placing a chair for the speaker in front of the lectern. There can be a great deal of flexibility in defining space in a public-speaking situation, or there may be no possibility for flexibility at all.

The effect of changes in the choice and use of space by the participants in a small group may be an important factor in stimulating active and enthusiastic participation. A small room is usually more suitable than a corner of a large hall for such communication. People find it easiest to communicate with those directly in front of them and hardest to communicate with those seated next to them. The person who sits at the head of the table is almost always looked upon as the leader of the discussion. Also, a strong feeling of cohesiveness or unity can sometimes be achieved if the members' chairs are grouped closely together.

The topic, the audience, the occasion, and the location are always significant factors in determining how other people will respond to your message. Seeking the greatest amount of control possible over these elements helps assure success. However, generalizations about one's use of space must be considered just that—generalizations. People behave differently and generalizing about their behavior is not always successful. To become more effective as a communicator or as a receiver, one has to be aware of both the generalizations and the possibility of exceptions.

TIME

Another factor that may have bearing on an instructor's first impressions of you concerns your use of time. When do you arrive for class? Are you the first one there or do you arrive after class has already begun? If you arrive late, you are probably noticed more than if you arrive early. Often, it is the extreme—the one who arrives very early or the one who arrives very late—that attracts attention, and of the two, the latecomer in our society, and especially on certain occasions, arouses the most negative feelings.

At one time or another we all use time for psychological effect. If you have a date with someone you don't know very well, you probably will not arrive too early because you might appear to be too eager. If you dent the family car, you wait for the right time to tell your parents about it. Our control of time is one of the most important forms of nonverbal communication.

As with space, we do not always appreciate the part time plays in our lives until control of it is taken from us. Just as patients in hospitals lose control over space, they also lose control over time and, like prisoners, are forced to do things when other people want them to. Tied to an institutional schedule, their lack of control over something considered second nature in other situations can cause anger, suspicion, and irritability. Students often feel similar frustration because so much of their time is spent doing other people's tasks. Teachers feel hindered and confined by the ritual of the fifty-minute class hour, which is often unrelated to learning activity. Workers, too, become frustrated by the five-day, nine-to-five, forty-hour weekly routine.

Status and Dominance

High-status people in our society have more control over time than those of low status. Doctors are examples of high-status people; they usually make patients wait in waiting rooms and then again, in various stages of discomfort and undress, in examining rooms. Even among doctors, however, patients are treated differently. Those asking for a diagnosis from a high-priced specialist will probably not have to wait very long, while those who go to walk-in clinics often have to wait for several hours for medical attention.

High-level executives in institutions such as corporations and government all have secretaries who control access to their time. If you are successful in getting to see executives, you are often told that the time they can spend with you is limited.

Those who have the lowest status in our society are forced to wait the longest. If you are an immigrant to the United States and have to solve an immigration problem in New York City, you are given a number in the immigration office and must wait your turn. If you are on welfare or unemployment, you must stand in line to make your application and to receive your check. If you are poor and can't afford a car, you have to wait in line for the bus.

Parents and children are other examples of low-status figures who have little control over their time. A parent with a small child must stop whatever he or she is doing to attend to the needs of the child. In the case of the mother, even when she is working full-time, she is most often the member of the family who must give up her time in order to prepare meals, take care of the children, and clean the house. Children have the least control over time. They eat at a specific meal time, they go to bed when they are told, and even when they are involved in fascinating activities, they can be interrupted by adults.

Formality and Informality

Business appointments and arrangements tend to be more formal than social get-togethers. You would want to be on time for a job interview, whereas you might not worry about being present at the beginning of a picnic or dance. The person who arrives early for a party scheduled for eight o'clock might find the host or hostess still preparing for the party—perhaps still getting dressed. On the other hand, someone who is late to a dentist's appointment may find that another person has been given his or her appointment time. The latecomer may be billed for the visit, too, despite the fact that he or she never saw the dentist. Considerations regarding time often change with the formality or informality of the occasion.

It is important for communicators to take note of the formality of the occasion when timing is important. A message designed for presentation on radio must be prepared with very careful consideration of time, whereas a message designed for most other occasions does not require the same concern. Being prepared to make wise use of a fifteen-minute job interview requires preparation and forethought because of the formalized time restriction, as does making good use of the five minutes allowed for a class speech exercise. It becomes a question of when you can loosen up and relax a bit and when you need to be highly structured and fairly rigid. With good preparation and a tightly planned presentation, most people can decrease the formality if the situation calls for it.

Tasks and Time

If you are interviewing someone for a television newsclip, you will handle the time you have differently than if you are talking with a member of the opposite sex to find out if you want to date that person. A group of people with a time limit and a problem to solve operate quite differently from a group of people who want to explore a variety of feelings or ideas about a particular topic with no time restriction. The central issue— whether one is speaking of interpersonal or small-group communication— is the relationship between the time available and the task at hand.

The time taken to complete an undertaking often depends on the communicator. Some people have the ability to get to the heart of an issue in a very efficient manner: the employer who learns all he really needs to know in a matter of three to five minutes; the teacher who finds out with one or two questions whether a student has read the material she assigned the night before. Efficiency in communication is often what makes certain situations exciting or engaging. The number of new, different, or relevant ideas, the extent of accomplishment, the number of quality ideas being generated are all likely to be a result of how well time is used. Test the theory that efficiency creates an interest by thinking about the last speech you enjoyed listening to and why you liked it. It is probably because the speaker used his or her time efficiently. This is as important in small groups as it is in giving speeches. Your decision to continue participating in a small group may depend on how efficiently the group uses its time.

Efficiency in the completion of a task is important, but different viewpoints and feelings should not be sacrificed for the sake of efficiency. In any endeavor, time should be allowed for exploration. Investigation and thorough inquiry provide a solid foundation for creativity, since a creative effort usually evolves when your thoughts or your imagination are stimulated by the ideas and opinions of others. Some tasks also take longer to complete than others and the task can involve other goals besides the solution of a problem or the completion of a decision. A task may include the gathering of information or the expression of personal feelings on a topic or issue. Thus, time must be related to the specific task at hand.

Choices about Time for Speakers

Although public speakers are bound by time restrictions, they frequently could present their ideas more efficiently and in less time. A half-hour speech to a group of forty people takes up twenty "people-hours." The longer a public speaker is allowed to talk, the more likely the audience will become bored and inattentive. A speaker's choices about time are likely to depend on the topic, the audience, the occasion, and the location. Just as in the case of space and its limitations, these factors will not always be clear-cut; they are directly related to each other in every communication setting.

The Topic   Select a topic that you can reasonably expect to cover with some depth and thoroughness within the time limit provided. You cannot expect to convince an audience to change the world in a ten-minute speech—nor the country, the city, or even the college. In a ten-minute speech your best bet would probably be to choose a manageable topic—to ask for a specific change in a class assignment, a library procedure, or a change in the menu at the student cafeteria. The shorter the amount of time allowed for a speech, the narrower, or more specific, the topic should be.

In planning the delivery of the speech, the communicator should also be concerned about timing. Strategic pacing of the information that supports the topic may make the difference between an exciting and a dull communication. The speaker may want to provide the audience some lead time—a prelude to the message or topic that is coming. Suspense can sometimes be created if examples and facts are stated first and the topic or essential message is delayed.

The Audience   Speakers should be sensitive to the audience's needs and expectations. A speaker who follows five other speakers will have a much better chance for a warm response if his or her remarks are brief and to the point. Even if there is only one speaker, a succinct and concise address will show respect for the audience. Nothing bores listeners more than repetition and rambling. One way to cure the habit of talking too much is by imagining that you are talking long-distance at day rates.

The Occasion   Perhaps the greatest influence on timing of a speech concerns the overall time restrictions for specific occasions. An after-dinner speech calls for brief, usually humorous comments. A commencement requires more lengthy, serious remarks. Think of a variety of different occasions where talks are given—club, assembly, student government, class, church—and you will become aware that certain standards are imposed to determine how long the speaker talks. In most cases, a certain amount of time is allotted for the speaker.

The Location   If you were giving a rallying speech to a group of students at the center of campus, you would probably give a short speech if the weather were bad or there were no place to sit. In the days of the American lyceum—a debate and lecture society formed in many communities during the nineteenth century—traveling lecturers often had to cut their speeches short because of poor heating or poor lighting in the buildings in which they were asked to speak. Ventilation, acoustics, lighting, and weather are some of the factors that might cause a speaker to speak for a shorter time, to increase his or her remarks, or to better adapt them to the situation.

BODY MOVEMENT

Jurgen Ruesch and Weldon Kees, pioneers in nonverbal communication research, divide nonverbal communication into three parts: sign language, action language, and object language.[4] We use *sign language* when we use a gesture or vocal tone to stand for a word, number, or punctuation mark. The clenched, upraised fist, for example, is a gesture often used by groups making strong demands. In the same way, a particular tone of voice may serve as an exclamation point, question mark, or period.

We use *action language* all the time; it includes all bodily movements that do not have the primary function of communicating. Walking, running, and sitting are examples. *Object language* communicates through the display of material objects on the human body. Both intentional and unintentional display are included. We wear an engagement ring or a wedding band with purpose. Our choice of clothing, on the other hand, may be without conscious intent.

Whether it is sign, action, or object language, we use the body for two nonverbal functions: to reinforce our verbal message—the words we use—and to reveal our attitudes and emotions. When you cannot believe what another person is saying, you might express your dismay verbally ("I can't believe you are saying that") and nonverbally by turning away from the other person, shaking your head, and sighing. You have not only reinforced your verbal message of disbelief, but you have revealed your frustration—your feeling—as well.

Much of nonverbal communication relates, in some way, to body movement. Space and time refer, in part, to the movement of the body in a setting. The manner in which any part of the body is moved relates directly to both space and time, for it is moved within a specified space and in a specific period of time. Ray L. Birdwhistell, a founder of research in the study of communication through bodily movements, called this study *kinesics.*[5] Our treatment of kinesics will cover the nonverbal aspects of eye contact, facial expression, gesture, and posture and motion.

Eye Contact

The last time an instructor asked a question that you could not or did not want to answer, what did you do with your eyes? You probably avoided the instructor's eyes by looking down at the floor or at the notebook on your desk. By shifting your eyes away from the instructor, you were attempting to break contact—to show that you did not want to respond. The degree to which this cue was effective may have been a result of how many others wanted to respond or how aware the instructor was of your motives.

In communication, eye contact works in three basic ways. It aids in giving attention and indicating inclusion; it shows intensity of feeling; and it provides feedback. In discussing attention, we will approach eye contact from both the source's and the receiver's viewpoints.

Attention and Inclusion   The last time you spoke intimately with another person, you probably maintained very direct eye contact at the same time. When you look directly into someone else's eyes, you reveal that you are attentive and that you want that person's full attention. When a communication is direct, eye contact is strong. By not looking at a person when you communicate, you effectively shut that person out of the communication. In small-group communication, stronger members can isolate weaker members by not communicating eye to eye with them. But with full attention to everyone and by everyone, feelings of inclusion are intensified, and cohesiveness—the state of being united—becomes greater.

Effective communicators both send and receive eye messages. Many of the messages we could receive are missed because of poor eye contact. There is no surer way to lose a receiver than by avoiding direct eye contact—letting your eyes wander to the floor, to the walls, to the ceiling, or to notes. As a communicator, you need to be concerned about all your listeners. Too often, for example, in public-speaking classes, students have a tendency to direct their comments to the instructor instead of to the whole class.

Since we spend more time receiving messages than sending them, eye contact has to be considered from the listener's side as well. A receiver who is interested in a communicator's message will listen attentively—revealing this attention through sustained eye contact. Receivers who do not look at the communicator often block the communication because the sender is cut off from the feedback he or she needs.

As the number of people with whom you are communicating increases, all must be included by your eye contact in order to feel that they have a part in the transaction. One neighbor can effectively give the "cold shoulder" to other neighbors by not looking at them as they approach. When you are engaged in a conversation with another person and a third person comes up to you, it is thoughtful and warm to shift your stance slightly to open toward the person who is joining you, and to look that person in the eye as he or she approaches. You are, in effect, receiving the other person and showing that he or she is welcome, even if you do not stop your conversation. In many cases, such eye contact can serve as effectively as if you had turned to the other person and welcomed him or her.

Intensity   Eye contact also reveals intensity of feeling. In intimate situations it often shows warmth, in other situations, coldness or anger. To say "I love you" or "I want to help you" or "I care about you" and to have the message received warmly, the one expressing concern must look the other in the eyes. One study found that happy newly married couples look at each other more frequently than unhappy newly married couples. Think of the courting behavior in our society. Boy meets girl—girl looks away and down. As the relationship grows and more familiarity is established, eye contact becomes stronger, more intense, even more meaningful. The officer, on the other hand, who is "chewing out" a subordinate may look the subordinate directly in the eye with the intention of revealing the intensity of his anger. The father who is reprimanding his child may use intense eye contact to reveal his utter dissatisfaction with the child's behavior. He may demand of the child, "Look at me when I am speaking to you!"

Sometimes the absence of eye contact can give an impression of aloofness that is misleading. For instance, if you feel a sudden rush of warm feeling for another person, you may avert your eyes to hide the intensity of your feelings—fearing, perhaps, that the other person will be overwhelmed by them. Strong disapproval or anger may also be conveyed by refusing to meet the eyes of the offending person. Thus, either the presence or absence of eye contact may indicate strong feelings.

Feedback   In addition to being an indicator of attention and feeling, eye contact also provides feedback. You have probably tried to talk to a person wearing dark glasses and found the situation difficult. You did not know if you had the other person's attention; you were not even sure he or she was looking at you. If you have experienced this problem—a barrier to effective communication—you know the value of eye contact.

An alert public speaker can get valuable feedback from an audience by maintaining eye contact. The audience will indicate if it is interested, confused, or content to listen for more. This feedback enables the speaker to restructure his or her message if it is not being received the way he or she intended.

You begin to understand how effective good eye contact can be when you realize what it is like to be left out of someone's eye contact. If you have ever been an outsider, put yourself in the position of the listener. As the communicator, you can make receivers feel wanted; you can set them at ease; you can even excite them. Your eyes serve as the first electrical connection with your audience—they turn on the current. Often, the amount of enthusiasm and interest you generate once you have made the connection is dependent on how much current flows.

Facial Expression

The face is one of the most expressive parts of the body. The way you move your forehead, eyebrows, eyes, mouth, tongue, lips, and chin communicates something about you. How others will react to these cues cannot be determined precisely, but they will react and they will react in different ways. Facial cues such as smiles or frowns can be controlled. Other facial characteristics caused by age or poor health are beyond our control. We have all made hasty judgments about a person based on facial cues and then changed our initial impressions after we got to know the person better.

Facial cues are important in any communication, and the closer the receiver is to the sender, the more important the facial cues are. In intimate situations, the receiver can probably see more expressions on the sender's face than in settings where the distance between the receiver and sender is great. At a distance, gestures often take the place of facial expression as far as indicating attitudes and emotions is concerned.

The best facial cues are natural ones. One does not, generally, practive smiling to reveal warmth or practice frowning to reveal unfreindliness. However, if one is aware that the cue being received by the listener is not the one intended, then the sender is in a position to at least find out the reason for the discrepancy and attempt to clear it up. A public speaker can analyze the facial expressions revealed during a speech in a videotape session. Seldom is criticism necessary, for the videotape speaks for itself. If the intention and the reception match, success has been achieved.

The importance of facial cues in communication is indicated by the number of colloquial expressions in the English language that describe the use of the face. The expressions, "poker-faced," or "two-faced" indicate use of the face to hide true feelings. A person may be condemned for telling a "bold-faced lie." When you are bold in another sense, one might say that you "have the face" to ask for or to do something; when you're in trouble, you may try to "save face." Facial expressions are important. Thus, you should try to "put a good face on the matter."

Gestures

Our use of gestures is often related to our personality and cultural background. Extroverts usually gesture more than introverts; people with a southern European or African background are likely to gesture more expansively than those who have a northern European background. If gestures are spontaneous and natural, they can make a message more lively and interesting. We can all recall the speaker who, by using gestures to describe a person or situation, made us "see" what he or she was talking about.

Gesture is important in public speaking. Often, because of the distance between the public speaker and the audience, gesture must take the place of facial expressions, which are lost because the listener cannot see them. Gesture is closely associated with emotion, for when the speaker becomes more involved in the material or seeks to reveal greater intensity, the gestures, too, often become more expansive or more intense. If a speaker stands before you immobile, how involved can you be with what that speaker is saying? The animated, vigorous, and enthusiastic speaker often stimulates the audience to respond in kind.

Using gestures before an audience is sometimes difficult; many people are inhibited in front of others. Although we may "talk with our hands" in interpersonal communication, we often cannot successfully transfer this important skill to a public-speaking situation. But if we make a conscious effort to use more gestures than we would normally, we may achieve the correct balance. Natural gestures that support and reinforce the verbal message will seldom be distracting.

Gestures should never distract from communication: When a listener pays more attention to what your hands are doing than to what you are saying with words, you are either gesturing too much or gesturing incorrectly. If the attention of a listener is distracted by a gesture—or anything else about the speaker's nonverbal behavior—that listener is not giving full attention to the speaker's verbal message.

Touch

We are all familiar with the use of touch in intimate situations. We kiss babies, hold hands with loved ones, and hug family members. In interpersonal relationships, however, touch is governed by a strict set of societal rules.

Nancy Henley, a researcher and writer in nonverbal communication, has presented considerable evidence to show that touch is a way of establishing dominance and status. The dominant person in a relationship is free to touch members of lower status.[6] A boss can touch a secretary, a priest can touch a communicant, a teacher can touch a student, and so forth. Since men are often viewed as dominant in our society, they are likely to touch women before women touch them. Any woman who works in a bar will tell you that she is often touched by men—something over which she has little control.

The reverse situation, however, is not true.[7] Most of us would not touch our boss, priest, teacher, or customer. Although adults can touch children they know, children soon learn that they are not free to touch adults until they are invited to do so.

An awareness of touching and the societal rules governing it reveal a great deal about status and power. Touch is not a random activity without meaning; it is an important communication strategy.

Posture and Motion

Posture is the arrangement and position of the body and the limbs as a whole. It can reflect your inner motivation and your intentions, as well as your attitude. When you first come into a class, your posture may very well reveal your feeling about the class. If you "drag" yourself into a class, reluctantly and with a great deal of skepticism and anxiety, your posture will probably reveal this lack of enthusiasm. This may be an exaggeration. Nonetheless, one of the best ways to reflect an I-could-care-less attitude is with your whole body. Have you ever wondered why the armed services encourages the military posture? "Stomach in, chest out, shoulders back!" The military is convinced that posture reflects attitude. It must be admitted that there is a certain amount of truth in the military's reasoning that the soldier who looks alert is alert.

Take a few moments sometime and observe the way people walk. It is

often possible to speculate about the importance of their mission by the way they move. The carefree person who has time to spare reveals an entirely different posture than the person who is running slightly behind in time in arriving at an important meeting. When you are relaxed, your whole body appears unconstrained and at ease; when you are tense, it is stiff and strained. The person who is a bundle of nerves, or who has an overactive thyroid, often manifests continual activity that one could interpret as the important pursuit of business, dedication to the task, or a "positive" use of time. The person who has time to spare is easygoing, often indifferent, and coolly unconcerned. It is the person's posture, in part, that provides the clue—even though we may not always be successful in reading the clue accurately.

Posture is important in communication because it can reveal the communicator's attitude toward the message and the receiver. The person who is interested in conveying a message may lean slightly toward the person or persons for whom the message is intended. A positive attitude toward the person with whom one is communicating may also cause one to lean toward him or her. A drooping, careless, awkward, or rigid stance could reflect a lack of interest and, perhaps, dislike. Albert Mehrabian, in a study of the transmission of attitudes by body posture, found that a communicator's body posture can reveal three different kinds of perceptions about the status of the person with whom he is comminicating: a relaxed body posture is assumed if the other person is perceived to be of lower status than himself; a less relaxed body posture will be assumed if the other person is perceived to be of equal status; and a tense body posture will be assumed if the other person is perceived to be of higher status.[8]

In the United States the word *slouch* has come to mean an inefficient or inferior person. Thus, the way you carry yourself will probably be responsible for the image you create when you are standing with another person, sitting in a group, standing before a group of people, or even reacting to another communicator. Just as the speaker's posture can reveal the speaker's attitude toward the topic, the purpose of the communication, or the listener, so, too, the listener's posture, according to Mehrabian, can reveal whether he feels threatened, whether he likes the communicator, and whether he feels the communicator's status is higher or lower than his own. Whatever the observations reveal, both communicator and listener should realize that the way they carry themselves can set the mood for the communication as well as determine its results.

Body motion is often as important as posture in providing cues. Movement on the platform, movement while talking to another person, or movement before a camera can be important. A skillful public speaker will, in general, try not to confine delivery to speaking from behind a lectern. Changes in thoughts and attitudes, as well as transitions from one idea to another, can be reflected by the body motion of a speaker. If you are developing a thought, moving in a new direction, or changing a mood, you may want to shift your body position. A change in body position may involve coming out from behind a lectern, turning to face another part of the audience, or taking a few steps one way or the other. Changes in body position suggest that you are comfortable in front of the audience. They also reveal that you are in command of the situation; you appear to know what you are doing. We often use these same cues when we are talking to another person. In addition, we may turn our body slightly to include another person who has joined us or turn our body slightly to those we are addressing. Interest and involvement in communication with another individual are revealed by facing that person squarely.

Body motions often reveal the intentions of a person to involve or exclude others—even if these are unintentional movements. Think of getting onto a bus or train and sitting next to a person you do not know. Your body motions will probably reflect coldness; you may cross your legs away from the individual or lean in the opposite direction. You will try not to impose any more than necessary on the other person's body space. If, however, you strike up a conversation with the person and receive a warm response, you may slowly change your position. You may uncross your legs for a moment and then cross them toward the other person. You may shift your position and even lean slightly toward the other person. Infringement of the other person's body space no longer seems inappropriate, for you have now shared each other's thoughts, and sharing each other's body space is a logical extension of that. In a small-group setting, as more participants contribute and more thoughts are shared, the corresponding tendency is for members to lean in toward the center of the group. The person who slouches in the chair, maintains a drooping body postition, or fails to move his or her body toward the center of the group may be overlooked or slighted in the discussion. A person who looks and acts alert invites others to react by moving toward him or her.

VOICE

There is a clear distinction between a person's use of words (verbal communication) and a person's use of voice. *Vocal nonverbal communication*, or paralanguage, includes such characteristics as pace, inflection, loudness, and tone. These factors coexist with the words and modify them in a variety of ways. In all speech, vocal nonverbal communication has tremendous potential for influencing the meaning of the speaker's verbal message as interpreted by the listener. Albert Mehrabian estimates that 38 percent of the social meaning in the communication process is stimulated by the vocal cues—not the words that are spoken but the way in which they are said.[9]

The *pace*—the rate or speed at which one speaks—can have various effects on the way the message is received. A very rapid rate for five minutes or more can dull the senses just as a very slow pace can have the same effect. Variety is important. A message of high emotional intensity may require a slightly faster pace, whereas a shift to a very important note or comment might require a slow and very determined rate. Mehrabian suggests that a communicator's pace is increasingly affected by speech errors as his anxiety increases. Anger, stress, and fear can be associated with faster speeds, whereas grief or depression can be associated with slower rates. The speaker will hold the attention of the listener best if the pace of speaking changes with the nature of the ideas, the mood, and the kind of feedback the speaker receives.

Inflection varies with the changes in pitch according to meaning. The phrase "That is great" can convey a whole range of meanings, depending on the relative pitch one uses for the different words in the phrase. You might say, "That is *great!*" (It really is the most exciting and interesting thing you've heard all day.) Or you might say, "*That* is great?" (You must be kidding; it's the dumbest thing I've ever seen in my whole life.) Or "That *is* great" (It is surprising and delightful to discover the significance and interest of this thing.) Note that the verbal message is the same in all three examples. The nonverbal use of voice inflection produces the intended meaning in each case.

Loudness is the strength with which the voice is used. No one likes to be yelled at, just as no one likes to have to strain to listen. A speaker who always uses high intensity must learn to modulate the voice to gain variety of tone. A loud voice is fine if used for a particular purpose and in moderation. Low intensity works the same way. Certain ideas, because of their importance, require more intensity or loudness of expression than others. If all of the speaker's points are delivered with the same intensity, the delivery will, like a fast pace, tend to dull the senses.

Tone is the quality or characteristic of a sound. It is a broad characteristic that generally varies according to the type of message being conveyed, the nature of the situation, and the kind of audience. A message of love being conveyed to a very intimate friend in the privacy of one's home has a very different tone from a message of protest delivered to the administration in a meeting hall. A funeral oration is different in tone than one given at a Fourth of July celebration. Finally, the audience may influence one's choice of tone. For example, a speech about women's liberation before an all-male audience would be different in tone from the same speech before an all-female audience. We talk differently in the dorm before friends than we do in the classroom before other students or at home before members of our family.

A sense of tone is something that develops as we grow up and is so much a part of us that we are barely conscious of it. There are few guiding principles. The effective speaker will vary his tone according to the message, the situation, and the audience—depending on what tone is most appropriate in reinforcing the communication and best conveys the attitudes and emotions of the communicator.

All the nonverbal cues often combine to tell the listener more about us than we want the other person to know. Although we have some degree of control over vocal cues, most of the time we do not give a great deal of thought to the way we use our voices. We are accustomed to them and often forget that others who hear us for the first time are making judgments based on them. No matter what the situation, the listener receives important cues from our voices whether we intend to convey them or not. Because voice is an important nonverbal cue, we should all be more conscious of its effective use.

OBJECTS

Ruesch and Kees define *object language* as the nonverbal cues that are conveyed through the display and use of material things, including the human body and the way it is clothed.[10] In addition to objects of clothing, we will also discuss objects worn with clothes and objects used in communication settings. The mere presence of objects communicates nonverbally.

When you enter a classroom on the first day of class, your clothing may be one of the cues to which others, including the instructor, respond in making initial assessments of you. What you choose to wear is an area over which you exert a fair amount of control, although your culture, your particular society, your peers, and sometimes even the school exert pressure on you to dress in a certain way. Whatever choices you make about the way you dress, these choices provide cues to which others can and do respond. The judgments that we make of others on the basis of their dress tend to reflect the norms of our particular subculture or peer group. Thus, what is perceived as an excessively tight sweater in one region of the country might be perfectly acceptable in another. Choices of clothing tend to communicate a great deal about the personality of the wearer, and interpretations of this nonverbal cue reveal a great deal about the viewer.

The objects we choose to wear with our clothes also have communicative significance. Lapel pins, earrings, fraternity or sorority pins, college rings, eyeglasses, or cosmetics all say something about us.

Most of us like to feel that we are not greatly influenced by what another person wears; we prefer to think that we judge a person by what he or she *is*. However, clothing is a powerful preoccupation in our society, and the advertising media encourage us to behave as if clothes do make the person. You can become more aware of the degree to which your own perceptions of other people are influenced by their clothing and also of the messages that you convey by your own dress by carrying out a simple exercise. Sit in some public area and observe the people around you, asking yourself what kind of people you think they are and to what extent your perception is colored by their clothing. What, for example, do you assume about a conservatively dressed man who is carrying a leather briefcase? How do you react to a woman who is wearing disheveled, unironed clothing? Then, take a look at yourself in a full-length mirror as you prepare to go out for the day. What are you saying to other people?

The objects we choose to handle as we communicate also convey nonverbal messages. Playing with objects such as pens or jewelry may reflect nervousness or boredom. Some distracting mannerisms become unconscious habits that are automatic and difficult to interpret. The way cigarettes and cups of coffee are handled can give clues about people. Pencils, papers, and sometimes anything that is handy may become distracting diversions as well.

In communication situations like an interview, the objects in a room can say a great deal about the interviewer. The arrangement of furniture, as discussed in the section on space, may reflect warmth or coldness. A nameplate on the desk—what it says and how it is made—can convey formality or informality. Pictures on the wall and a carpet on the floor might reveal a cozy informal atmosphere. Magazines on the desk can disclose that the interviewer is informed of current happenings in his or her field or in the world. These objects may have been deliberately chosen, but whether chosen or not, they do convey a message to those who see them.

When you are communicating in a public situation, you may have an opportunity to control the objects around you, or the objects may be controlled for you in such a way as to convey an impression that someone else desires. Whether or not you use a lectern may determine the degree of formality of the presentation. Whether a meeting is held in a classroom, a church, a large hall, a school, or in someone's home may determine the tone of that meeting. Whether you are seated in a chair in front of an audience or seated on a table certainly makes a difference. Flags, banners, and signs have a great deal of communicative significance. They add, for example, to the pomp and pageantry of a speech before a national party convention, just as picket signs help to provide some of the mood for protest speeches.

The objects you select to wear, to handle, and to use in a particular setting convey a message. As with all other nonverbal cues, you should make sure that the impression they give is the one you intend, for their impact may, in part, determine how another person responds to you—even to the extent of determining whether that person wants to listen or respond at all.

MIXED MESSAGES

Many messages are sent simultaneously by verbal and nonverbal means. When these two methods of expression confirm and complement each other, the total message is clearer because one reinforces the other. However, trying to make a correct judgment about the meaning of a message is often difficult if the message being sent verbally and the message being sent nonverbally contradict each other. Such a contradiction between the two will be referred to as *mixed communication.*

Perhaps on the first day of this class you heard your instructor say something like, "I feel that instructors should make themselves available to their students. Thus, you can see me anytime." As soon as the class was over, you went up to the instructor to ask a question about the course. As you watched him or her pack away the lecture notes, snap shut the briefcase, and nervously look at the clock while talking to you and moving toward the door, you realized that he or she was saying one thing but meant another. You were caught in the contradiction of a mixed communication.

What does a person really mean when he says, "I like you" in a cold tone of voice? What is a child to believe when the parent talks about the importance of honesty and then cheats on his income tax? What is a student to believe when the professor encourages disagreement but gets very upset when she receives any?

Anyone can pay lip service to a belief, a creed, or a cause; it is what a person does that counts. Actions *do* speak louder than words. We tend to believe the nonverbal communication—not the words—because the nonverbal behavior is harder to counterfeit. It is more powerful in communicating feelings, and because it is more natural—that is, more a part of us—it is more difficult to control. To communicate our messages clearly and accurately to others, we need to be skillful in both the nonverbal and the verbal means of expression. It is also important to make the nonverbal and verbal agree with each other.

Certain social situations may dictate that the nonverbal and verbal messages need not be in agreement. When you ask another person, "How are you?" the inevitable reply, no matter what the other person's actual physical or mental condition is, will be "Fine" unless, of course, the person is a very close associate and you have asked the question with deep concern or interest. We have many similar verbal formulas that we use in a variety of situations: "It's a pleasure to meet you"; "You look nice"; "That was a good speech"; "Thank you so much, we had a wonderful time"; "You will come again, won't you?"; "See you later"; "Take care." The list is nearly endless. Such responses fill a need. They often serve as an acknowledgment of another person. They might provide a brief introduction for a more extended relationship. They often serve to terminate an encounter and let everyone know: "That is all there is; there isn't any more," even though the literal content of the verbal message is often meaningless or even false.

CULTURE AND THE NONVERBAL

Much of our nonverbal behavior is learned from childhood, passed on to us by our parents and others with whom we associate. Through the process of growing up in a particular society, we adopt the traits, mannerisms, and activities of our societal group. The ways of living that are passed on to succeeding generations are known as a society's *culture*; they are a major factor in why people communicate as they do. A society, however, also contains subunits or *subcultures*. Although we may exhibit the traits of the larger unit, smaller groups with which we may associate become more specific frames of reference for certain ways of communicating.

A person's membership in a youth subculture, the radical right, a black subculture, an ethnic subculture, the WASP middle class, the anarchistic left, or the "jet set" is communicated to others nonverbally by the cues that we have discussed in this chapter. Members of activist groups, for instance, have special ways of dressing, a special vocabulary, and even special mannerisms that enable members to identify and to communicate with each other. Such systems of communication provide rewards for those within the subculture, because using common terms and experiences gives members a special sense of identity and permits the group to unify.

In most communication situations, you have at least some control over your body movement, voice, and use of objects, but you do not ordinarily think of controlling the cultural aspects that have influenced you. The various pressures to conformity that a culture imposes exert a great deal of influence on your behavior. Those cultural elements that are revealed to others are permanent and inseparable, for the most part. Changing or controlling communication behavior that is culturally determined is extremely difficult. It is useful, however, to become more aware of those behaviors that are a result of social training, especially when one is involved in intercultural communication. Nonverbal behavior is most noticeably affected by culture in the way we control space, time, eye contact, touch, gesture, and voice.

Space

When you talk to another person, how far away do you stand? It is usually about an arm's length. The space is not consciously controlled every time you speak with someone because the appropriate distance is determined by your culture. In some cultures, the accepted distance between two people engaged in communication is smaller. In the United States we tend to interpret distances between people that are smaller than an arm's length as reflecting a need for privacy or indicating a close relationship.

Test the theory that an arm's length apart is the general, acceptable space in which most Americans operate most comfortably by slowly reducing the distance between you and another person with whom you are talking. You will find that the other person will unconsciously withdraw to find the acceptable distance. Remember that in our culture, moving in on someone is often interpreted as being pushy or overbearing. (You are "coming on too strong.") If you move away slightly, your behavior may be interpreted as avoidance or concealment or that you do not like the other person.

Time

Time affects communication between people in different cultures in various ways. An American, for example, does not like to be kept waiting. Often, five minutes is enough to make one edgy, and waiting for ten minutes might make one very angry. Anyone who keeps us waiting, according to our cultural standards, shows no concern for us and treats us with contempt. But in some countries, keeping a person waiting is one method by which influence or importance is indicated. The social codes of a culture often dictate how we are supposed to regulate our time. Although the use of time varies among various subcultures of American society, everyone has a pattern and that pattern is understood by most people with whom one associates. Violation of the pattern to which your group conforms may mean that other members will look upon you unfavorably.

Eye Contact

Eye contact is also governed by culture. In Pakistan it can be insulting to a woman if a man looks her directly in the eye. A woman who follows traditional customs still wears a veil covering all or part of her face so that a man cannot cast his eyes upon her. An American who was to receive an award for outstanding performance in tennis in Thailand was instructed not to look the Queen directly in the eye when he received his award. Such an act would have been insulting. In the United States we communicate with others directly eye to eye, but in Nigeria prolonged eye contact is disrespectful. Not to look another directly in the eye in our culture may mean that you are not telling the truth. It may also mean that you are not interested in the other person or that you are shy. Prolonged eye contact such as staring, however, is considered rude in our culture.

Touch

Touch, too, is heavily influenced by culture. In Southeast Asia, parts of Africa, and some Arab states one often finds men holding hands. This behavior has no sexual overtones in these cultures. You have probably seen leaders of the Soviet Union hugging and embracing each other when they meet; yet you would undoubtedly find it peculiar if you turned on your television set and saw the President of the United States hugging and embracing the Vice-President upon his return from a foreign country.

In some foreign countries, it is still not permissible for a man to have any physical contact with a woman before marriage. Holding hands in public in these countries might be taken as a contemptuous affront of one family to the other. Our culture also regulates touching behavior between unmarried couples to a certain degree. During the early stages of dating, there are definite and understood standards of behavior that vary according to the community and the age of the couple. A man who wishes to go beyond a mere kiss on an early date may be regarded as too aggressive. Under certain circumstances, however, a woman may touch a man without generating the same kind of response. When standing next to him, for instance, she might touch the man lightly to indicate that she likes him or would like to date him.

Gesture

Many gestures are behaviors that are absorbed through cultural influences, and often we do not think much about them. In Pakistan, the gesture that Americans use to wave "Good-bye"—the up and down motion of the hand—is used to beckon others to come. In Ethiopia, people put one finger to their lips to gesture for silence to a child but four fingers for an adult. To use one finger for an adult would be disrespectful, just as shaking an index finger from side to side to an adult in the United States would be disrespectful. Certain African groups point with an outstretched lower lip; they consider pointing with the index finger, as we do, rather crude. In Greece, the gesture we use to signify "Stop" is used nonverbally to curse another motorist. In southern India, people shake their heads from side to side to mean *yes*. These are gestures we learn from childhood, and most of us would not give their use a second thought, no matter where we were.

Voice

Voice varies from country to country, perhaps more than it does from one segment of a country to another. But it is important to realize that a dialect in one part of the country might be found peculiar by some people in other areas. A news reporter with a strong Boston or Brooklyn accent would probably not be acceptable as a network newscaster, since his voice would be broadcast throughout the country. A southern accent, midwestern twang, or western drawl are vocal traits over which many of us have little control. We are not likely to realize the extent of our accent or peculiarity unless we travel to or meet people from other regions. An Englishman would probably be ruled out as a network news announcer even more quickly than one with a regional accent, although he might have more opportunities as an actor or a talk-show host in our country.

SUMMARY

Nonverbal communication is extremely important in communication, no matter what the context. More than 90 percent of the social meaning of a communication may be projected by nonverbal elements. These elements include space, time, body movements, voice, and the choice and use of objects. Social meaning is also conveyed by cultural components, and cues regarding one's culture are reflected through most all the other elements. A person's cultural background largely determines the nonverbal factors expressed in communication.

When we communicate with others, we should attempt to integrate nonverbal elements so that they support and reinforce the words we speak and the attitudes and emotions we wish to convey. When we communicate with others, we should be aware of nonverbal as well as verbal elements and attempt to analyze them as they relate to each other.

What we communicate nonverbally in different situations is often similar to what we have communicated nonverbally all our lives. In communicating with others, it may be more important to be aware of the nonverbal elements than the verbal ones, since many of them are used unconsciously. Often, our nonverbal cues provide information about our personality. These cues allow others to "read between the lines." As our understanding of the roles and functions of nonverbal communication grows, our capacity to influence and to adjust to our surroundings will increase. The old saying "What you are speaks so loud I cannot hear what you say" indicates the importance of nonverbal communication in our lives.

FURTHER READING

Flora Davis, *Inside Intuition*. New York: New American Library, 1973.
   A good introductory book about intuition and the role it plays in nonverbal communication.

Ralph Ellison, *Invisible Man*. New York: Vintage Books, 1972.
   This now classic novel is about a man who seems invisible to those around him because of his race. The book illustrates brilliantly how a person's self-concept is defined on the basis of how people react to his physical appearance.

Edward T. Hall, *The Hidden Dimension*. Garden City, N. Y.: Anchor Books, 1969.
   In this paperback book, the author deals with spatial experience as it is dictated by culture. The "hidden dimension" is man's use of space, and the author is very convincing in presenting the idea that virtually everything a person is and does is associated with the experience of space. This is an immensely interesting and exciting book full of examples and illustrations that develop the concepts of social and personal space and how they are perceived.

_____, *The Silent Language*. New York: Fawcett, 1959.
   This paperback book examines the cultural component of nonverbal communication, especially how American behavior differs from that of people in other cultures. The author is an anthropologist and uses numerous examples and anecdotes to examine the world of human nonverbal communication that occurs around you. This book will stimulate you to make your own observations and analysis of the nonverbal behavior of others.

Wilson Bryan Key, *Subliminal Seduction*. New York: New American Library, 1972; *Media Sexploitation*. Englewood Cliffs, N. J.: Prentice-Hall, 1976.
   This author's thesis, which is somewhat overstated, is that advertisers are attempting to influence us with messages that appeal to our subconscious. Of particular interest in these books is the idea that subconscious messages are another form of nonverbal communication. .

John T. Molloy, *Dress for Success*. New York: Warner Books, 1975.

This book reinforces the importance of clothes as a significant non-verbal element. The focus is on the dress of the business executive, but Molloy proves that the clothes one wears evoke conditioned responses from people.

NOTES

[1]Paul Watzlawick, *How Real Is Real?* (New York: Vintage Books, 1977), pp. 30–36.

[2]Albert Mehrabian, *Silent Messages.* (Belmont, Calif.: Wadsworth, 1971), pp. 42–47.

[3]Edward T. Hall, *The Silent Language.* (Greenwich, Conn.: Fawcett, 1959) and *The Hidden Dimension.* (Garden City, N. Y.: Anchor Books, 1969).

[4]Jurgen Ruesch and Weldon Kees, *Nonverbal Communication: Notes on the Visual Perception of Human Relations.* (Berkeley: University of California, 1956). See also Jurgen Ruesch, "Nonverbal Language," in *Small Group Communications: A Reader,* Robert S. Cathcart and Larry A. Samovar, eds. (Dubuque, Iowa: William C. Brown, 1970), p. 260.

[5]Ray L. Birdwhistell, *Introduction to Kinesics.* (Louisville: University of Louisville, 1952). Also see his "Background to Kinesics" in *ETC: A Review of General Semantics,* 13 (Autumn, 1955): 10–18.

[6]Nancy M. Henley, *Body Politics.* (Englewood Cliffs, N. J.: Prentice-Hall 1977), pp. 94–123.

[7]*Ibid.*

[8]Albert Mehrabian, "Communication Length as an Index of Communicator Attitude," *Psychological Reports,* 17 (1965): 519–522; "Influence of Attitudes from the Posture, Orientation, and Distance of a Communicator," *Journal of Consulting and Clinical Psychology,* 32 (1968): 296–308; "Relationship of Attitude to Seated Posture, Orientation, and Distance," *Journal of Personality and Social Psychology,* 10 (1968): 26–30.

[9]Mehrabian, *Silent Messages,* pp. 42–47. See also "Communicating Without Words," *Psychology Today,* 2 (1968), p. 53.

[10]Jurgen Ruesch and Weldon Kees, *Nonverbal Communication: Notes on the Visual Perception of Human Relations* (Berkeley: University of California, 1956). See also Jurgen Ruesch, "Nonverbal Language and Therapy," in *Communication and Culture,* Alfred G. Smith, ed. (New York: Holt, Rinehart and Winston, 1966), pp. 209–210.

chapter 4

Verbal Communication

Think, for a moment, about the last time you communicated something in words to another person. Was it just a minute ago when you told a friend you had to study? Was it at dinner when you asked someone to pass the salt? Was it when you asked someone in your last class what the reading assignment was? Whatever the situation, we all know the importance of language. If we were to go through the day without speaking, most of us would feel frustrated. Travelers in a country where they do not know the language not only feel frustrated but exhausted from the effort of trying to communicate without having a common language.

Even when we are not talking, we use language. It would be difficult to think something through without using the symbolism of language. Our dreams and daydreams, undiscernible to observers, consist of images that depend on language.

In ideal situations we use language understood by other people and hence achieve our goal of communication. In less than ideal situations, however, language is often manipulated by its user. A real estate development named "Woodland Heights" implies that the land has woods and hills. If it has neither, language is being used to create the impression of a pleasant atmosphere rather than to reflect reality. Lan-

89

guage can still be used in such subtle ways that even when it is accurate, it can still distort meaning. McDonald's, for example, calls one of its hamburgers the "Quarter Pounder." Any calorie counter can tell you that a quarter of a pound is only four ounces, which is not a very large quantity.

It is important to remember that even though we use language in most communication situations, what we mean to say is conveyed not only by the words themselves. We usually add all sorts of nonverbal communication to our words, and the two become so interrelated that it is difficult to tell where one begins and the other leaves off. Although language consists of sentences, clauses, and phrases, these elements might have a different meaning for the user than for the listener.

This chapter is largely concerned with the language behavior of communicators and listeners; to divorce words from how they are spoken and how they are heard is to look at them in isolation—and words are never isolated in oral communication. It is impossible, for this reason, to discuss language behavior without discussing the people who are using the language. This applies equally to the communicator and to the listener. If you speak perfect French to someone who does not understand the language, you will not be understood, no matter how clear your words are. Successful communication depends upon the completion of the transaction, and much of our emphasis here will be on the two ends of the communication chain: the speaker and the listener.

Part of the communicator's effectiveness in conveying thoughts and emotions is derived from his or her language. In this chapter we will first discuss the language environment in order to understand the context in which language appears. Following this section, we will focus on language style to provide a broad base for understanding the importance of language choices. With this foundation, we will then examine how words work. Finally, we will briefly note several ways you can improve your language and style.

An understanding of language will help you to express what you really want to say, honestly, clearly, and straightforwardly. When messages are misunderstood or when a communication has no effect on the listener, it may be that the language of the communicator is, in part, at fault. The grandiloquent style of early orators has yielded to a modern communicative style that is direct, efficient, and vigorous. The speaker who says, for example, "the waves beat against the shore" has a better chance of being understood and appreciated than the speaker who says, "The rapacious waves beat against the virgin shore." Communication that is not clear is likely to be unsuccessful no matter how skillful it may be in other ways. Some understanding of language is therefore necessary to every chapter in this book in which oral communication is a factor.

THE LANGUAGE ENVIRONMENT

All language takes place within a particular environment. A minister speaks in the environment of a church, two friends have a conversation in the student center, and a teacher gives a lecture in a classroom. Language that is appropriate to one environment might appear meaningless or foolish in another. A discussion about killing people, for example, would differ greatly if it took place on military maneuvers rather than in a church.

According to Neil Postman, a writer about language, the language environment is made up of four elements: the people; their purpose; the rules of communication by which they achieve their purpose; and the actual talk being used in the situation.[1] To illustrate these elements let's take the simple example of John and Mary passing each other on the street. Their main purpose in communicating is to greet each other.

Mary: "Hi. How are you?"
John: "Fine. How are you?"
Mary: "Good."

The rules for this sort of conversation are well known to all of us, since we often participate in it ourselves. If John had failed to follow the rules, however, and had stopped to give Mary a five-minute talk on the condition of his gall bladder, Mary would probably have felt annoyed because John had gone beyond the limits of this sort of conversation.

If we followed the rules and purposes for a language environment, we would probably not have much difficulty in communication. Often, however, people violate these rules. Let's take the example of the Curriculum Committee—a committee that exists in every college and university. Generally, the purpose of the committee is to approve new courses and programs. For purposes of discussion, let's assume that the committee's rules state that it will approve new courses if the courses function for the good of a particular departmental program. Yet, even when the rules and purposes of the committee are clear-cut, it is doubtful whether its members will adhere to them. In deciding whether to permit a new journalism course, the member representing geology is likely to argue that she has not had a new course for three years and, therefore, journalism should not be permitted to have one either. The member from English argues that the journalism course might decrease enrollment in English courses, so he is also opposed to the proposed course. In this situation, then, people are ignoring the purpose of the language environment in order to promote cross-purposes of their own.

All language environments demand different responses. In some cases, the milieu itself demands the response. We all know, for example, how we should dress and talk at a funeral home, a church, or a formal dinner party. The roles we play in the environment might also tell us how to respond: a student in the second grade soon learns to raise her hand if she has a question; a wise Army captain doesn't give advice to the major.

Some language environments have vocabularies that are unique. Computer scientists, C.B. users, cooks, and publishers all employ a language that is special to their particular environment. The language used in one environment usually does not work in another. A marriage will not last very long if the wife insists on communicating to her husband with the command "over and out." A romance can be dampened when a computer scientist asks for "more meaningful input" from his girlfriend.

Many language environments use specific kinds of sentences. In religion, sentences tend to be prescriptive, judgmental, and evaluative, while in science, sentences are largely descriptive, predictive, and explanatory.[2] If a scientist uses the language of science to talk about faith to a priest, a breakdown in communication is almost inevitable. In fact, this difference in language environments might explain why countless discussions and writings about science and religion have never resolved any of the crucial questions.

The important thing to remember about language environments is that they demand appropriate language. If we think about the environment, we will ask ourselves whom we are talking to and in what context our language is going to occur. If we don't adapt to the environment, our language will not work and we will lose our chance for communication.

STYLE: YOUR VERBAL IMAGE

The words you use are determined by all your past experiences, by everything in your individual history. You learn words in order to express thoughts, and thought and language develop together. The way you think and the way you talk are unique; they form a distinctive pattern. In a sense, you *are* what you say because language is the chief means of conveying your thoughts. Neither language nor thought can be viewed in isolation. They are related and constantly growing. Together, they determine your verbal style.

Style is the result of the way you select and arrange words and sentences. Everyone chooses different words to express his or her thoughts, and every individual has his or her own personal verbal style. Styles not only vary among different people; each person also uses different styles to suit the situation. In the pulpit, a minister often has a scholarly and formal style. At a church dinner, however, his or her style is likely to be informal and casual. When an actress meets her fans, she might speak in a style similar to her best-known role—even though this is not her natural style among friends.

Sometimes style can negate a communicator's other good qualities. We all know someone who remembers every joke he has ever heard and then retells them so badly that we feel embarrassed. A person who demands that we use a rational style in discussing an emotional issue is a person who is unaware of the language environment. Style, because of its power and influence over us, is as important to the acceptance of ideas as all the other aspects of communication. Even if we have the proper information, the right occasion, and a listener interested in our message, what we have to say may be lost if our style is inappropriate.

Impressions of personality are often related to verbal style. When you characterize a person as formal and aloof, part of your impression may result from the way that person talks. We sometimes consider others crude, vulgar, or trite because of their verbal style. Since your style partially determines whether others accept or reject you as a person, it also influences how others receive your messages. Style is so important that it can influence a person's opinion of you, win the friendship of another, lose the respect of a neighbor, or sway a teacher.

A young man in a pickup truck stopped next to a group of college students at a prominent New England college and said to them, "Hey, ya'll, kin ya point out how a fella' kin geet to tha main bildin' 'round cheer?" Confused for a moment, the students decided he meant the administration building and pointed out the direction. "Thanks a heap, ya'll," they heard as the man departed. The looks and the comments of the students in the group following his departure revealed their amused contempt. The stranger's verbal style had made a very definite impression. We generally think less of a person who uses poor grammar. We show scorn for a legislator who cannot make a reasonably fluent explanation of a policy that he is advocating. We wince when we hear an actress we have admired in films show poor command of the English language on a late-night talk show. On the other hand, an adolescent boy who uses words far above his level of sophistication surprises us and earns our admiration.

We are most critical of style when it is used in the wrong setting. The man in the pickup truck was not using a style that is generally accepted on a college campus. When he uses this style with friends, however, it is appropriate. The adolescent boy might impress adults and teachers with his large vocabulary, but if he uses it with fellow baseball players, he will probably be ridiculed. If we give a speech in class or write a paper, we aim for a style that is grammatical and literate, but among friends, our style is often more colloquial. Those who are skillful in their use of language are able to change their style to suit the situation.

Dialect

Americans speak a variety of dialects. We are all familiar with the differences in speech between Southerners and those who live in the North. When we travel, we are often surprised to discover that people use different words for the same thing. A large sandwich, for example, is a hoagy, a grinder, a submarine, or a hero; the name you use depends on where you live.

A *dialect* is the habitual language of a community. It is distinguished by a unique grammatical structure, certain ways of pronouncing words, or even by figures of speech. The community members who use the dialect may be identified by region or by such diverse factors as education, social class, or cultural background. In many cases, dialect may change as people move to new regions and are influenced by new experiences. A Northerner who has moved to the South might, for example, decide to substitute the colorful expression "Say what?" for the more formal northern expression, "I beg your pardon?"

One recurring question on the subject of dialect is whether one dialect is preferable to another. This question can be answered only by examining the situations in which the dialect is used. Because language is used for communication, it is appropriate to use the form of language that can be understood and appreciated by the people with whom you are communicating. If you share a similar background with these people, it is natural and sensible to use the dialect that you have in common.

The real problem occurs when you move out of your dialectal area. In some cases, your dialect may be perceived as "inferior" by others. Although linguists do not like to consider dialects as "inferior" or "superior," they do agree that some dialects have more prestige than others and that "... prestige comes from the prestige of those who use it."[3] In other words, if you want to be accepted and identified with people who use a dialect different from your own, you might have to adapt to their dialect. You should know, however, that the prestige of a dialect is elusive and transitory. For years, many Americans did not consider a southern dialect as very prestigious. When Jimmy Carter became President, however, Southerners, and their dialects, acquired a new prestige.

Speaking and Writing

The English language includes many more words than most of us will ever use. The largest English-language dictionary contains about half a million words, but most of us will use only about 2 percent of them in our everyday reading, writing, and speaking. As Figure 4-1 shows, we use only about ten thousand words in our day-to-day transactions.

We use fewer words in speaking than we do in writing. Speech is intended to be understood as soon as the listener hears it; there is no

The English Word Pyramid

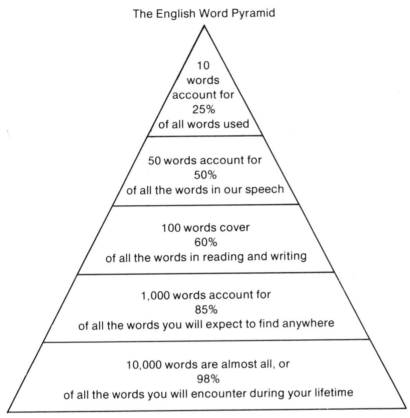

10
words
account for
25%
of all words used

50 words account for
50%
of all the words in our speech

100 words cover
60%
of all the words in reading and writing

1,000 words account for
85%
of all the words you will expect to find anywhere

10,000 words are almost all, or
98%
of all the words you will encounter during your lifetime

Source: *Writers Workshop Handbook.* (Syracuse:
National Affiliation for Literacy Advance, 1977), unpaged.

Figure 4-1

opportunity to go back and listen to a conversation or a speech again. In spite of this fact, we *can*, however, ask questions, respond to feedback from our listeners, and rephrase our message if we are not being understood.

The writer has more time to choose words, phrase sentences, and check grammatical construction. Because of this increased time and the possibility that the reader will reread the material, the writer can deal with more complex and difficult ideas.

Perhaps the most important difference between speaking and writing is that the speaker is dealing with people who are listening and reacting to the message as it occurs. In writing, part of the meaning is lost because the communicator does not have a direct relationship with the reader. Even if the same words are used in writing and in speaking, the meaning can be different.

Words work best in the oral communication process if they are kept relatively simple. It is more important that your communication be understood than that you strive to use a large vocabulary. The listener has a limited amount of mental energy, and this energy should be expended on comprehending the ideas rather than in trying to understand the words or the language construction. You should not insult the intelligence of a listener, but you should provide a stimulus—language—that is immediately understandable. This may involve building up a greater reserve of words from which to draw upon as well as doing a better job of drawing upon an already existent pool of words.

HOW WORDS WORK

When you use a word orally, you are vocally representing a thing—whether that thing is a physical object like your biology textbook or an abstract concept like peace. The word is a *symbol*; it stands for the object or concept that it names. This is what distinguishes a word from a random sound. The sounds that are represented in our language by the letters c-a-t constitute a word because we have agreed that these sounds will stand for a particular domestic animal. The sounds represented by the letters z-a-t do not make up a word in our language because these sounds do not stand for anything.

When you study a language, whether it is your native tongue or a foreign one, you must learn what the words stand for in that language; that is, you have to know the vocabulary. Another thing you need to know is how to put the words together to make the clauses and sentences that express relationships among the words. This is the grammar of a language.

When you say that another person understands your language, you mean that he or she knows what your words stand for and how the words are put together to express ideas and relationships. You both interpret the verbal sound that is being made as meaning approximately the same thing. Each of you has learned the connection between the sound and what it represents and each of you can use the sound intelligibly.

Notice, however, that your idea of an object or a concept is never exactly the same as another person's, because each individual has different experiences. Your notion of what *cat* means comes from all the cats you have ever known, read about, seen on television, heard others talk about, and so on. This *cat* is unique to you, but you can use the sound to communicate to someone else because cats have general qualities in common and are recognized by the other person from all of his or her experiences of cats. The fact that language works at all means, therefore, that those with whom you speak have had a certain number of experiences similar to your own. If this were not true, the other person simply would not know what you were talking about.

Sometimes we assume that others know what we are talking about when, in fact, they have very little common experience with us. When you say that you *love* another person, for example, you use a word that represents your experiences in being loved and in loving. Since these experiences, and their interpretation, vary a great deal from person to person, someone else may mean something very different when he or she uses that word. The meanings of words also change as our experiences broaden. A twelve-year-old girl who says she is in love is speaking from a very different range of experience than a woman of twenty-five who says the same thing.

Words can be very easy to understand, or they may be very difficult. Distortions and misunderstandings often occur, because people assume that everyone means the same thing with a particular word. To you, *music* may be the latest folk-rock record, whereas *music*, to your parents, may mean a Strauss waltz or a popular song interpreted by Lawrence Welk. To some, *vacation* means camping in a remote spot in a forest and roughing it; to others it means calling ahead and reserving rooms at Holiday Inns. Just as we have various reactions to things, we also have various reactions to words—the symbolic representations of those things.

In our use of words, we often do not say what we intend to say. You have undoubtedly caught yourself replying, "No, that's not what I meant" or "I know what I mean, but I just can't say it." The problem of not using words clearly and precisely is a common one. We do not select the "right" words; we omit words; we say too much; we are vague; we are ambiguous; we jumble our words. Difficulties in verbal communication occur for several reasons: it may be that you are not sure of what you want to say; perhaps you do not have the verbal skill to express your message in the most concise way.

PEOPLE DETERMINE MEANINGS

For the listener to understand what the speaker intends, the speaker should have something definite in mind. The more general the idea or impression the communicator wishes to convey, the more likely that catch-all words or words that are hazy, vague, or ambiguous will be used. *Understanding* is the core of meaning, and understanding is a two-way process; that is, the speaker is responsible for presenting the idea clearly, and the listener is responsible for trying to understand it accurately. Meanings are determined by people, not by words.

Even though an idea is clearly presented, it may still be misinter-

preted. Meanings develop in individual ways throughout our lives. From earliest childhood we build up a complex set of meanings from our associations and relationships. Since each person grows up in his or her unique world, it is easy to see why meanings differ. For this reason, a communicator who thought he or she was being clear might not have been able to communicate in a way that has meaning for the listener.

One example of different interpretations often occurs in communication between parents and children. The world of a parent or another adult is different from the world of a child or student. A parent might wish, for example, that his or her child were popular. "Popular" to the child means being able to stay out late and to use the family car—both unacceptable terms to the parent. Because the experiences of the child and parent are so different, their values and vocabulary also vary.

New meanings are continually created by all of us as we change our ideas, our feelings, and our activities. As we think, read, travel, make friends with others, and experience life, the associations and connections that have certain meanings for us are changed. The word *ghetto* is likely to mean something quite different to a black person who has experienced ghetto life and a white person who has never been inside a ghetto. The white person's understanding of the word would change if he or she read Claude Brown's *Manchild in the Promised Land.*[4] If the white person were to become familiar with the ghetto, further changes in his or her understanding of the word would probably occur. As he or she talked with others there, additional changes might take place, and if he or she had the opportunity to live there for a while—experiencing ghetto life—even more changes might be effected. Talking to this person before, during, and after such a series of experiences would undoubtedly reveal that his or her interpretation of a ghetto had changed a great deal as a result of these experiences. As the white person's understanding of what ghetto life means increased, he or she would become more and more likely to be able to exchange meaningful messages with a black person who has experienced ghetto life.

There is still another reason why understanding may be difficult between two people. As we noted in Chapter 2, *Interpersonal Communication*, listeners often perceive messages selectively. Listeners tend to filter the messages they hear according to their needs, expectations, attitudes, and prior knowledge. Two neighbors were discussing the grand opening of a local supermarket. Early in the conversation, the woman who had actually been to the store mentioned the number of "free" items available. Because of the other woman's concern about finances and the rise in prices, nothing her neighbor said after the mention of these "free" items registered. Even though the woman who had visited the store mentioned that she had had to wait thirty minutes to get into the store, was obliged to push through crowds and crowds of people, had to wait while clerks restocked ravaged shelves, and stand in long check-out lines, her neighbor filtered out the hardship part of the message and reconstructed what she heard in accordance with her personal predisposition—the desire to obtain something for nothing. In a way, she created her own message. She did not hear about the tremendous expenditure of time, energy, and frustration that getting the "free" items would entail. In a similar manner, we all hear parts of a communication that agree with our feelings and are likely to filter out other parts with which we do not agree.

Levels of Meaning

There are different kinds of meaning, and misunderstanding can occur on any of the various levels. Hubert G. Alexander discusses four distinct meaning levels in *Meaning in Language.*[5] There is, first, meaning as the communicator intends it, or *intentional meaning*. Intentional meaning is what is in the communicator's head before he or she says anything. *Content meaning* comes from the content of the message itself, as it is expressed. The meaning that comes from our signs and symbols —including language—is called *significative meaning*. Finally, there is *interpreted meaning*, the meaning given to the message by the listener. Although each of the four kinds of meaning will be discussed briefly here, it should be clear to the reader that all are part of a simultaneous and continuous process.

Intentional Meaning   At any given time, we can have several intentional messages in our minds. We intend to tell our roommate that he or she should help clean the room; we intend to tell our instructor that we will not be in class on Friday, and so forth. Whenever we intend to convey a message, three elements are present: the desire to say something, a listener to say it to, and the language to express our message.

Misunderstanding can originate at the intentional stage if the communicator is unclear about any of the three elements. If you are confused or unclear about the idea you want to express, if you do not know the person with whom you are trying to speak, or if you can't find the right words to say what you mean, the message is liable to be misunderstood. The clearer you can be about your intention, the more likely you will be to send a message that will be well-received.

Content Meaning   The content meaning of your communication consists of the ideas and feelings you communicate in the message. When any verbal communication is attempted, more is conveyed than the actual words. Both you and your listener will also have feelings and sensations associated with the ideas. Sometimes the message is primarily about feeling; at other times, the intention of the communicator is to be quite objective, to express very few of his or her own feelings in the message. The emotional associations of both the speaker and the listener will, however, color the content of the message, no matter how objective it is intended to be.

The feelings associated with an idea may be the most interesting part of the message. However, feelings are a primary cause of misunderstanding. Individual emotions differ widely; feelings are subject to many different influences, and they are often beyond our immediate control. The feelings that a speaker associates with an idea may prevent him or her from expressing that idea clearly. They may also distract from the objective part of the message. A particular emotional association may lead the listener to the message according to his or her own feelings. The listener's strong negative feelings associated with an idea may prevent him or her from considering it according to the speaker's point of view.

✗ Significative Meaning   The chief function of the symbols of our language is to express meaning. Significative meaning is that part of the communication conveyed verbally. Thus, significative meaning excludes nonverbal communication. The meaning of a verbal communication depends upon how the language is interpreted, and some words are usually interpreted with greater fidelity than others. A word that stands for a fairly concrete and emotionally neutral thing—such as the word *mailbox*—can usually be interpreted with good fidelity because most people respond primarily to its *denotative meaning*, the dictionary-definition meaning that designates the thing for which the word stands. Other words stand for concepts about which most people have strong feelings or extensive associations of a personal, individual nature. Words like *freedom* or *moral* are easily misunderstood because they carry a lot of *connotative meaning*, the feelings or associations that we have about an idea.

When there is a fairly direct relationship between the word and the object that it stands for, the significative meaning will usually be clear. Conversely, when the speaker uses words with strong connotative meanings, there is a good chance that misunderstandings will occur. This is to say that it is easier to be sure that you will be understood when you talk about mailboxes than when you talk about morals. We do not mean to suggest, however, that the best conversations are those which are limited to the mailbox level. Some of our most important messages have to do with ideas that have strong connotations; they are important precisely because we feel strongly about them. It is important to remember, however, that when what you say has strong emotional feelings attached to it, you are more likely to be misunderstood.

Because significative meanings are dependent upon the way the words are interpreted, there is a strong likelihood that misunderstanding will occur at this stage. In addition to problems raised by the emotional associations of some words, interpreting what another person means by the words he or she uses is difficult for several other reasons. The meanings of verbal symbols are not fixed. Many "fad" words are extremely short-lived. Slang and jargon operate this way. Words like *hassle, rap, rip-off,* and *uptight,* to name a few, have come into being within the last few years. Other words tend to change their meaning over time. Words such as *heavy, swinger, decent,* and *trip* have taken on new meanings. The meanings of words also change quickly according to the context in which they are used. Words like *love, liberated, conservative, religion,* and *sensitivity* have different meanings in different contexts. Thus, one can see how understanding can be affected at this stage.

Interpreted Meaning Once you learn the fundamentals of a language, interpretation is automatic. You are no longer even aware of the fact that you are interpreting—fitting meanings to words as quickly as you hear them. You make connections with previous experiences and prior knowledge in order to identify words, and you tend to assume that your meanings for those words are identical to those of the communicator who spoke them. As we have seen, this is never literally so, and misunderstanding can occur in the interpreted meaning as well as in any other.

In addition to the inevitable differences between the experiences of the listener and the experiences of the speaker, there are other factors that can cause misunderstanding at this stage. A receiver, for example, who cannot identify the sounds he or she hears as verbal symbols will be unable to understand the message. Listening to Shakespearean lines delivered by a great actor would have little or no meaning for most of us if the actor were an Israeli speaking in Hebrew. Words may be garbled when they are received because the listener is inattentive or distracted by outside noise. Different backgrounds and differences in frames of reference between the source and the receiver can also cause errors in interpretation.

The responsibility for fidelity in communication rests with both the speaker and the listener, since misunderstanding can be the result of failure at either end of the transaction. Whenever misunderstanding occurs in the process of spoken communication, both people can help to clear up the misunderstanding by giving a second interpretation. He or she can repeat the point or elaborate upon it by giving further instances and examples. The speaker can restate his or her idea, phrasing the same idea in a different way by using different avenues, presenting it to the listener in varying perspectives. The effective communicator will make use of these devices during every communication. In addition to using these methods, the communicator might also strive to make better language choices, following the suggestions in the next section.

The most important thing the listener can do is to question the message that he or she does not understand. A speaker can work to correct misunderstanding only if he or she realizes that the message has not been received. Sometimes the listener can also help the speaker to understand what is causing the lack of fidelity in their communication. Comments such as "I can't hear you" or "I think that you and I have very different meanings for that word" can clear up a communication problem.

To Whom Are You Talking?

When you seek a specific response from a listener, your words have to have meaning within the person's experience. This entails a fundamental principle that underlies many other parts of this book—the principle of audience analysis. The communicator must have *some* knowledge of the audience in order to draw upon a common fund of meaning; otherwise, it is impossible to communicate. The more the communicator knows about the listener, the easier it will be to select an appropriate vocabulary. Words are one means of conveying meaning from one person to another. The desire of the communicator is to create understanding in response to a specific stimulus—the words which he or she uses. This requires flexibility in vocabulary. The communicator cannot use the same words to communicate a similar idea to two very different people. As listeners vary, so must words. You might tell your instructor that you weren't in class because you didn't feel well. To a close friend, however, you might admit that you had a hangover. Expressions such as "laid back," "getting your act together," and "hang loose" are more appropriate in conversations with your friends than in a formal speech. You may have to sacrifice some of your choicest phrases, discard some trivial details, or give up highly technical and professional words in order to communicate with a particular listener. In conveying ideas to your parents, you may generally avoid most of the slang and colloquial terms that you use in talking to another student. You know your listeners well—through years of analysis—and you alter your words accordingly. *Discourse*—the words you choose to use—should be designed for the hearer.

LANGUAGE CHOICES

Although we are often told that we should use clear and precise language, this recommendation is somewhat similar to the demand that we stop snoring at night. We would all like to break our bad habits—whether they are poor language usage or snoring—but we don't know how to do it. Command of the language requires years of practice and study. It is impossible to lay down strict rules that govern the choice of language for all occasions and for all circumstances. Therefore, we are going to limit ourselves to a few particularly useful recommendations. Specifically, we will discuss clarity, energy, and vividness.

Clarity

Sometimes we do not speak clearly because of the sentence structures we use. Although the ideas may be clear to us, we don't always express them very well. The restaurant manager who posted the sign, "If you don't like our waitresses, you should see our manager" did not express his message clearly. The sign did not mean that the manager was worse than the waitresses; it meant that restaurant patrons could complain to the manager about the waitresses.

Many times in oral communication we have a chance to straighten out the confusion we cause by poor sentence structure. If our listeners look baffled or ask us a question, we can try again. There are other times, however, when the need to speak as clearly and precisely as possible is more urgent. If we are saying something of special importance or if we are in a formal speaking situation, clarity is essential, since there will probably not be the opportunity to make our point again.

Some language is so specialized that it is inappropriate to use it outside the field where it has come into use. "Input" and "output," for example, are computer terms that do not work very well in describing human relations or activities. "I would like your ideas for this project" is a more appropriate phrase than "I would like your input." "Interface" is a useful word in the natural sciences, but it should not be used to describe human interaction. Although specialized words and phrases can be effective in their appropriate settings, we do not need them—nor should we use them—in everyday communication.

We also warn against the pseudopsychological jargon that is so widespread in our society. In a novel satirizing this kind of language, the author had this to say about her main character: " . . . she had decided to play the whole scene off the wall, to just go with the flow. Everybody knew, in these days of heightened consciousness, that the rational mind was a screw up; the really authentic thing to do was to act on your impulses."[6] Other phrases that occur in the same novel include "heavy trip," "get your act together," "dump on you," "schizzed out," "freak out," and many others.

The problem with this jargon is that it gives the listener or reader very little idea of what is really going on. What does it mean to "freak out"? Is it to go insane? To start screaming? To be frightened? If you don't know precisely what the expression means, how do you respond? Another problem with this jargon is that it can become boring. If everyone were to use the expression "heavy trip" to describe a bad experience, all the different words and expressions in our language that describe these experiences would fall into disuse.

One of the delights of language is that it has so many subtleties and shades of meaning. Choosing jargon to express all our ideas is like eating Big Macs for dinner every night. Language is a marvelous banquet and a wide variety of choices is available to us.

Energy

When there is energy in our communication we give our listeners a feeling of excitement, urgency, and forcefulness. Energy, or the lack of it, can be communicated both verbally and nonverbally. Although a lack of energy is obvious in such nonverbal cues as slouching or speaking slowly, most of us are not as aware of how language can convey a lack of energy.

In English a sense of energy is communicated mainly by verbs—the action words of the language. "She slapped him" and "He jumped up and down" are both sentences that have energy and excitement. Adjectives and adverbs, however, slow the language down. If we say, "The outraged Judy slapped him soundly," our sentence is not nearly as energetic. Another way to add energy to language is to put sentences in the active rather than the passive voice. The active "The boy hit the ball" is more energetic than the passive "The ball was hit by the boy."

Many of us slow down our speech by using complicated words when simple words would be more vivid. The weather forecaster who says "There is a 10 percent chance of rain" sounds much livelier than the one who says "The probability of precipitation is 10 percent." "Fire" is a more active word than "conflagration" or "holocaust." The verb "left" has more action than the verb "departed."

Language also has more energy when the speaker avoids tired, worn-out phrases. "Blushing bride," "Mother Earth," "busy as bees" are all examples of clichés that have been used so much they have lost their impact.

Energetic language is active and direct. It expresses ideas in the simplest and liveliest way possible. Forceful language is one way of telling your listener, "Hey look. This is important. Listen to me!"

Vividness

Vivid language appeals to the senses. It enables us to smell the musky scent of perfume, to taste crisp french fries (with a light sprinkling of salt), and to hear and feel the vibrations of a concert.

Think back on some of the ghost stories you heard when you were a child. The best ones were the ones that filled you with terror. Ghost stories are filled with deathly shrieks, bloodcurdling moans, and mysterious howling. They are usually set in dark places illumined only by an occasional ghostly light or a streak of lightning. If any smells are mentioned, you can be sure they're dank and musty.

A ghost story is usually told by the person who had the experience. Any narrative told from the point of view of "I was there," "It happened to me," is particularly vivid. By re-creating the experience for your listeners, you can often make them feel what you feel. Thus, the quality of vividness in communication is a result of the re-creation of a personal experience.

Vividness also comes from unique forms of speech. Some people would say that a person who talks too much "chatters like a magpie," a phrase that has become a cliché. To a southern speaker, however, this person made a lot of "chin music." When we say that language is vivid, we often mean that someone has found a new way of saying old things. Children often charm us with the uniqueness of their language because they are too young to know all the clichés and overused expressions. One of the best places to look for vivid language is among poets and musicians. Although more words have been written about love than any other subject, Bob Dylan, John Prine, and Joni Mitchell have all given us new expressions and therefore new ways of looking at the experience. Their unique perspectives make an old idea sound original and exciting.

IMPROVING YOUR VERBAL STYLE

Improving language usage and verbal style continues all through life; skill and sensitivity in verbal expression are not developed overnight. We tend to take language for granted, but a person who wishes to improve his or her style *can* do something about it through conscious effort and practice. Improved style does not result from the memorization of formulas and rules. Because your use of language is such a clear reflection of your self, the project of improvement will be continued throughout your life.

The following three suggestions have proved useful for communicators in trying to improve their verbal style. You can become actively involved in one or all of them during the normal course of everyday human interaction.

1. *Increase your vocabulary.* Since you hear thousands of words every day, you can benefit from this continual access to other people's vocabularies. When you become more conscious of the words of the television advertiser and how he skillfully and subtly tries to sell his product, or of the politician and how he presents his ideas, or of the teacher and how she teaches a lesson, you are simply taking advantage of a situation already present and available.

When you hear a new word, strive to understand it in the *context* in

which it is used—from the parts that precede or follow and are directly connected with it. Although you may not always be able to stop another person to ask what he or she means by a certain word, sometimes it is helpful to do so, if possible. People sometimes use words incorrectly, of course, and contexts can be deceiving or misleading. When you hear a word that is unknown to you or when you hear a word in an unfamiliar context, check its meaning. You can also develop sensitivity to the meanings of words by paying attention to people's feelings as they are revealed in verbal expression and in nonverbal cues. This will help you to become more aware of the emotional level in the expression of others.

Another way to build your vocabulary is by reading, looking up the meaning of new words, and remembering them. When you are reading, just as when you are listening to your friends talk, try to be aware of new words—then try to fit them into your own conversation. A word that is not actually used will not be remembered for long.

If you increase your vocabulary, you will increase the possibility of getting your intended meaning across to your listener. The more words you have at your command, the more likely you will be accurate and precise. This does not mean that you should search for big words—short, familiar words are often the best. By increasing your vocabulary, then, you will enrich your conversation. The beneficial by-product of reading and listening critically with an eye toward building your vocabulary is the broadening of your thinking. Words are the building blocks of communication, and you can form a foundation that will help to assure a meaningful, intelligible, and expressive edifice.

In addition to building your vocabulary, note how the words you read and hear are used in combination. It is the combination of words that make style effective or ineffective. Thus, you should not just examine the individual trees—the words—but the way the trees combine to make the forest—the sentences, phrases, and the ideas themselves. Thoughts are expressed in groups of words—seldom as words alone.

2. *Adapt your oral language.* As you talk to people, become conscious of them as particular people for whom you need to adapt your message. Note the language environment in which your conversation is taking place and make those adaptations that are necessary. Also, note the topic you are discussing, since it, too, can influence your choice of words. Be aware of what you are saying. This added consciousness will increase your sensitivity to other people as well as your awareness of language choice and use.

Sometimes people confuse personal authenticity with inflexible language usage. "Telling it like it is" becomes an excuse for allowing the first words that come into your head to spill out, a stream-of-consciousness that could be labeled "verbal diarrhea." Our feeling is that such language choices can reflect a kind of self-centered indulgence that says to your listener, "Never mind who you are; listen to me." Adapting your language to the individual with whom you are talking can result in an authentic exchange.

⅄ 3. *Practice*. There is no substitute for practice. Communicate with others as often as you have the opportunity and as often as you have something worthwhile to say. Be your own critic; that is, be sensitive to your own performance. We all talk, but most of us do not stop to reflect on what we have said and how we have said it. If you practice using language, your verbal style will improve.

SUMMARY

We all use language to communicate. Language is tied into our thought processes, and without language, we would not be able to think. In an ideal setting, language is used to achieve understanding; in other situations, it is used to deceive and to manipulate.

Language occurs in a language environment, and to be successful it must be appropriate to that environment. We should try to understand and adapt our language to each particular situation. Otherwise, our language will be inappropriate and the quality of communication will be affected.

Style, the way we express ourselves, is an important aspect of language. Our style often influences the judgments other people make about us. An inappropriate style often ruins our chances for clear communication.

Speaking and writing differ in that oral communication is more spontaneous, personal, and immediate than written communication. Our speaking vocabularies are smaller than either our reading or writing vocabularies, and spoken discourse is most effective when it is simple and direct. Words are effective when the speaker and the listener both know what the words stand for. Distortions and misunderstandings occur when we assume that everyone else has had the same experiences, and therefore interprets the words in the same way that we do. The responsibility for achieving fidelity in oral communication rests with both the speaker and the listener. Our ability to send and receive clear messages depends upon our experience, our frame of reference, our perception, and our knowledge of the person with whom we are communicating. There are four different levels of meaning—intentional, content, significative, and interpreted—and misunderstanding can occur at any of these levels.

It is impossible to lay down strict rules for making good language choices. Language that is clear, energetic, appropriate, and vivid will be most effective, however, and you can improve your use of language by making a conscious effort to become more aware of these qualities. Your efforts to communicate more accurately will surely make life easier—for yourself as well as for those around you.

Language is a dynamic process. Personal experiences and the experiences related to us by others affect the way we use words. Thus, verbal communication is really a stirring-up process, changing understanding within, between, and among people. It is a human process, the ability that distinguishes us from all other forms of animal life. It is also a personal process, for language usage is unique to each individual and, thus, varies with each individual.

Language gives your experiences and feelings a form that can be understood by others. It is the vehicle for the most precise communication possible in human relations. Language brings ideas to life.

FURTHER READING

Robert L. Benjamin, *Semantics and Language Analysis.* Indianapolis: Bobbs-Merrill, 1970.
    This brief paperback textbook investigates the working of language as a coherent system; it is a study of "how language means." The author looks at instances of the effective communication of meaning as well as examples of failure in communication.

Ivor Brown, *Mind Your Language!* New York: Capricorn Books, 1962.
    In this brief paperback, Brown takes the reader on a witty and enjoyable journey through the linguistic tangles created by over-worked adjectives, slang and dialect words, scientific and technical words, as well as clichés and vogue words. His ideas are useful for those interested in avoiding the pitfalls of language, and for those who are interested in developing their own natural style.

S. I. Hayakawa, *Language in Thought and Action*, 3rd ed. New York: Harcourt Brace Jovanovich, 1972.
    Here is a comprehensive examination of the relationships among language, thought, and behavior. Language and people's linguistic habits are examined as they reveal themselves in thinking, speaking, listening, reading, and writing. This paperback book is very useful for the serious language scholar and includes "Applications" sections that are useful and interesting extensions of the concepts in each chapter.

Cyra McFadden, *The Serial.* New York: Alfred A. Knopf, 1977.
    This novel, available in paperback, offers a biting satire about people who talk only in pseudopsychological clichés. Many episodes of the novel first appeared in comic strip form in a California newspaper.

Edwin Newman, *Strictly Speaking*. New York: Warner Books, 1975; *A Civil Tongue*, Indianapolis: Bobbs-Merrill, 1976.
Both of these books are intended for people who have some sophistication in using language. Written by a television newscaster, the books offer many examples of the misuse of language in contemporary American life.

Neil Postman, *Crazy Talk, Stupid Talk*. New York: Delta, 1977.
This paperback book describes crazy talk (talk that promotes unreasonable or evil purposes) and stupid talk (talk that is inappropriate). It is easy to read, entertaining, and filled with suggestions for analyzing and improving language.

William Strunk, Jr., and E. B. White, *The Elements of Style*, 2nd ed. New York: Macmillan, 1972.
Although designed for the writer, speakers, take note: for the brevity, clarity, and truth it contains, this little book is worth considering. It treats the fundamentals—the rules of usage and the principles of composition most commonly violated. It will make you more conscious of the words you use.

NOTES

[1]Neil Postman, *Crazy Talk, Stupid Talk*. (New York: Delta, 1977), p. 9.

[2]*Ibid.*, p. 68.

[3]Raven I. McDavid, "Sense and Nonsense About American Dialects," in *Language*, Virginia P. Clark, Paul A. Eschholz, Alfred F. Rosa, eds. (New York: St. Martin's Press, 1972), p. 359.

[4]Claude Brown, *Manchild in the Promised Land.* (New York: New American Library, 1965).

[5]Hubert G. Alexander, *Meaning in Language* (Glenview, Ill.: Scott, Foresman, 1969), pp. 5-13.

[6]Cyra McFadden, *The Serial.* (New York: Alfred A. Knopf, 1977), p. 14.

chapter 5

Small-Group Communication

Contemporary American culture has been referred to as a "tribal society" because of our dependence on groups. We are born into a group; we go to school in groups; we worship in groups; we play in groups; we are laid to rest in a ritual group meeting. Our society itself is a large group composed of many small ones. It would probably be impossible to survive without participating in group activities.

As a college student, you may spend several hours in a single day communicating in small groups of various kinds as you take part in a seminar discussion, argue for change in a student government committee, and chat with friends who meet for coffee after class.

People join a group to complete a task; for personal growth (as in sensitivity or encounter groups); in connection with their work with the PTA, the League of Women Voters, their business, religion, or local government. An individual may be part of the research and development section of a corporation, a long-range planning committee of a university, an ad hoc committee to study pollution problems, a standing committee of a social club, or an on-the-job group where he or she earns a living. We are all part of a family, which is another group. There are, then, task-oriented small groups, therapeutic groups, short-range and long-range work

groups, social groups, and discussion groups. The concepts and characteristics in this chapter relate to groups such as these—groups of a variety of different types.

Groups function to increase understanding, to render judgments, to heighten sensitivity, to facilitate social give-and-take, and to solve problems. Many times, one group will serve several of these functions at the same time. The executive committee of a social group, for example, needs to keep members informed, render evaluations about the progress and health of the organization, and solve the problems of the group—all in addition to providing the social give-and-take which is the organization's primary reason for being and the function that makes all the work seem both worthwhile and enjoyable.

A *small group*, in the way we are using the term, has several characteristics that distinguish it from other communication settings. These characteristics are determined by the relationships and the interaction among the listeners and speakers who are members of the small group: 1) There should be some similarity and interdependence among members —as Kurt Lewin, an early researcher on groups, pointed out.[1] Similarity, according to Lewin, refers to an awareness by all members of the existence of every other member as an essential part of the total group. Interdependence means that members influence each other; one member's behavior is modified by the action and behavior of all other members of the group. 2) Another prerequisite is that there be interaction and communication among members. Interaction means reciprocity—the influence of members on each other. Communication in a small group involves the mutual interchange of thoughts, opinions, and information both orally and nonverbally. 3) Members of a small group share common needs or goals. The desire to complete a task or work out a problem in a joint and united way is an example. Finally, 4) there is a set of norms—or expectations—for the group as a whole or for specific members. A *norm* is simply a standard. A group may set standards that regulate behavior, participation, interaction, or almost anything else. Norms that refer to specific members are called roles. A *role* is the part that a member plays or the function he or she performs in the group.

Every small group is a social event because every person involved in a group's process plays the role of inquirer—wondering how he or she will relate to the other people of the group as human beings. When people share ideas, an important social dimension is present that should not be overlooked in analyzing small-group behavior—no matter what task the group is pursuing. To achieve full participation and full productivity, a congenial atmosphere of trust and understanding is needed. For this reason, attention must be given to certain group norms that treat the human side of small groups. Encouraging behavior that makes members feel liked, admired, and respected and producing a climate that allows each member to enjoy the company of others and to consider the ideas of all important and worthwhile are essential. The establishment and maintenance of this norm should override all other considerations because the closer all groups come to this ideal, the more successful they are likely to be.

The communication models presented in the introduction to this book describe *bilateral* situations in which messages are sent and received from one person to one other person. Small-group communication is *multilateral*—that is, it takes place between one person and several others, and any one of those several others is free to respond. Thus, feedback occurs between a number of individuals, each person responding to all of the others as potential sources of communication. All members speak and listen with equal responsibility because the primary source of communication is constantly changing. Individuals switch from speaker to listener and back to speaker again, instantaneously. This multilateral communication gives small-group members a shared purpose and stimulates the development of a structure of roles and norms.

In this chapter we we will investigate five major aspects of small-group communication. We will first examine some of the variables that affect the success of small groups. Secondly, we will examine the kinds of communication that occur in small groups. In the third section we will examine small-group leadership and the components of effective leadership. We will then consider several methods of evaluating small groups. Finally, we will discuss the problem-solving group as a case study of the small-group process.

WHAT MAKES A SMALL GROUP WORK?

The factors that affect small-group success include size, spatial arrangements, roles, norms, and cohesiveness. These essential variables will affect the amount and quality of the communication that is likely to occur as well as the ability of a group to complete its task successfully and the likelihood that leadership will be effective. These factors form the foundation for good group functioning and will help determine the outcome of group work. No matter what type of group it is—social, business, educational, legal, scientific, literary, or religious—and no matter what its task may be—making arrangements for a party, discussing a company's sales, learning about biochemistry, deciding on an interpretation of a law, talking over a new discovery, arguing about an author's approach, or conversing about church doctrine—the factors discussed below will affect that group's success.

Group Size

The amount and the quality of the communication that occurs between members of a small group are affected by the size of the group. Group size will also affect the way that members relate to each other, since relationships are developed by communicating.

Think about how you would react in a group of three individuals discussing your experiences in looking for a job. In a group of three, you would likely be fairly open and communicative, revealing those times when you had to search the classified ads for weeks or when you were interviewed by a tough personnel manager. Now, add two members to the hypothetical group and imagine the changes that might occur. You have fewer responsibilities for holding up your end of the conversation because you now have four other members to do it instead of two. You are not looked at as often; your ideas are not sought as much. You retreat slightly—but you still feel very much a part of the group, showing your willingness to contribute if you want to. If you double the number of members in your hypothetical group—making it ten instead of five—the likelihood of your participating in the group's activities diminishes even more. "Why should I contribute when there are nine other people?" might be your feeling. Your responsibility is decreased, and perhaps you begin to feel that your experiences do not mean so much to the group—they might even sound ridiculous if presented. You "clam up."

This description reflects the behavior of many people when group size is increased. Larger groups do not give you as much time to speak. When more people are involved, you cannot maintain social relationships with all the members. Anxiety, fear, and inhibition become more likely because members find it harder to express their true feelings—particularly dis-agreements—and feel the threat of other group members' attitudes and feelings on their own. Passivity results, and the communication becomes a bilateral experience rather than a multilateral group sharing, since two or three of the more forceful individuals carry the burden of the communi-cation. The other group members begin to behave like an audience, and the situation resembles public speaking more than the small group. As an audience member, an individual becomes anonymous—losing himself or herself in the group. Willingness to communicate, thus, is replaced by eagerness to conceal and retreat as groups get larger.

To maintain quality communication in a small group, the group's size has to be controlled. The ideal size will vary within certain limits according to the task of the group and the personalities of the members. A task that involves far-ranging and extensive gathering of information such as a town government's task force committee to investigate the effects of a proposed bypass—might, of necessity, require more members simply to accomplish the task than, perhaps, a policy-making subgroup of a larger organization—such as a constitution-revision committee set up by the student-government association.

There are other factors, that will influence decisions about group size. Robert Freed Bales, a researcher of small-group interaction, suggests that members of small groups should be able to meet face-to-face.[2] He also points out that members should be able to receive a distinct impression of every other member of the group—an impression that can be recalled. Face-to-face interaction could, conceivably, involve from three people to upwards of fifty people—depending on the size and flexibility of the room. A circle of fifty people might be called a small group by this standard. The second factor is more limiting, however, since it is unlikely that anyone except a person with a photographic memory could recall a vivid impression of many more than fifteen or twenty individuals. Recalling that many would be possible only with concentration on the task of remembering and only after meeting together over a period of time.

Acquiring a vivid impression of others depends on extensive interaction and communication with them. This occurs most successfully in groups of three or more and nine or less. Members of groups with less than five complain that their group is too small. When the size is greater than thirteen, the tendency is to form smaller groups—to splinter. Groups composed of an odd number function better than groups totaling an even number, since a majority decision can be attained in an odd-numbered group; thus, groups of five or groups of seven are generally more efficient than groups of four, six, or eight. Research indicates that five is an ideal number for most small groups. Larger groups often end up with a core group of five or so, among whom talk becomes centralized anyway. Bales recommends committees composed of more than three but less than seven. Our class experience demonstrates that students prefer collecting, exchanging, coordinating, analyzing, and evaluating information in groups of five—as opposed to groups of three, four, six, or seven.

Spatial Arrangements

One of the influential factors in determining the flow of communication during a small-group meeting is eye contact—the extent to which group members communicate eye-to-eye with other members. Just sitting and talking around a table in the local hang-out with a bunch of friends may reveal some of the effects of eye contact. Even in this small group you will probably interact more with those whom you can observe directly and readily, and you will likely direct most of your comments to those seated opposite from you. Also, in this same situation, the closer the chairs are arranged to each other, the more likely that communication will be facilitated rather than inhibited. Note the intention of inhibiting communication revealed by the arrangement of chairs in a library—chairs are often removed from the heads of tables, and some distance is often put between the chairs around a table. Erving Goffman, Edward T. Hall, and Ray Birdwhistell—all writers and researchers on nonverbal communication—agree that direct visual contact can be uncomfortable and disconcerting under ordinary conditions, and even produce feelings of anxiety. It is sometimes difficult for people to "break through" their customary reactions to sustained visual contact.[3] For some, it takes concentration, but the effort is worth the value gained in small-group situations, where dependence on the quality and the quantity of communication is at a premium.

The expected psychological relationship among members of a group may also affect choices about the spatial distance. In an encounter group, for example, physical closeness is preferred because it is the intimacy of the group relationships that aids in increasing individual understanding of group process and personal potential. In a conference where members represent different points of view, on the other hand, distance is often preferred.

Small-group communication is also affected by the task. Members who engage in a task that requires a high degree of cooperation generally select spatial arrangements that facilitate interaction—adjacent, side-by-side, corner, or face-to-face arrangements. Distant seating is preferred when no cooperation is required, when members are working on different tasks, or when members are competing.

Member Roles

The function of role-playing in the communication of self and in interpersonal relationships has been discussed in Chapters 1 and 2. Role-playing is also commonly found in small-group situations. Most of us play a role of some kind much, if not all, of the time, no matter what context we are in. These roles are a kind of public self and reflect our cultural training, our expectations of our self, our reactions to the expectations of others, and so on. In small groups, as in other communication settings, playing a role can be positive or negative.

One of the positive functions of roles in small groups is to allow division of labor among the members according to their capabilities and specialized knowledge. As groups begin to operate—whatever their function—certain people begin to specialize. When a member and the group discover that this is occurring, the member establishes a role in that group. Such roles are not necessarily consistent from one group to another. Roles change from group to group just as personalities do. For example, a person could be the leader of his religious-study group but show no leadership tendency in his classes. Your role will be determined by the situation, by the people around you, and by the task at hand, as well as by your own personality. It will be negotiated by you and the group.

Some people are more skilled or talented than others in certain areas or when it comes to special fields of interest. A group faced with a task that involves math, for example, will likely have at least one member with some skill in mathematics. A group faced with a creative task will probably have at least one member with creative talents. In circumstances requiring their special skills, such members will play the role of group expert; in other circumstances they may fade into the background. Inherent capabilities cannot always be estimated or anticipated, and groups need to stress their need for specialized knowledge and to encourage this kind of positive role-playing by talented group members.

Roles also are related to specific group responsibilities; for certain groups to operate efficiently, necessary tasks must be performed by someone. One such role is the coordinator of group activities. Sometimes, the coordinator will be the president, the chairman, or the program director. Sometimes, it will just be one member to whom the others look for leadership. There is also likely to be an energizer, who gets the group moving and pushes it toward greater activity. There is often a recorder, who keeps track of group progress and notes accomplishments and defeats or agreements and disagreements. There might also be an evaluator-critic, who examines the productivity, the decisions, or the reflections of the group and seeks to render some judgment of the worth of such activities. These roles or functions are likely to overlap, and several may be fulfilled by the same person. They vary with the group and with the task.

In a group that meets briefly for coffee between classes, such task-oriented roles are inappropriate, but even in groups whose chief function is social, individual roles do come into play. Think about the last time you shared coffee with a group of friends. Did you find that someone was more aggressive than the others? Did someone seek recognition? Did someone play the role of self-confessor? Playboy? Dominator? Help-seeker? Special-interest pleader? In such a group, these roles are not necessarily irrelevant to the group's behavior. They can make the group experience interesting and exciting as they stimulate conversation, provide a sounding board of ideas, and generate new ideas for consideration. Individual role-playing may have a negative effect on the group, however, because the roles that some people assume get in the way of the group's progress. Whether members of the group meet simply for the social purpose of getting to know each other better or whether there is a specific task that the group is trying to accomplish, certain individual roles can short-circuit the group's functioning.

We have catalogued a number of roles that are commonly found in human relationships. When these roles are played in small groups, they can significantly hinder the group's process.[4] We have listed below those that we have observed being played most often. It is not a complete list, nor are the roles necessarily listed according to frequency or importance; those we have noticed occurring most often are near the beginning of the list. Many times, a person will play several roles or a combination of roles. Think about yourself and those with whom you associate, and note the effects that such roles have had in groups in which you have participated.

The Anxious Participant   These individuals often make others in the group feel tense because of their own uneasiness. Sometimes, these people are disturbed just by being in a group because they are feeling apprehensive about working with others. Such group members may also be concerned about making personal feelings known, or the topic or task at hand may cause worry. A relaxed, informal atmosphere in which feelings are readily shared does the most to relieve unnecessary anxiety. If such people are encouraged to participate and are made to feel part of the group, anxiety soon disappears.

The Authoritarian   These members want to control all the other group members and everything that happens in the group. Not surprisingly, they often generate quite a bit of group hostility since the rest of the group is likely to see them as selfish and thoughtless. An authoritarian can create an atmosphere in which other group members suppress their feelings and reduce their communication. An informal group may show the authoritarian that such behavior is not welcome, especially if the group establishes a norm of cooperation. In more formal task-oriented groups, thorough preparation by all may create equality among members. Indicating the need for ideas from all members may serve to tone down the influence of the dominator.

The Silent Participant   Because of certain fears, many people are reluctant to be open with others; they prevent communication by saying very little. Left alone, the silent people will retreat further and further until they become hostile and bitter and either leave the group or become antagonistic and unhappy. Individuals who are silent suffer from the need to be supported by the group so that they can feel safe in expressing their true ideas and feelings.

The Intellectual Some intellectuals avoid full emotional relations because they are uncomfortable with feelings. These people are likely to stress rational procedures in group process and to discount affection, anger, and other personal feelings as irrelevant. Effective small-group communication requires human beings who can express emotion as well as ideas. To help make intellectuals more comfortable, emotions can be played down if the group is involved in a problem-solving task. Some intellectuals work best independently; thus, they can be given a task of responsibility that can be accomplished alone. Since many group members value emotional expression as part of the group process and since all groups need opportunities to develop member relationships through emotional exchange, often the emotional issue must be faced squarely. Failure to permit expressions of feeling may cause hostility or anxiety. Also, dealing with intellectual issues separated from emotional issues causes sterility in group deliberations; that is, the deliberations become dull, dry, and boring, lacking both depth and feeling.

The Know-It-All These individuals care more about winning the arguments than about evidence, listening, or learning from others. The know-it-alls can be quite uncomfortable in groups that have problem-solving as a major function because such groups require cooperation and a willingness to suspend judgment until all the evidence is in. Clarifying group goals, stressing cooperation, and delegating specific responsibilities to the know-it-alls may encourage such members to become more responsive to the needs and wishes of others.

The Verbose Participant Verbose members fill every void in communication by saying so much that nobody can possibly sort out all the words and figure out anything about these members' ideas or feelings. More than anything, verbose members need the support of the group. Feeling accepted and wanted, they will express their true ideas and feelings.

The Conformist These people need the acceptance of others more than they need individual expression. Since conformists are unwilling to disagree, most small groups have little interest in what they say. Conformists need to be encouraged to offer personal viewpoints. Reinforcement of their ideas will often call forth more ideas and more positive behavior.

✗ *The Indecisive Participant*   Indecisive people avoid making decisions as long as possible for fear that the decision will turn out to be wrong. Remaining indecisive is safe—a means of self-protection—but serves little useful purpose in a small group, especially a group in which decision-making, policy-formation, or problem-solving is the standard operating procedure. Uncertain members become roadblocks to effective small-group operation when there is a need by the group for the ideas, efforts, and contributions of everyone. Delegating individual responsibilities by giving task assignments and stressing the importance of deadlines and "due dates" may help the indecisive people. Respecting their contributions may also be helpful.

✗*The Rival*   Rivals in a small group make every situation a contest and every other member a competitor. They become hostile to anyone else who strives for superiority. Discussions become debates, because in debates someone wins and someone loses. Setting a tone of cooperation at the outset may help to "steal the thunder" of members bent on competition. Aligning these members' goals with those of the group- the desire of the group to excel and succeed—may also help integrate their efforts with those of other group members.

✗ *The Cynic*   Cynics distrust everybody else in the group. Often, these people have been disillusioned by some profound disappointment, and they are dissatisfied with life. Cynics have trouble being neutral about any idea or proposal. They are likely to belittle, to argue for the sake of arguing, and to dismiss any constructive suggestion as naive. Cynics are difficult members for a small group to contend with, and they often affect the whole atmosphere in which the group works. Showing a sincere interest in cynics and their ideas and demonstrating that people really do care may help to make these people more receptive to the group members and the group's ideas.

✗*The Comedian*   Group members who play this role are seeking visibility; they want to be seen by the group. If, in this role, these people would provide comic relief, the role could supply a badly needed characteristic that many groups lack. Unfortunately, comedians often take nothing seriously and hinder the work of the small group by constant laughing, jokes, and playing the role of fools for others. Pointing to the importance of the group's task, the seriousness of the matter at hand, or the need for full group attention to the problem may help gain these members' help.

There are other roles, but the important thing here is to recognize that such roles can be destructive in small groups. Often we act out roles unconsciously, but once we are aware that we are doing it, we can look for ways to change our role or the role structure of the situation or of the group so that the total resources of the group can be used. We can stop and talk about problems that occur because individuals in the group are playing roles that are causing problems. Becoming aware of the roles that we and others play and being able to discuss these roles in relation to the group's process will go a long way toward helping all the group members to reevaluate and change their role-playing behavior.

In the social circles in which you move, you can probably think of friends of yours who always seem to fulfill certain roles when your group gets together. Some of these roles are positive and some are negative, but when this group of people gets together, the roles are generally predictable. The more groups in which you participate, the more likely you are to observe a variety of different roles in others and to play a wide range of roles yourself.

Group Norms

Sometimes roles are determined by norms—standard, accepted ways of behaving, of participating, or of thinking that govern membership relationships and modes of operating. Pressures in the group cause members to conform. Norms are acceptable when they result from the collective wisdom of the group. In some cases, when a person chooses to enter a group, he or she also agrees to accept the norms of the group. In other cases, tension is created between individuals and the group because of disagreements over norms. Deviation from a group's norms will result in the norm being changed or overlooked, or in the deviate member leaving the group by pressure or by choice.

Cohesiveness

The extent to which members assume positive roles, the degree to which negative roles are minimized, and the extent to which members willingly subscribe to the norms of a group will often determine the group's cohesiveness. *Cohesiveness* is simply the group's ability to stick together, to work together as a group, and to help each other as group members. Group size is related to cohesiveness since the larger the group, the less likely that it will be cohesive and the more likely factionalization, the opposite of cohesiveness, will occur. A group that has "pulled itself together" spatially is also more likely to create cohesiveness because physical closeness generates close feeling.

Cohesive groups generally display high motivation and morale, positive group performance, and greater possibility for success. When group members are united behind a common cause or need—even if that need is simply conversation or the pleasure of each other's company—members are more cheerful, confident, and eager to expend more energy on behalf of the group. With more enthusiasm, positive group performance naturally follows. Members of a cohesive group willingly interact conversationally, which provides pleasure, a measure of positive performance in any group.

Positive performance may also be related to a task. Because cohesiveness often results in increased pressure for all members to agree, task completion is facilitated by strong cohesiveness. This can be negative when pressures to conform prevent, hinder, or otherwise obstruct tendencies to disagree. All sides of an issue are often best presented through disagreements, as evidence and ideas are challenged and questioned by nonconforming members. This strength should not be sacrificed—even if it means some loss of cohesiveness.

High motivation and good group morale may also be valued by some group members. If individuals derive pleasure from such feelings, it is likely that cohesiveness will increase in a cyclical manner—building on itself. Better decisions, freer participation, and even high motivation to carry out and support group decisions are likely to result.

Cohesiveness does not mean total uniformity or total agreement. As a matter of fact, those groups that demonstrate high cohesiveness are often noisy, full of good-natured teasing, disagreement, even argument—all characteristics of strong interaction and a healthy group atmosphere. Individuals in such groups enjoy being together, sometimes disregard time limits, discuss issues even after the meeting is over, and raise important questions, which they discuss thoroughly. There is cooperation, consideration for others, some defined group goals, some discipline, and some differentiation among roles as well.

X A group *personality*—the aggregate of the individual personalities combined together at a particular time and for a specific purpose—depends upon the size of the group, the way the group arranges itself, the roles the members play, the norms of the group, and the degree of cohesiveness achieved. Together these factors can create a group that is greater than the sum of its parts. In successful small groups, the personalities of the individuals in the group combine with, intensify, and

complement each other as the members interact in the group setting. No group experience can duplicate another; every meeting of the same group is different just as every group is different because the personality of the group develops and changes as the group works together.
develops and changes as the group works together.

PATTERNS FOR COMMUNICATING IN SMALL GROUPS

Much of the communication that takes place in a group results from an individual's need to learn what the others believe, to modify his or her own opinions, to try to change the beliefs of the others, and, thus, to bring his or her view of reality into line with that of members of the group. *Group process*—the carrying out of the group's functions—depends upon this communication. Unity within the group is created as group functions are negotiated, appraised, and agreed upon. Decisions regarding size, spatial arrangements, individual roles, and group norms are reached through communication just as cohesiveness is achieved through communication.

Ineffective communication can result if the size of the group is too large, if the spatial arrangements do not allow for close face-to-face interaction, if the members' roles do not support the group effort, or if the norms are broken or disregarded. Successful group process also depends upon establishing constructive patterns of communication among group members and utilizing good communication skills.

The patterns of communication between individuals in a group are produced by the flow and direction of message exchange. Effective communication involves everyone; messages flow among all members rather than resting statically with one or being exchanged by only a few. Communication is dynamic—continually circulating and proceeding smoothly among members in a spontaneous manner—unprogrammed and unstilted.

The direction of the message flow is often affected by the roles of members or by their status in a group. If one member's role is considered important for the situation or for the task, the others in the group are likely to direct comments to that member and to acknowledge his or her contributions more than those of others. A group of friends deciding to go to the movies may, for example, recognize the suggestions of one member who is a film major in school or is known to keep up with movie reviews. In this group, this member plays the role of a knowledgeable source. The direction of communication in such a group is represented in the pattern in Figure 5.1.

The direction of the communication may also be influenced by member status. If a manager calls together a group of employees to discuss

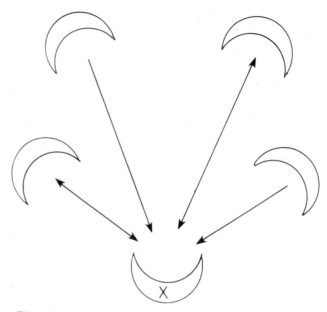

Figure 5.1

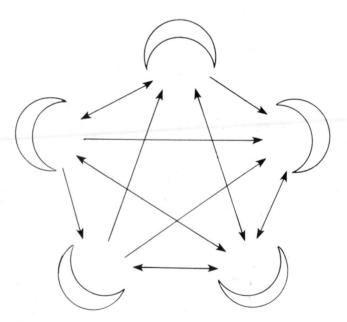

Figure 5.2

changes in company policy, their communication would probably be directed according to the pattern in Figure 5.1. If, instead, the manager is not present, and the employees decide to get together as a group to prepare a slate of grievances, the communication patterns would be more like Figure 5.2.

This second pattern for the direction of communication is more likely to encourage a free exchange of ideas and to result in members feeling that they have had a chance to express themselves because participation is fairly equal, with communication directed to all members of the group.

Patterns of communication in small groups should not be static. Direction and the extent or degree of flow in any single discussion are likely to change as the group functions. The group of friends who are selecting a movie, for example, will use the pattern in Figure 5.1 while they get suggestions from their knowledgeable source; they will use the pattern in Figure 5.2 when they decide which showing of the film is the most convenient time for most members.

The best communication patterns are those that encourage widespread participation in fulfilling the group's task. Thus, the manager-directed meeting is really not a small group at all. It is a public-speaking situation because the manager is not interested in receiving messages from the group of employees in order to change his views; he is simply interested in sending a prepared message. When employees meet to exchange grievances, on the other hand, the pattern of their communication involves all the group members in the transaction; this is a true small-group situation.

Effective small-group communication depends upon the same speaker and listener skills that produce effective interpersonal or public communication. Each speaker should be audible, use variety, be clear and fluent, and coordinate the verbal and nonverbal channels of communication so that they support each other. Each listener should give attention to all channels of the message and should provide clear feedback so that the speaker will know his or her message is being received. These skills are crucial in small-group situations because the whole group process depends upon a continual flow of clear messages among the group members.

It is important for both listeners and speakers in small groups to be flexible in their use of communication. Sometimes it is best for the listener to interrupt—to say that he or she does not understand the message, for example. At other times, it is more helpful to allow the speaker to complete his or her message before imposing another message on top of it. Sometimes the best way to communicate in a small group is to say nothing, to send an I-am-waiting-to-see-what-the-others-say message nonverbally, and to wait. Small-group communication sometimes requires such restraint. Each member should be sensitive to what is happening with all the others as well as to the effect of such nonverbal factors as room size and extraneous noise on the quality of the communcation.

Good communication is an important factor in cohesiveness; the cohesive group will likely demonstrate effective use of communication skills because all members make every effort to cooperate with each other—which means sending and receiving messages in a way that does not obstruct or build barriers to the exchange of meaning. They will interrupt others and willingly be interrupted by others to help generate the spontaneity good discussion requires. Cohesiveness encourages good communication, too, because as members begin to care about the group, they will speak up, ask questions, and seek more information.

LEADERSHIP

Some people see all leaders as coercive, inflexible, dogmatic tyrants. To others, leaders are impotent, "wishy-washy," ineffectual opportunists who got where they are by accident. The effective small-group leader resides somewhere in between, revealing characteristics of both extremes when the context calls for it. He or she is a leader, perhaps, because of special training or ability, because of the purposes of the group, because of pressures put on the group from outside, or because of the way the people in the group relate to one another. People do become leaders by accident; they are also appointed, chosen, and voted into office. Often, too, they rise to the occasion in a group because of some specialized knowledge or ability that is appropriate at the time.

X A *leader* performs actions that direct the group toward achieving a desired goal. A group may, thus, have one leader or many—as many leaders as there are members—depending upon the situation, the participants, and the task. Any member who influences a group is, in a sense, leading it. For a group to have a leader, then, someone need not be designated to perform the leadership task; it is rather a question of the degree to which members of the group are willing to lead. We are all leaders since even a member's silence may influence the group. However, some people will, very likely, lead more than others.

Understanding leadership and how it operates in small groups helps in two ways: it makes us more aware of what leaders in general do, and it helps us to know what is expected when we play a leadership role in a small group. To provide this understanding, we will examine the emergence of leadership, the function of leaders, and the styles of leadership.

The Emergence of Leaders

There are, basically, two ways that leaders become leaders. They appear in a group because they are imposed on it—such as the employee who is asked by an employer to "head up" a study group to determine how the company can educate employees in ways of using their leisure time. They may, on the other hand, emerge from the group during its deliberations. A group of tenants, for example, may meet to discuss what steps they should take as a result of their landlord's raising everyone's rent. Each of the members has his or her own alternative, which is considered in turn by the group. As each tenant suggests and defends a particular alternative, he or she is leading the group. A group that operates without an imposed leader is likely to experience *functional leadership,* in which the role of leader is distributed among the group members in this way. If the group selects one of its members as a leader, the group is imposing a leader on itself.

Just because a group has an imposed leader, does not mean, however, that functional leadership cannot also occur. When an individual senses at a particular time that he or she can best mirror the group's needs and influence its behavior, that person may take a leadership role, even if another person has been designated group leader. An effective imposed leader will create a permissive atmosphere by supporting free discussion and, thus, provide an environment hospitable to, and encouraging of, functional leadership.

Leadership is a role that is given by the group; it is not a property of an individual. A leader cannot function in that role without the group's permission, in spite of the fact that groups often do not realize this and leaders do not often acknowledge it. Leadership is conferred upon various individuals by the group during the process of interaction. How this occurs is not always clear, since the process varies with the task, and the role of leader may move very quickly from individual to individual. But leadership is likely to remain with an individual who is most influential at a particular time until he or she no longer meets the group's needs.

The Functions of Leaders

There are, essentially, four major leadership functions that need to be filled in a small group. These functions can be fulfilled at the appropriate time by anyone in the group. A group with a strong imposed leader may look to him or her to satisfy most of these needs whereas a group with no imposed leader will, very likely, find that these needs are satisfied by a variety of individuals. The four major functions of a leader are establishing procedures, raising questions, focusing on answers, and encouraging social-emotional growth.

X *Establishing Procedures*   A small-group meeting is conducted according to a plan that structures the group's work; establishing and maintaining this structure are procedural functions. If an effective procedural framework is established, the task of the group will be easier and more efficiently fulfilled. Procedural functions include beginning the communication, selecting and ordering the topics, encouraging participation, achieving progress, and calling for self-assessment. The need for procedures such as these varies with the task of the group, but the leadership of any group includes providing a structure within which the group can best function.

A strong start sets the precedent for effective group process. Just as first impressions count in interpersonal relationships, they also influence group procedures. The group leader who begins with a brief introduction, makes his or her remarks clear and interesting, and shows the group through manner and responsibility that the task is worth considering and capable of solution will stimulate the group to productive activity. Any member who helps to get the group off to a good start is fulfilling this leadership function.

When no order is agreed upon by the group, chaos may prevent the group from making any progress with its task. Some sequential ordering is necessary for most discussions just as road maps are for traveling long distances. The pattern should result from group deliberations and, generally, should not be imposed on a group. The leader's role here is simply to point out the need for order and to encourage the group to discuss the structuring of its work. Order should be flexible—able to change as a result of the actual discussion—and the leader may also warn the group about imposing too rigid a structure on itself at the beginning.

The leader who makes all group members feel that they have adequate opportunity to speak will also create a positive group atmosphere. Participation cannot be completely equal, of course, and the silent member often feels satisfied with the group. However, contributions from as many members as possible will be solicited by an alert and conscientious leader.

The best way that contributions can be clarified is by using the mirroring response, in which a person seeks to find out from a communicator whether or not he or she understood what the communicator said. A leader who is skilled in paraphrasing the contributions of others will keep all group members informed on the comments of other members and keep the discussion on the topic. Through paraphrasing, the digressions and extraneous material can be weeded out. When misunderstanding occurs, it should be cleared up at once. Full participation is generated when all members realize that they are being listened to by the rest of the group.

Groups cannot move ahead when members spend excessive amounts of time dealing with trivial matters or dealing with only a certain phase of a problem. An effective small-group leader will move the group toward another phase of the problem when the leader feels that a sufficient amount of information has been presented, when information is being repeated, when a point being discussed is trivial, or when members engage in purposeless conversation and small talk. Often, achieving progress requires some aggressiveness on the part of the leader. The leader must be willing to interject himself or herself and the group's agenda upon its members. This requires some discretion and diplomacy because group members do not like to be bossed; it also requires the ability to recognize useful digressions, which can promote harmony, encourage humor, or permit the expression of new ideas within the group.

It is often necessary for a group to take time out to find itself. Misunderstandings occur, material is omitted, direction loses focus, and digressions take place. Many such problems can be solved if the group feels free to take time out from the task to discuss how it is progressing. An effective leader will call for this self-assessment when it is needed.

Summarizing is one good way to provide self-assessment. It serves to alert the group to where it has been, what it has accomplished, where it is now, and where it is going. Conciseness and brevity require that only basic ideas are stated in a summary—not complete details. It is essential that the leader who summarizes be accurate; if a leader reports what he or she wishes the group had said instead of what it actually said, conflict will result from the summary and time will be lost instead of gained. Summaries do not need to be given only by an imposed leader; they should be provided as needed by anyone in the group who feels that clarity, efficiency, and understanding will be promoted by summarizing the group's progress.

Raising Questions Questions are asked by the leader during small-group deliberations for specific purposes: to identify goals, to gain information, to evaluate information, to find solutions, to resolve differences, or to ask for a plan of action. Leaders who are effective in getting answers to such questions are able to ask them in such a way that the leader does not place group members on the defensive or make a member feel that the question is designed to "catch" him or her off guard or to challenge his or her integrity.

Group members who are not clear about the nature of specific group goals are likely to direct their efforts toward different objectives. Goal-seeking questions provide a common focus. Changes that occur during a group's deliberations often require modifications in the goal or changes in previous commitments to goals. A leader who asks group members about limiting the discussion to the goal at hand, who inquires about making clear certain aspects that have been previously discussed, and who comments that the group appears to be off the track is focusing on group goals. This leadership intervention may help individual focal points to become group focal points.

Seeking information is an integral part of many kinds of groups. If the task of the group is to solve a problem, the group should be encouraged to delay a consideration of solutions until all the facts are in and have been analyzed. When there is insufficient information, profitable discussion is impossible since a pooling of ignorance is ignorance. In encounter groups, the most important information has to do with what members are feeling or how they are reacting to something that another member has said. Once the information is discovered, it should then be shared to the fullest extent possible.

Often, a group receives information that must be evaluated. Effective leadership can be exercised if a member asks questions such as these about information: How recent is the information? Who is the source of the information? Is he or she biased? Is he or she an expert? Under what circumstances was the information collected? Does the information mean what it appears to mean? Is there contradictory information? These questions are as appropriate for information about personal feelings and judgments as they are for information about objective knowledge. Facts and opinions should be scrutinized carefully for possible errors or misinterpretation.

When the group is seeking solutions, leadership can be exercised to encourage members of the group to be flexible in their thinking. People often become prisoners of their own thinking because they suffer from "hardening of the categories." Questions can be designed that will free these prisoners from their stereotyped, typical, or common-knowledge responses. Roadblocks to discovery can be overcome when a leader is prepared to offer alternative courses of action that will motivate group members to achieve a higher level of critical thinking. This is equally vital whether the group is discussing a political topic or a personal one.

Solutions should be evaluated with consideration for their advantages and disadvantages. Some solutions rejected earlier in the discussion can be offered again as new insights are gained and new combinations seen. A useful leadership role is played by members who ask questions such as these: What are the consequences that are likely to occur? What are the costs that are likely to accrue? What barriers have to be overcome and how serious are they?

Good leadership includes allowing for disagreements to occur and encouraging their expression by all members of the group. If the group establishes a norm of permitting differences to be expressed, questions about various positions and statements of opposition will not appear offensive. The energy that is generated by conflict in a group can be a strong and positive force for pushing toward the fulfillment of the group's task, but conflict is difficult for many people to handle. Careful leadership is required if disagreement is to be used constructively by the group. The leader can mediate controversies by phrasing questions about opposing views in a neutral manner that focuses on the points of difference; this is clarifying behavior. Leadership is also exercised by the member who distinguishes between the controversial idea and the person who expresses it; when possible, members should avoid attaching a controversial position to a particular speaker.

Complete unanimity is seldom possible in small-group process when minds are actively operating in a mature and intelligent way. The success of the group depends on satisfaction with the process—not whether everybody agrees all the time. If the atmosphere is warm and friendly, conflict can be tolerated by the group and members are less likely to become angry or embarrassed about the statement of controversial ideas.

In some groups the task includes formulating a plan of action, a group commitment to do something to solve the problem with which the group has been struggling. If you decide in a group that the only course of action is to demonstrate against the administration for its unfair practices, your group will be faced with making plans for that demonstration. How are you to publicize your grievances, get recruits, and carry out the protest so that it will effect the changes your group wants? Effective leadership includes helping the group to plan carefully for the action that it has decided to take. It is important to remind the group that a superior plan for action that is ineffectively implemented is of less value than a mediocre plan that is well executed.

X *Focusing on Answers* To accomplish its task, a group needs answers. If the function of the group is to solve a problem, members need to keep their attention on solutions. One of the most frustrating discussion-group experiences is to be a member of a group that just talks and talks without seeming to come to any closer clarification of the issue under discussion. In groups in which social-emotional growth is the main task, members need to feel that they are finding some answers to the personal difficulties that brought them into the group. Effective group leadership in each of these situations involves focusing the group's attention on the need for answers and supporting members who work toward answers without imposing the leader's answers on the group or any individual in the group.

In a group composed of definite factions, where intragroup conflict is strong, or in which the potential for controversy is great, the leader should exercise restraint—assuming a position of neutrality and playing the role of receptive listener. His or her answers should be scrutinized to the same extent as the answers of other members. It is very important in such a group that all positions are heard and that summaries and interpretations be given fairly.

When conflict is not as great, the leader can make more frequent substantive contributions. He or she should place greatest emphasis on the substantive contributions of others, however, assuming primary concern for the procedural aspects of leadership. The leader should not excel in providing answers at the expense of others but should provide facts, evaluations, and solutions whenever these would be helpful to the group.

Encouraging Social-Emotional Growth   Personal growth is one of the by-products of any effective small group. This growth is achieved when people are recognized and accepted by others, when they feel secure, and when they are valued. The main task of encounter groups is to encourage personal growth through accentuating humanistic values, which emphasize the dignity and worth of the individual. The group engages in supportive behavior that builds a person's sense of worth and importance. But the need for these feelings is not confined to encounter groups; any group to which a person belongs needs to provide that person with the same reinforcement. The more friendliness, mutual trust, respect, and warmth exhibited, the more likely the member will find pleasure in the group and, too, the more likely he or she will work hard toward the accomplishment of the group's goals.

The development of an informal group atmosphere will aid in the reduction or elimination of anxiety, discomfort, embarrassment, and strain. Status differences can be minimized by the arrangement of chairs. The leader can encourage the use of "we," "us," and "our" to show group spirit, and he or she can use the first names of all persons.

The effective leader will strive to reinforce desirable traits, worthy cntributions, and helpful additions to group deliberations. Rein-forcement simply means strengthening. When behavior is rewarded, we can expect more evidence of the same desirable behavior in the future. The leader who understands others, provides conclusive proof of his understanding—through paraphrasing, for example—agrees with others, and helps others, goes a long way in promoting higher levels of participant satisfaction.

Styles of Leadership

In a successful small group, members know that others in the group are behaving in accordance with the demands of the situation for a certain style of leadership. In some situations, complete freedom for full participation by all members is desired. There are other situations, however, in which forceful, unchallenged leadership is expected. These are the opposite ends of a continuum. There are, essentially, three kinds of leadership styles: authoritarian, democratic, and laissez-faire. In addition, some groups function best with no leader at all.

Authoritarian Leadership Using the authoritarian style, the leader determines all policies, dictates the particular work task, and, generally, remains aloof from active group participation. One would expect this style in the military establishment. At times, too, one sees signs of it in elected political officials or in business bureaucrats. They appear to possess virtue, realize that justice resides with the strong, share leadership with no one, insist on deference and respect from others, and treat others as means to an end.

Although one would think that a person who demonstrated such characteristics would be easy to identify, these characteristics are probably not all demonstrated by one person in a small group. Sometimes two or three members in a group exhibit authoritarian leadership styles; if they are strong enough or remain unopposed by other members with different styles, these individuals establish the leadership style for the group. Often such persons play the role of dominators. The authoritarian may well be a skillful manipulator who engineers consent in a subtle and unforceful manner. Cleverness is often a trait of the leader who seeks to control by authoritarian means.

Democratic Leadership Using the democratic style, the leader encourages and assists the group in the determination of policies. The group is also responsible for determining the general steps required to meet the group goal. The leader maintains objectivity by giving the group choices, suggesting alternative procedures, being fact-minded in praise and criticism, and in trying to be a regular group member rather than dictating procedure on courses of action, praising or criticizing members themselves instead of their information, and maintaining aloofness.

Democratic leadership lies between the extremes of authoritarian

and laissez-faire leadership. The democratic leader draws characteristics from both these extremes. Some control and guidance from the leader is necessary to obtain order, efficiency, and forward progression, and some permissiveness is also beneficial—with the minimum amount of restraint—to encourage full participation and the widest possible range of suggested alternatives—ideas, suggestions, feelings, courses of action, and so on.

Democratic leadership is also beneficial for the group members. Members like to share in the process—in the way things are accomplished. Members reveal greater degrees of friendliness, more willingness to work as a team, and more satisfaction with the group as a whole because of democratic leadership. When they have been an integral part of the process, they not only speak positively of other members and of the way things were done, but they are also more willing to support conclusions, decisions, or other group results and products.

Laissez-faire Leadership Using the laissez-faire style of leadership, the leader will participate in the group very little, allowing complete freedom for group or for individual decisions. The laissez-faire leader is still a leader because he or she will provide information when asked. He or she takes no part in the discussion, however, and this leader's usual behavior could be described as almost complete nonparticipation. There is, thus, no attempt to appraise, regulate, question, or direct except for occasional spontaneous remarks on member activities—unless otherwise requested by the members.

The Leaderless Group In contrast to these styles of leadership is the leaderless group. There appears to be a trend toward such groups because of the reactions people have toward leaders in general and because of some of the negative models presented for us by those in high administrative places. Much communication and discussion occurs in groups without the presence of a chairperson or other high-status person to take over the leadership role. When a group of students meets casually to plan a program, a petition, a platform, or a presentation, no single member may be recognized as the leader.

Robert Freed Bales found that in leaderless groups there are usually two complementary types of individuals who appear, one who tends to specialize as a task-oriented person and one who becomes a social-emotional specialist. He also found, in asking group members to rate one another, that the "best-liked" individual was the one who most actively initiated social-emotional interactions.[5]

Discussion may occur in which no one emerges as a leader. All the functions are diffused among all the members but with no division of labor or specialization. Feelings of equality, of freedom, of informality, and of activity are sometimes experienced in such groups. However, one may soon discover, depending upon the situation, the participants, or the topic or task, that procedure breaks down. Minority views may be slighted, perhaps, even unknowingly; progress toward a specific goal may be absent; efficiency may deteriorate. when minority views, goal-orientation, and efficiency are unimportant or irrelevant—as they may be when a group of students who have had some training in group methods meet to discuss politics, religion, or sex—then a leaderless situation may work well. It may work, too, with a group that meets casually with no particular purpose except sociability or compatibility.

Choosing the Appropriate Style of Leadership   Styles of leadership often result from the style of the group. Often, a group composed of members with strong personalities needs to be democratic—the preferred leadership style for most groups. Members will either press for or provide an atmosphere for their leader to operate democratically. Leadership is often contextual as well as personal; it can be determined by the context of the group as well as the individual personality of the leader, although it is likely that both affect each other. A group leader will probably not be able to operate democratically if the members are unwilling to receive his coercion, help, protection, or restrictions in the benevolent manner in which they are proffered. Benevolence—the desire to do good for others—distinguishes the democratic leader from the undemocratic leader in his or her use of power.

There are other characteristic ways in which groups behave that have a tendency to inhibit the operation of democratic leadership. Members, for example, would not be recipients of democratic leadership if they became excessively task- or productivity-oriented rather than concerned with the degree of representation of group members. If the pressures toward conformity—inducing members to go along with an idea because everyone else is—become too great, democratic group functioning may discourage democratic leadership. Efficiency, too—being overly concerned with the time element—may cause a group to dispense with democracy in favor of more efficient procedures. Thus, one can see that the needs of the group will determine the appropriate leadership style for that group.

EVALUATION IN SMALL-GROUP PROCESS

Evaluation sometimes occurs spontaneously after an interpersonal communication when you find yourself thinking, "Oh, I wish I had thought to say that." After you have given a speech, you often find yourself delivering in your head the speech you wish you had given. In the same way, you are likely to evaluate the small-group situations in which you participate; you may think about how you behaved as a group member, and you probably have an overall reaction to the group, labeling it "good," "bad," "a waste of time," "productive," or "fun." Criticism and evaluation are bound to happen. Thus, it is worth considering briefly useful techniques for judging small-group communication. For groups that continue to meet over a period of time, evaluation can improve the process and product of the group. For groups meeting only once, evaluation will facilitate better understanding of what happened in the group and why it happened. In addition, members may acquire information that might enable them to become better participants or leaders in other groups.

X There are, essentially, two aspects of the small group that can be evaluated. The first is the process—the things that occurred while the group was carrying out its task. Analysis of the process includes examination of the development of relationships in the group, the degree to which members got along with each other and formed a group, as well as cohesiveness and attitudes; problem-solving patterns; the quality, quantity, and spread of communication; and the leadership. In evaluating leadership, you could ask: Who was leader? How did he or she perform? What style was exhibited? What effect did it have on the group? What functions were fulfilled by the leader?

X The second focal point for evaluation is the product—the end result of the group's work together. You might examine the quality of the product: how satisfied group members were with it; the feasibility of the solution, if one was reached; the amount of information obtained by group members; possible changes in attitudes; the quantity of the product, or the extent to which the group achieved its goal.

Individual group members may also be evaluated separately in an analysis of their effectiveness as participants in this particular group. We can look at the participants and the way they handle information, reason, structure their contributions, use language, relate to others and communicate. We can also look at the leader and the group to determine how the various parts combined to make the whole.

Evaluation can be undertaken by the group members themselves —although members may not be as objective as they might be if they were not focusing on themselves. Self-evaluation is a useful exercise for each individual, especially when performed along with other kinds of evaluation. Evaluation by other group members is also useful. However, a great deal of variation often occurs between ratings, and averages are useful to achieve a balanced criticism. Trained observers sitting on the sidelines are often more objective than we can be ourselves or than other group members can be about us. A final type of appraisal may be made by people who have had nothing to do with the discussion and who see it on film or videotape, or hear it on tape recording.

Evaluation during the group process allows members to see problems when they occur, to halt the discussion while in process, and to act before a serious difficulty gets in the way of the group's functioning. The group can thus alter its process or change its direction to a more fruitful course of action.

Perhaps the most useful time to evaluate is immediately after the discussion or meeting, when the whole picture is vivid and the proceedings are still clear in the minds of participants. To delay the evaluation is to blur the images somewhat, which may spoil the sharp contrast of the picture even though delayed evaluation may allow time for reflective thought and for testing the decisions reached by the group.

There are several methods of evaluation. One useful method is to discuss what took place. Another method is to use rating forms that might include such items as knowledge of the subject, analysis of the subject, reasoning ability, familiarity with the process, communication skills, and awareness and concern for others. Another type of form is the open-ended one, which allows the evaluator complete freedom in response. In some groups, one can test the feasibility or workability of the group's decision as a method of evaluating it. Simply raise the flag to see if it flies! Finally, one can judge the holding power of a group by finding out who comes back. If members keep coming back, there is no question that they feel they are engaged in a worthwhile activity, an enjoyable experience.

THE PROBLEM-SOLVING GROUP: A CASE STUDY

Much of the communication that occurs in small groups is directed toward solving problems. For example, all groups must determine procedures, set norms, and negotiate individual member roles, and each of these decisions may be seen as a problem that the group needs to resolve if it is to function well. In addition, some groups are created specifically to find the solution to a particular, predetermined question. A work group such as a committee that is formed to investigate an issue and bring back recommendations to its authorizing body is an example. Since problem-solving is such a common group task, we will consider in some detail the functions of a successful problem-solving group.

The main form of communication in problem-solving groups is discussion. The group meets to exchange information and ideas in an effort to gain better understanding of particular issues or situations. Discussion, in this sense, is restricted to situations characterized by free interaction among members in which specific objectives are outlined by the group, relevant information is offered to substantiate ideas, consideration of the ideas is thorough, and group responsibility is directed toward moving from conception of the idea to its disposal or solution. It is, thus, different from communication that normally occurs in bull sessions, coffee klatsches, encounter groups, and sensitivity sessions.

In 1910, John Dewey wrote a book entitled *How We Think,* which provides a guide to reflective thinking—a scientific pattern of thought requiring a high degree of rationality, a deep respect for evidence, and a careful consideration of possible answers or solutions to problems.[6] Dewey's reflective pattern includes five steps in a sequence that leads from the determination of the problem to the determination of the solution: 1) recognition of the problem; 2) description of the problem; 3) suggestion of possible solutions; 4) evaluation of solutions by reasoning and the discovery of the best solution; 5) development of the plan of action. The reflective pattern provides a useful structure that can be put into practice—in part or *in toto*—in small problem-solving groups. The entire pattern, which is presented here, is probably best suited to formal, task-oriented groups. The structure may be adapted, however, for use in less formal group situations in which problem-solving is part of the group's process.

Recognizing the Problem

One of the most difficult tasks for students involved in practicing discussion techniques is the selection of a topic. In real-life situations, topics arise naturally out of the situation: school boards are faced with formulating a policy about the "open classroom"; company administrative committees must make a decision about the four-day work week; a group of town selectmen try to determine how to handle the problem of sewage disposal. Students planning for in-class situations may find fruitful topics in the areas of business or education, in the social or political arena, or in considerations of personal opinion about local issues. Such topics include business monopolies, educational grading policies, the social problem of crime, political scandal, and a person's right to privacy.

After the topic has been selected, it should be formulated as a proposition. *Propositions* are simply formal presentations of any subject selected for discussion; they may be in statement or question form. There

are three types of propositions: fact, value, or policy. Propositions of fact allege the existence of something an object, an event, or a relationship. They are found to be either true or false, based on the evidence that is accumulated to affirm or deny them. Propositions of fact are most appropriate for groups whose primary purpose is the accumulation of information or evidence—fact-finding groups. For example, seeking to encourage shopping in a downtown area, a group of businessmen may get together to resolve a proposition that might be phrased "Business in the downtown area can be expanded." The businessmen might wish to present information on this topic such as the *likelihood* that it can be expanded, current sales this year versus last year at the same time, parking availability, and so on, before deciding that something should be done. They may find that business is operating at near peak capacity, considering the parking spaces available, or they may find that most businessmen are not at all dissatisfied with the present level of business. Either of these findings would make their proposition false.

Propositions of value express evaluative judgments concerning the goodness or badness of some person, institution, or idea. This kind of proposition involves making a judgment only; it is not concerned with recommending a policy or action. "Business in the downtown area is good" is one example. Another might be "Is the present system of electing the President truly a democratic process?" Commissions selected to determine the possible harm of a current trend or a proposed change treat value propositions: "Is pornography harmful to society?" "Pollution is damaging our environment." "Will the proposed bypass be harmful to downtown business?" "Will the pass-fail grading system be detrimental to future employment?" Questions regarding judgments of value are often resolved before a group takes action on a policy.

Propositions of policy are the types of questions most often discussed in small-group problem-solving discussions. Such propositions are concerned with a new policy, a change of policy, or some other specific action. A proposition of policy asks, should this be done? "Should business in the downtown area be advanced?" "Should our system of electing the President be changed?" "Should pornography be legalized?" "Should pollution be controlled?" Almost any topic can be phrased as a proposition of policy. Policy questions often can be detected by the presence of the word *should*, or one of its synonyms: *ought, has to,* or *must.*

Knowing whether you have a proposition of fact, value, or policy is only part of recognizing the problem. The actual phrasing of the problem is also important, for a poorly worded proposition can affect every other stage of its resolution. The proposition can be phrased as a question or as a statement, but a question often attracts more attention and provides more impetus for active discussion, since it challenges rather than just declares. The proposition should be clear. Ambiguous wording will cause discussion time to be wasted in figuring out what the words of the proposition mean. The proposition should concentrate on one aspect of a broad topic, one that can be reasonably handled in the time allotted for the discussion. Trying to treat "Should stricter measures be employed to reduce crime?" in a one-hour discussion is certain to be frustrating because the necessary information cannot possibly be covered in that amount of time. Discussing a single subtopic such as recidivism, rape, or shoplifting in an hour is a bit more feasible.

Good discussion can be encouraged, too, if the proposition invites many-sided responses rather than simply a yes or no. It is better to begin with "To what extent should . . ." or "What should be the role . . ." than simply to begin with "Should. . . ." Finally, the proposition should not reflect the biases of the formulators. You should try to avoid using words like *irresponsible, unnecessary, irrelevant,* or *unreasonable* in a policy proposition. Let these judgments be discovered in the discussion of the topic and be supported with evidence.

Early consideration of these problems in finding and phrasing topics encourages productive discussion. A group that finds an exciting and stimulating topic and phrases it precisely and clearly is well on its way toward generating effective communication and strong group cohesiveness. If everyone agrees with the topic choice and its phrasing, a healthy group spirit and atmosphere will probably accompany all group deliberations. A well-phrased proposition also provides the foundation for the remaining steps in the Dewey reflective-thinking procedure.

Defining the Problem

One way to define a problem is to look at its effects. To study the proposition "Should television violence on children's shows be reduced?" you would need to find out the immediate effects of violence on the children who watch it. Do children who are exposed to televised violence commit more aggressive acts than children who are not exposed? What is the relationship between juvenile crime and televised violence? Your group might also look into long-range effects such as the extent to which violence in children's shows affects those who, later, as adults go to prison for committing violent crimes.

Often, it is difficult to determine cause-effect relationships of this kind. If the group is unable to link a particular effect with televised violence, the group has still uncovered useful information since it may conclude that no such relationship exists. Thus, no information is sometimes as helpful as positive information in the description of the problem.

Another way to define a problem is to examine its underlying causes. Some consideration of the history of the problem is often helpful. How long have children's shows depicted violence? Has there been an increase in juvenile crime or in aggressive acts by children since television has become widespread? These sorts of questions will help to place the problem in historical perspective.

Finally, in defining the problem, specific information about the immediate causes should be sought by the group. Who writes television shows depicting violence? Why is it depicted? Why do advertisers support shows with violence in them? To what extent is violence ignored by parents? Learning about the immediate causes of the problem will help the group to clarify exactly what the problem is; it will also prepare the group to consider solutions.

Finding Solutions

Following a thorough and complete defining of the problem, discussion should turn to the discovery of solutions. Information gained from the definition phase will help the group to determine the conditions to be met by an acceptable solution. A solution to the television-violence problem, for example, would have to be agreeable to writers, advertisers, and audience members. In another example, a solution to our transportation problems would have to satisfy the needs of automobile users, be reasonably inexpensive, and be efficient.

With conditions outlined, possible solutions—including a variety of alternatives—can be determined. A high degree of creativity is desirable in this step. New solutions, or unusual approaches, often result from the combination of individual contributions. Group members who try to integrate and synthesize are often the ones who see the big breakthroughs, the uncommon, the unpredictable, and the new. Such combinations, however, result from a base created through careful study and preparation, the accumulation of knowledge and methodical planning as well as imaginary wandering, hunches, intuitions, and the ability to juggle many different responses.

Realistic discussion of solutions includes consideration of the kinds of attitudes that exist regarding the problem. If the topic is abortion, it is important for group-discussion members to understand the Roman Catholic position on abortion. The degree to which a negative attitude is held toward a topic—and the number of people who hold such an attitude—could determine the workability of a particular solution as well as the plan of action to be used to institute it.

Evaluating Solutions

Once a number of solutions have been discussed, they can be evaluated and the best one accepted by the group for action. The best solutions come out of group discussions in which evaluation of the various possibilities is delayed until all solution alternatives have been discussed. Sometimes a solution that would have been rejected by premature evaluation eventually becomes part of the accepted solution because the group delayed a too hasty judgment of it.

In evaluating solutions, members should discuss their merits and weaknesses, keeping in mind that each solution may offer a partial answer. It is essential that disagreement as well as agreement be expressed so that the group can come up with the best possible response to the problem. Often, a multiple solution—one that has different parts, phases, or steps, and combines several responses—is the best answer. The final judgment of a solution will be determined by whether it has the potential for changing present undesirable effects, whether it corrects the causes of the problem, and whether it satisfies the other conditions to be met by an acceptable solution, conditions that have been agreed upon during the phase of discovery of solutions. Some initial testing might be necessary.

The Plan of Action

The final step involves the plan of action—the determination of how the accepted solution will be put into operation. What group or what individuals will carry out the solution endorsed by the group? How will they do it? How will they be contacted? How will they be supervised and evaluated? What barriers need to be overcome? To consider the solution in light of how it can be put into action is to look at it in the light of reality—what really might happen when it is publicized and promoted.

It is easy for a group to be idealistic, especially a group of students sitting in the classroom, generating creative and interesting ideas that look good and sound good. There is, no doubt, merit in the consideration of such paper policies—but often the test of a group's success is whether they come up with ideas and courses of action that can be practiced, utilized, or implemented. To consider the plan of action is to keep an eye on the real world.

Using Dewey's pattern of reflective thinking encourages active, persistent, and careful consideration of ideas. It also promotes the investigation of the evidence that supports ideas and the conclusions that lead from them. Discussion characterized by the use of this structural format reflects definite purpose; systematic and logical procedure; effective oral communication; consideration of all available ideas, facts, and opinions that bear on the topic; group cooperation; and leadership in one form or another. This is what successful problem-solving small-group communication is all about.

SUMMARY

We depend upon various kinds of small groups in much of our living. These groups have different kinds of goals, from the solution of a specific problem to the pleasure of social interchange, but all of them have certain characteristics in common: the members are similar and interdependent; there is interaction and communication among them; and they share common needs or goals.

Small-group communication is multilateral in that members play the role of speaker and of listener interchangeably. Successful small groups have between three and nine members in most cases to permit maximum interchange among the members. The arrangement of space for small-group communication depends upon the expected psychological relationships of the members and also upon the group's task. Members of small groups play roles that may be either helpful or destructive of the group's purposes. Each group also develops a set of norms for the group's behavior. The degree of cohesiveness in a group depends upon the group's size, its spatial arrangements, the roles that members assume, and the extent to which the group develops and adheres to group norms.

Constructive patterns of communication in small groups permit the greatest flow of messages among all the group members. The direction of the message flow in a group is affected by the roles of the members and by the relative status of various group members. Among the most important communication skills in groups are the ability to listen, the ability to give good feedback, and the ability to be flexible.

A leader directs the group in performing its task. Any member who influences the group may be said to be leading it. Leaders may be imposed on a group, or they may emerge from the group in response to a need felt either by ths leader or by others in the group. Among the functions of a leader are to establish procedures, to raise questions, to focus on answers, and to encourage social-emotional growth. Of the three leadership styles —authoritarian, democratic, and laissez-faire—the democratic style works best for most groups. Some groups also function successfully without leaders.

Evaluation need not always occur in small-group communication. However, if one intends to improve group behavior, evaluation should be part of the group's operations. Evaluation may center on the group's process or on the end result of the group's work. It may be carried out by the group members, collectively or individually, or by trained outside observers. Good timing is important. It may be useful to stop during the group's work to evaluate; evaluation is also effective right after the group has met or later, when the results of the group's decisions are known.

Communication in small groups is often directed toward problem-solving. Following Dewey's pattern for reflective thinking, a problem-solving group can move from recognition of the problem to definition of the problem to discovery of solutions to evaluation of solutions and, finally, to a plan of action.

Many of the skills discussed in the chapters on interpersonal and public communication also apply to small-group communication. A person who is effective in any one setting is likely to find success in other situations as well. However, each format has special characteristics and makes special demands on the communicator functioning within that format. In small groups, perhaps the single most important characteristic of a good communicator is his or her ability to interact constructively and clearly with all the others in the group. Since small groups are a large part of our everyday existence, some knowledge of how to perform better in them will make our lives more satisfying and rewarding.

FURTHER READING

Eric Berne, *The Structure and Dynamics of Organizations and Groups.* New York: Ballantine Books, 1963.
> This paperback book discusses group process from a psychological perspective; one section treats group relationships from the transactional point of view. Although the book is intended for both professionals and laymen, it uses a fairly complex vocabulary for the beginning student. The glossary is very useful. Written in an informative and interesting manner, this work is required reading for those interested in the psychological aspects of group behavior.

Erving Goffman, *Relations in Public: Microstudies of the Public Order.* New York: Basic Books, 1971.
> This is a collection of six articles in which the author details the social understandings necessary for the orderly conduct of the larger group—society. His thesis is that there are delicate connections between social relationships and public life. The book makes clear that almost all activity in which we engage is group-regulated.

John Huenefeld, *The Community Activist's Handbook: A Guide to*

Organizing, Financing, and Publicizing Community Campaigns. Boston: Beacon Press, 1970.

A realistic, straightforward, practical book for those who want to become more active in their community. The author outlines essential techniques for sharpening performance and preventing blunders and oversights in coordinating community efforts.

Irving Janis, *Victims of Groupthink.* Boston: Houghton Mifflin, 1973.

Janis characterizes the effects of group behavior on the participants. Many of his "victims" are people with whom we are all familiar. He categorizes those people who are negatively affected by strong group spirit, momentum, or loyalty. He causes the reader to be on guard for various influences that occur during group discussions.

Thomas C. McGinnis, *Open Family Living: A New Approach For Enriching Your Life Together.* Garden City, N.Y.: Doubleday & Company, 1976.

Perhaps the group with which we are most familiar is the family. McGinnis analyzes personal, marital, and family circumstances on an intellectual, emotional, and behavioral level. An open family living style encourages growth as well as mutual strength and encouragement. His chapter, "Learning to Communicate," is excellent.

Clovis R. Shepherd, *Small Groups: Some Sociological Perspectives.* San Francisco: Chandler, 1964.

Here is an introduction to sociological and social-psychological theory and research dealing with the small group. Designed for the serious student with little or no background in sociology or social psychology, this paperback includes a thorough bibliography and provides a stimulating starting point.

Henry and Elizabeth Swift, *Community Groups and You: How to Manage and Participate Effectively in Boards, Clubs, Committees, Fund Drives, Charities, Etc.* New York: The John Day Company, 1964.

This book is written for everyone who is a member of an organization or group. It is a practical resource that covers running meetings, handling money, public relations, committee work, and choosing people. The authors also explore ways of working more effectively with other people.

NOTES

[1]Kurt Lewin, "Field Theory and Experiment in Social Psychology: Concepts and Methods," *American Journal of Sociology,* 46 (1939): 868-896.

[2]Robert Freed Bales, *Interaction Process Analysis: A Method for the Study of Small Groups* (Reading, Mass.: Addison-Wesley, 1950), p. 33.

[3]See Erving Goffman, *Behavior in Public Places* (Glencoe: Free Press, 1963), Edward T. Hall, "Silent Assumptions in Social Communication," *Disorders of Communication,* 42 (1964): 41-55, and Ray Birdwhistell, "Field Methods and Techniques," *Human Organization,* 11 (Spring, 1952): 37-38.

[4]Kenneth D. Benne and Paul Sheats, "Functional Roles of Group Members," *Journal of Social Issues,* IV, No. 2: 41-49, reported in Robert S. Cathcart and Larry A. Samovar, *Small Group Communications: A Reader* (Dubuque: William C. Brown, 1970), pp. 137-138.

[5]Robert Freed Bales, "Task Roles and Social Roles in Problem Solving Groups," in *Readings in Social Psychology,* Eleanor Maccoby, *et al.,* eds. (New York: Holt, Rinehart and Winston, 1958), p. 441.

[6]John Dewey, *How We Think* (Boston: D. C. Heath, 1910), p. 72.

chapter 6

Public Speaking: Content

Public speaking has been practiced for thousands of years. People have always made speeches, and generations of authors have written books about the art of speech-making. More than two thousand years ago, Aristotle wrote *Rhetoric*, a philosophical and practical book about speech, which scholars still read and use. In more modern times, anywhere from twenty-five to fifty new books about speech/communication have been published every year.

Public speaking has been regarded in a variety of different ways throughout the ages. Some have seen it as a useful art in that it is a means of social control. Others have argued that it is a fine art because speeches often offer beauty, permanence as a literary form, and insight into human experience. In the twentieth century many see it as a science, and they use behavioral science methods to measure its impact and to determine why some speakers are more effective than others. Regardless of the approach, most authors and speakers agree that public speaking is necessary to democratic decision-making. A public speech still provides a setting for people to meet and talk about their problems, and it encourages people to unite and act.

Throughout history the function of public speaking has gone through little change. The Greeks saw it as a means of persuasion, just as twentieth-century politicians do. In this century, however, there have been changes in form. Now public speakers must compete with the technology of the mass media. In a country of instant communication, the long, leisurely speech is dead. An old-time minister thought nothing of a two-hour sermon, but if a modern minister tries to speak more than twenty minutes, his church membership will probably decline. An African politician can give a two-hour campaign speech and hold attention, but most American politicians find they are more effective with television spot announcements. Influenced by a constant barrage of commercials, we now expect all of our persuasive messages to be short and to the point.

Historically, the study of speech has revolved around the interaction of the speaker with the audience. Now the new technology has given us an entirely new phenomenon to study—many modern speeches are delivered to an audience whom the speaker never sees, and the interaction is delayed, if it occurs at all. When the President addresses the nation, for example, he does it in his office to the television cameras, and public reaction is delayed. Although pollsters seek immediate responses to the speech from the public, as do radio and television commentators, full public reaction often requires a longer period of time.

Public speaking is in a transitional period. We still have the speaker at the Lion's Club luncheon as well as the nationwide television address. These two kinds of speeches are similar in many ways. In this chapter we will examine the more traditional public speech, since that is what most of us will deliver during our lives. Still, we must keep in mind that the new technology is influencing public speaking. For example, some advertising tactics for getting attention and creating concise messages may be useful to us as public speakers. Therefore, our speech-making becomes a combination of the old and the new.

In this chapter, we will consider the "content" aspects of public speaking, that is, the actual preparation of and format of the speech itself. We will discuss audience analysis (identifying the type of audience before whom the speech will be delivered), choosing a topic, gathering information, and organizing the speech. In the next chapter we will consider the "delivery" aspects of public speaking, including some suggestions about what to do for speech anxiety—the fear that is often associated with speaking in public. Although we have divided the process into two parts for the purposes of discussion, the end result is the synthesis of both content and delivery.

THE PUBLIC-SPEAKING SITUATION

Interpersonal, small-group, and public-speaking situations all share the same communication components: speaker, message, listener, and feedback. Within the public-speaking situation these components are more strictly defined than they are in most other communication settings. In public speaking, a single speaker plans and sends a message for the specific purpose of evoking a precise response from his or her audience. Although one or more of these elements, the single speaker, for example, may be present in interpersonal or small-group communication, they are all found in public speaking.

The speaker is almost always the only person who plans the message, and the speaker determines the desired response *before* the message is sent. Since the speaker is the only person who is speaking, he or she has a heavy communication responsibility for the message. Whether the message is accepted or rejected will depend on the communication strategy that the speaker uses. Impressions of the speaker (and, therefore, of the message) are based on prior knowledge of the speaker, the content of the message, and how the message is delivered.

The message also has certain characteristics in a public-speaking situation. It has a specific purpose, is prepared and structured, and is generally static and unchanging. The message, however, does not stand alone; it is closely identified with the speaker. You have probably used the phrase "consider the source," which means that we can discount the message because we don't like or respect the source. The phrase illustrates the fact that source and message are practically inseparable.

The audience is also different in the public-speaking situation. Generally, audience members are not known to the speaker as individuals, and therefore the speaker relates to them as a group. When the speaker plans a message to affect them, he or she makes broad assumptions about the group. For instance, if the audience is predominately Republican the speaker may assume that they will probably be conservative and plan the speech accordingly.

The feedback in public speaking is limited and specialized. If the members of the audience approve the speech, they may laugh or applaud; if they disapprove, they may sit in silence or leave. There is often little feedback that tells the speaker whether or not the message is being understood in the way he or she intends it to be. Some speakers *do* get immediate feedback, such as the speaker who arouses a crowd, solicits funds, receives a vote, or asks for a decision, but they are the exception to the rule. Feedback limitations put a burden on the speaker to prepare messages that are clear and can be understood within the context of the single speech.

One unique characteristic of public speaking is that it usually occurs for a specific occasion or a planned event—it seldom occurs spontaneously. The occasion may be informal such as a college class or a basic-training lecture in the army. Other occasions may be very formal—a President's inauguration, an after-dinner speech, or a graduation speech. There are situations, of course, when a speaker will speak both informally and spontaneously. For example, a speaker may wish to reveal feelings on a public issue, support a position on one side of a motion, or express an attitude on an issue or a belief. In these cases, the speaker will likely have done no formal preparation. The majority of public speaking, however, tends to be more formal than informal, and it is the degree of formality that determines the nature of the speaker, the message, and the audience.

All communication is part of an ongoing process. No speech occurs in a vacuum. Audience response to a public speech is determined by the attitudes, values, and prior information they have brought with them, for these attitudes, values, and prior information form the reference base into which the speaker's ideas are introduced. In addition, after the audience leaves, its members will get more information from other sources. There are few one-time communications that have the power to shake audience members to their very foundations, and a speaker who works to this end will probably not succeed. It is disappointing to discover we cannot be earthshakers, but as public speakers this perspective is the only realistic one from which to work.

ANALYZING THE AUDIENCE

A good speech is audience-centered; it is planned, structured, and delivered with a particular audience in mind. In order to get the audience to respond to the message in the way the speaker intends, he or she must know as much as possible about the audience. Thus, much of speech-preparation time is spent in audience analysis.

A speaker will find many variables in any audience analysis, but the key to good analysis is identification. The more the speaker can identify and relate to the background, experience, interests, and attitudes of the audience, the greater the chance for speech effectiveness. Generally, we can put audiences into three different categories: those who share common experiences and interests with the speaker; those who have different experiences and interests; and those audiences that are so large that it is impossible to discover common experiences and interests.

Identification is easiest when the speaker shares a common background with his or her audience. A Baptist minister has a good idea of the values of his congregation, because the very fact that they are Baptists implies certain values and attitudes. A college student has little problem identifying with his or her classmates. They are basically in the same age group, probably examining various life styles, deciding on future careers, and sharing common interests in social activities.

In many speech situations, however, a speaker is unlike his or her audience and must spend time finding a common basis for understanding. A helicopter pilot must work to discover common ground with a bricklayer, and a college student must spend time to discover what experiences and interests she shares with the local Rotary Club.

The most difficult audience analysis comes when an audience is so large that no common interests can be found except for the desire to hear the speaker. Politicians face this kind of audience in large political rallies as do people who speak on television. Usually they solve their audience problems by making their message appeal to values that are widely held.

Several approaches are useful whenever we analyze an audience. The first approach is to look at the audience variables of age, sex, socioeconomic class, racial-ethnic background, religion, occupation, and education. These variables can be important if one or more of them separate the speaker from the audience. For example, the white dean of a college for black students always mentioned in his speeches to the student body that he had grown up poor. His attempt to identify with his students was a failure because the students knew that growing up poor is considerably different from growing up black. The dean picked the wrong thing to identify with. Age is a critical factor if an adult is speaking to children, and the sex of the speaker may be important when a male is speaking to an all-female audience or vice versa.

In other situations, these variables may not be important. If a Presbyterian is speaking in favor of better schools, his or her religion is probably not an important factor, even though the audience is predominately Methodist. The speaker's sex should not be an issue when a member of the League of Women Voters is giving information about forthcoming municipal elections to the Lion's Club.

Every speaker must consider each of these variables as a possible factor in the success of the speech. If the speaker and the audience are significantly different, the speaker must find a way to bridge the gap within the speech. A speaker should not pretend that he or she has the same background and experiences as the audience, but the speaker can overcome differences by emphasizing common experiences. "I know that you are white and I am black and this has caused problems in the past, but our topic today is not race. Our topic is working together to get our street paved, and I hope that that will be our concern."

All the variables we have been discussing—race, sex, age, class, religion, and so on—determine our beliefs and attitudes. These overall attitudes are more important than any single variable. How can a speaker determine the beliefs and attitudes of the audience? It is impossible to discover or deal with the thousands of individual attitudes that may be present in any one audience. Again we will say that if audience attitudes are basically the same as your own, you will not have any problem. But what if they are different from yours, and your speech purpose is to change some of these attitudes? How do you prepare your speech with this goal in mind?

First, you must remember that your speech is one event in a continuing communication. It is not the only time that your audience will hear about your subject—they have probably heard it before and they will likely hear it again. Attitude change happens over a long period of time. Very few people will change their attitudes after hearing a single speech. They will consider what they already know, and they will consider what happens after your speech. When Jimmy Carter ran for President, many people had never heard of him. He established his popularity and support as a result of active campaigning. Victory appeared certain. Yet as election day grew closer, his support dwindled, because of a variety of circumstances, and he managed to win only by a narrow margin. If the campaign had continued a few more weeks, he might have lost the election. Here we can see attitude change occurring over a period of time.

There has been considerable research in the area of audience analysis. Some general review of the findings may be useful to beginning speakers. The first area of research deals with *self-esteem,* the opinion that a person has of himself or herself. People who have high self-esteem tend to be confident about their judgments and opinions and are therefore not easily persuaded.

On an interpersonal level it is often easy to discover whether a person has high or low self-esteem, but determining the collective self-esteem of a large audience is more difficult. If the audience is made up of professional people, you are probably meeting with a group that has fairly high self-esteem. An example of such an audience might be a group of lawyers. The best strategy for dealing with such an audience is to give it an examination of facts, both pro and con, and let the listeners make up their own minds. An audience with low self-esteem could be made up either of people who are not accustomed to making decisions or people who have had many failures in their lives. A group of people who have spent long periods of time in prison would probably fit this category. Low self-esteem audiences are more responsive to speeches that represent what they perceive to be the majority position. Therefore, the best tactic is to show that what you are proposing is what most people want.

The second area of audience research deals with *dogmatism,* the extent to which individuals are committed to certain ideas. People are most dogmatic when their own lives are closely tied in with the issue under discussion. For example, someone in rural Indiana might be quite objective and liberal in a discussion about increasing low-income housing in urban centers. On the other hand, someone who is living in center-city Philadelphia might be quite closed-minded and strongly opposed to such housing since he or she could feel the housing as a personal threat. In planning message strategy, we know that open-minded individuals will listen to logical and rational approaches and closed-minded individuals may change if they perceive the change as proposed by a respected authority. George Wallace, for example, is a hero to many white Southerners. If he so desired, he could probably influence many people toward better race relations in the South.

The last area of audience research deals with *prior commitment,* the way the audience feels about an idea before it ever comes to hear the speaker. If the audience is on the side of the speaker, then there is no problem, but if the speaker is on the "wrong" side of the issue, he or she must take care in planning the message. The speaker should work to convince the audience that although the message may seem to be unacceptable, it is really keeping with the general philosophy of the audience. If a Roman Catholic speaks to a group of Baptists about the Catholic church, he would be wise to play down issues of doctrine—the virgin birth and papal infallibility, for example—and emphasize the ideas that all Christians have in common.

A Case Study in Audience Analysis

Let's see how these theories about audience analysis work in a practical speech situation.

A college-educated woman in her late twenties is interested in the subject of abortion. She had an illegal abortion while she was still in college, and the experience was so unpleasant that she has decided to work for greater public understanding and acceptance of abortion. Through her reading and experience she has become an expert on the subject, and she is willing to give public speeches about abortions throughout the community. Several groups have asked her to speak, and she has agreed to talk to four audiences: a group of radical feminists, a convention of the American Medical Association, a group of interested citizens at the city auditorium, and a group of Roman Catholic priests. How can she handle these diverse audiences? Each group must be analyzed separately.

1) The radical feminists are the easiest group for the speaker to relate to because they have taken a well-known public stand in favor of abortion. The speaker's main problem is not in identification but in her approach to the topic. She knows that her audience is on her side and agrees with her premise that abortion should be available to all women who desire it. Therefore, her best strategy would probably be to get them to organize and to spread information about abortion, to join her in her own crusade of spreading public information and gaining wider acceptance of abortion.

2) The speaker has a moderate amount of identification with the AMA because they share a common interest in the medical problem of abortion. In this speech situation, the sex of the speaker is important; she is a woman speaking on a problem of women to a predominately male audience. Her education may also be a factor to this audience, and it would increase her credibility if she were to use correct medical terminology. The speaker realizes that doctors are crucial to the issue of abortions, and she decides to ask them to provide psychological support to patients undergoing the operation and to provide inexpensive abortions. In asking for psychological support she relates her own unpleasant experience of undergoing an abortion and points out that this would not have happened if she had had more sympathy and understanding from the doctor performing the abortion. The issue of inexpensive abortions is a delicate one, since most people—including doctors—like to make money. Therefore, she spends time describing well-run, efficient abortion clinics that are operating throughout the country and making profits for doctors as well as providing low-cost services. She has assumed that her audience will be generally in favor of abortion, and she has given them information about ways to improve abortion services.

3) The speaker has less information about the citizens at the city auditorium than any of the other audiences. She can only assume that they have come to hear her because they are interested in the topic. In this speech, the speaker spends time in the introductory part telling why she is interested in and qualified to speak on abortion; she gives the audience a reason for listening and believing what she has to say. Since she does not know how the audience feels about the topic, she gives a general objective account of the status of abortion today. She discusses the present abortion law and the procedure a woman must follow to get an abortion. She concludes her speech with a discussion of the facilities that are available in the city and state of her audience.

4) The Roman Catholic priests are the toughest audience of all and,

therefore, this speech requires the greatest advance preparation. The speaker knows that most of the audience has definite ideas about abortion and that these ideas are contrary to her own. She must deal with both dogmatism and prior commitments. Again, she decides to be as objective as possible, and she covers many of the points discussed before her audience in the city auditorium. The speaker is not able to find any high authorities in the Catholic church who have supported abortion, but she has found a group of liberal Catholic theologians, who support the idea that individuals can and should make individual decisions regarding morality. After quoting one or two of these theologians, she cites examples of women who have chosen to have abortions, not for selfish reasons but for the welfare of their families. She knows that she has little chance of changing anyone's mind, but she hopes to leave the priests with the idea that in some circumstances, abortion may be the best solution.

As you can see by these examples, the speaker has made a number of choices. In every speaking situation, she has adapted and changed her speech to meet the particular needs of the audience. This need for adaptation is present in most speaking situations. Giving a speech is somewhat similar to shopping for a gift. You don't go out and buy everyone the same thing—you take time to choose what is right for each person. If you take the time to make these choices for your audience, you have a greater chance of affecting your audience in the way you intend.

CHOOSING A TOPIC

Many people are asked to speak because they have expertise in a particular area. A civil engineer may be asked to speak to local businessmen on the need for a new city sewage system, and a member of the National Organization for Women might be asked to speak to a school assembly on the Equal Rights Amendment. Other people may choose to speak because they have a desire to accomplish a certain goal. Politicians speak to win elections, and Billy Graham speaks to save souls. Since these people are speaking for specific reasons, they do not have a problem of choosing topics because the speech occasion dictates the topic. Their main problem is their approach to the topic and, again, the key to their approach is audience analysis. As speakers they ask, "How can I best reach the audience with this topic?"

Classroom speeches, however, fall into another category. A student is not necessarily an expert, and the speech occasion is somewhat artificial because the student speaks to fulfill an assignment. Students are usually not given specific speech topics, but they may be asked to speak within a

broad framework, for example, a speech to inform or a speech to persuade. Once you know your speech framework, how do you go about
choosing a topic? It will probably help you to consider two questions:
What will interest you, and what will interest your audience?

Students sometimes deliver speeches on such broad and important
social issues as poverty, tax reform, or inflation. Undoubtedly, these are
important topics, but they are not very good subjects for five-minute
speeches. Chances are that you have very little knowledge of or experience
with such topics and that you would do well to stay away from them. You
would probably be better off directing your attention to topics that you
know something about and that can be reasonably discussed within your
time limit.

Knowledge and *experience* are key words. What do you know about?
How do you spend your time? What really turns you on? The best way to
answer these questions is to look at how you spend those sixteen or so
hours that you are awake each day. Do you spend your time working on
your car? Buying new clothes? Playing cards in the student union?
Working out a chemistry experiment in the lab? All of these activities
could lead to very good speeches. In fact, with the right approach, almost
any subject can be turned into an interesting speech.

Your audience is another important consideration in choosing your
topic. Speeches are more than exercises for speakers to hear themselves;
thus, it is important for you to ask how you can present your knowledge
and experience in a way that will interest the audience. There are several
good ways of doing this.

Let's say you spend most of your free time working on your car, and
so you have specialized knowledge about cars. You can assume that most
of the members of your audience do not share that knowledge; if
something is wrong with their car, they take it to a mechanic. Since you are
limited to a five-minute speech, what approach can you take that will be
effective? A good approach would be to apply your specialized knowledge
to help the audience deal with problems about cars. You could speak on
"How to Avoid Getting Ripped Off in the Body Shop," "What to Look for
in a Used Car," or "What You Should Do to Keep Your Car Running
Well." All these topics demand specialized knowledge on the part of the
speaker, and each speaker adapts this knowledge to the needs of the
audience.

Maybe you are a chemistry major, and you spend all your time in the
lab. Many students barely manage to struggle through their chemistry
classes, and they will probably never think about the subject again. How
are you going to interest them? Think of it this way—every day of our lives
we are touched by the impact of chemistry. Most of your audience is

wearing clothes created by chemistry. Anyone who cooks is causing a chemical reaction. Chemical additives in foods and their effects on the human body are vital because they have life-and-death implications. Every kitchen and bathroom has a wide range of chemical products. All these aspects of modern chemistry could well lead to an interesting speech.

If you are someone who spends much of your time playing cards, then you have another possible topic at your fingertips. Have you ever wondered where all of those cards come from? Why do we use the terms *jack, queen, king?* Why do all decks have fifty-two cards? You can find the answers in a quick trip to the library. Interesting questions lead to interesting answers, and interesting answers lead to interesting speeches.

If you have several ideas for a topic, try placing yourself in the role of an audience member: Which topic would be the most interesting to you? Which would reach out and grasp your attention? When you think you have a workable topic, sit down and try to plan an approach. Most of your preparation time can best be spent working on your speech rather than choosing your topic, but choosing a good topic will make preparation easier.

GATHERING INFORMATION

After you choose your topic, you should start gathering information. In the beginning it is not necessary to know just exactly how you are going to use it; you can arrange it later. You may find that some of the material will not fit into your speech and so you will want to eliminate it.

Your first source of information should be your own experience and the experiences of people you know. Personal experiences are effective because they have greater meaning for you and for your audience. It is easier to identify with personal experience than with any other kind of material. Using your own experience also enhances your credibility. In essence you are saying, "I have experienced this. I know what I am talking about."

One student used her own personal experience very effectively. She got up and said, "Today I am going to talk about contraceptives. I believe that this subject is important to all college students. If I had known about contraceptives, I probably wouldn't have had a baby in my sophomore year of college." From that point on, she had the full attention of her audience.

Information can also come out of your own community. If you are planning to talk about urban decay, be cautious about building your speech around New York City slums (unless you live there). Every city in the United States has slums. If your own community has lakes and rivers that can no longer be used, why discuss pollution in the Atlantic Ocean? Shoplifting occurs in all American cities and towns. Suicides happen in Big Ten universities, small private schools, and community colleges. Used-car salesmen use many of the same "come-on" gimmicks in every city. Your own community probably has all the social good and evil of the entire country, so consider it as a starting point.

Another source of information is local experts. Policemen, firemen, welfare officers, health department officials, doctors and lawyers—all of them are experts in certain areas, and they know a lot about your particular community and the problems in that community. Talk to them and quote them. A local authority will carry much more weight than some far-off figure in another city.

You don't always have to go to the top to get your information. If you decide to speak on the working conditions in the sanitation department, you will probably learn more from the man who picks up your garbage than from the Commissioner of Sanitation. If you want to find out about Sanitation Department policies, on the other hand, the commissioner will be the best person to help you. A prostitute will be able to say more about the life of a prostitute than all the sociology instructors in your school. However, the story of one prostitute does not tell us very much about the state of prostitution in the United States, and to get this information, you will have to go to more traditional academic sources.

One of these academic sources is the faculty at your school. Instructors all have specialized knowledge within their given fields of study, and often they know how to get information in places that would not occur to someone who does not know about that field. If your topic is a fairly academic one—the history of prostitution, for example—you can probably get some information and leads to good sources from members of the faculty.

The library, of course, is the traditional source for information found in books. You have probably been using libraries since you learned to read, but most of us know about only a fraction of the sources and services that are available. Since you need to use these sources all the time, it would be worthwhile to spend an hour or two in the library just looking around and asking questions.

Several library resources are particularly useful to people who are gathering information for a speech. The reference section will give you the facts, or the bare bones, on any subject. Encyclopedias, although limited, are useful for general information and for short historical summaries. If you need information about people and their achievements, you can look in the *Dictionary of National Biography, Who's Who in America,* and

Current Biography. The World Almanac and *Book of Facts* and the *Information Please Almanac* are good sources for current facts, since new editions are published every year. If you want a quotation, look in *Bartlett's Familiar Quotations* or the *Oxford Dictionary of Quotations,* where quotations are listed by subject. The best source of statistical data for the United States is the *Statistical Abstract of the United States.* If you browse among the reference shelves, you will discover a wide variety of sources of information.

For a more detailed discussion of a topic, look in the card catalogue under the subject. There you will find the titles and authors of all the books in this library on the topic you are researching. Many of the cards may have similar call numbers because the books are shelved together in one of two sections of the library. If you go to that section, you will find several different books that handle the topic in different ways. Sometimes, this kind of browsing will help you find a unique approach to your particular topic.

The Reader's Guide to Periodical Literature is another useful source. this publication, which is found in the magazine or periodical section of the library, lists all the articles in popular magazines that have appeared on your subject. Magazine articles are good sources for current information, and often you will find recent statistics and other material that you can quote in your speech.

After you have gathered all your information, ask yourself again if this information is suitable for your particular audience. Will it help them to see, identify with, and understand the subject better? When you have gathered the best possible information, information that will work for you and your audience, then you are ready to begin building your speech.

ORGANIZING THE SPEECH

Earlier in this chapter we said that the purpose of a public speech is to elicit a specific response from the audience. One of the best tools available in helping you to get this response is good organization of your speech, which will be instrumental in obtaining the response you want.

Most speeches have the general purpose of informing or persuading the audience. An *informative speech* is one that presents the audience with information about a subject and lests it draw its own conclusions. A *persuasive speech* may also give information, but it tries to move the audience toward a specific commitment or action. There are some differences in organizing the two types of speeches, but their basic organizational pattern has greater similarities than differences. Both types of speeches require that material be organized into a statement of purpose, an introduction, a body, and a conclusion.

The *statement of purpose*, or the thesis statement, may clearly state the reason for your speech in one sentence: "I am going to persuade the class to vote for Martha Smith"; "I am going to explain why meat prices are so high"; "I am going to convince the audience that excessive suntanning is dangerous." This thesis statement is particularly helpful in speech planning because you can test all your speech material against it. If a particular piece of information supports your thesis statement, then you know that material is relevant. Although you may never actually state your thesis to the audience, it is implied and obvious throughout a well-organized speech.

The speech *introduction* has two purposes: it makes the audience feel comfortable with the speaker, and it creates interest in the topic. If an audience does not know you, you will want to make them receptive to you and hence to your speech. Many speakers use humor for this purpose. Sometimes a speaker needs to reassure an audience. For example, one speaker was scheduled to speak at a conference just before lunchtime. She knew that the conference had gone on all morning, that the audience had heard many speakers, and that they were probably both tired and hungry. She began her speech by saying, "I know you are ready for lunch, and I have not prepared a long speech because I am hungry, too. If any of you want to keep time, I am going to speak for exactly twelve minutes." Reassured that lunch was not a long time away, the audience sat back and listened with interest and attention.

You have already done an audience analysis and chosen a topic that is important in the lives of your audience. Point out this importance in your introduction—this is the best way of building interest in your speech. A college student began his speech to a group of classmates in this way: "You probably all know that the greatest epidemic in the United States is the common cold. Today, I am interested in the second greatest epidemic, one that involves a disease that is common among college students. This disease does not cause sneezing and minor discomfort—it causes insanity and blindness and finally death. I am speaking about venereal disease."

There are several kinds of material which are appropriate for your introduction. The guide in each choice should be whether it is *relevant* to the speech, makes the *audience feel comfortable*, and creates *interest* in the topic. Some good choices are:

1. *a startling statistic*
2. *an example or illustration*
3. *a personal experience*

4. *a quotation*
5. *expert opinion or testimony*
6. *immediate reference to the present situation*
7. *a summary of the major ideas in the speech*
8. *historical background of the topic*
9. *a humorous story, anecdote, or joke (the use of humor, however, is not easy and should be avoided if you have no prior experience with it)*
10. *a combination of these*

The organization of the *body* of your speech will depend on the type of speech you are giving. In an informative speech the best organization can be achieved by putting yourself in the position of an audience member. Assume that you know almost nothing about the subject and ask yourself how it should be presented so that you can understand it. For instance, Julia Child, who appears on a television cooking-instruction program, always explains what she means by terms such as *baste* and *sauté* before she goes on to the complicated aspects of cooking. The student who speaks about venereal disease realizes that his audience probably knows something about the subject, but he also might assume that some of the information they have is colored by fear and superstition. The best organization pattern for information is one that will present your material in a clear and comprehensive form to your audience. If you keep this in mind, you will discover a structure that will work for your speech.

Your speech might have a persuasive purpose; you are asking people to change in some way. One of the best ways of organizing a persuasive speech is to divide your subject into the problem and the solution. For example, some schools have dormitory curfew hours for women but none for men, and you want to change this. In explaining the problem you point out the present conditions, and you tell your audience that these rules discriminate against women. Your solution to the problem is to organize a five-person delegation from the class to approach the student government association and the dean of students to ask that these rules be changed.

Some speakers work to change an attitude rather than to ask for direct action. Again, you can use the problem-solution order. In a speech named "What Do Women Want Anyway?" a student pointed out that there is wide-scale discrimination against women. In the problem part of the speech, she used statistics showing that women earn less money for doing the same jobs as men, that they are promoted less often, and that employers often refuse to consider them for promotion because they are afraid of the possibility of pregnancy. In her solution, she said that women want the same chances and opportunities in employment that are given to

men. She knew that the men in her class were more likely to be students than employers, but she also knew that some of these same men would be employers some day. She hoped to bring about a change in attitude that would have long-term effects.

All speeches, whether they are informative or persuasive, will benefit from an outline. The purpose of your outline is to list the main points of the speech followed by the supporting material. Generally, a short speech should have from two to four main points. Let's say you are going to speak on "Common Sense About Pot." Your points might be: 1) how pot is different from hard drugs, 2) the effects of pot when it is smoked, and 3) the laws in your state regarding pot. All these main points should be supported by material substantiating them.

Supporting material includes examples, facts, statistics, illustrations, and opinions. It is based on your experience, the experience of others, and the information you find in your research. This supporting material and the way in which it is structured will reinforce your message. Sound judgment and good sense are conveyed when ideas are developed and when they are arranged in a specific order.

Forms of Support   Forms of support are the means whereby the communicator's main ideas are sustained or reinforced. They make up the "meat" of a message. Without forms of support, messages become assertions and generalizations—unsupported declarations and statements. Ideas can be developed with several different forms of support; they should, however, be supported appropriately—in a way that can be understood by the listener.

One form of support is the *example*, that is, an instance or case in point. A woman talks to another woman about the problems of dating. She cites her own experience for support of the assertion that one of the problems is with the fellow who wants "to go too far" on the first date. She is using an example. In this case the example comes from the speaker's personal experience, an excellent support because the details of the example are well known to the communicator and because many people may have a similar storehouse of examples on which to draw. Examples from one's personal experience are also revealing of the self and, thus, invite empathy from the listener.

One can also draw examples from the experience of others. Citing the experience of a roommate concerning the problems of dating might be useful. The well-read person will also have a storehouse of examples on a variety of topics derived from books, magazines, and newspapers. Another kind of example is hypothetical—the kind that is created by the communicator for a specific reason. Again, the person with a great deal of experience is often skillful at using such examples because they can be constructed by combining parts of many other examples. On the other hand, it can be totally fictitious. If you use hypothetical examples, it is important that the listener be aware that you are doing so.

Facts, another form of support, are those verified statements or propositions that can be checked against reality. If something is not disputable, it is a fact. We use facts all the time to lend greater emphasis to our ideas. When you talk to another person on any subject, you are likely to mention in your conversation a fact that you recently read; talking to another on marijuana, you might point out that a recent fourteen-year study linked continual smoking of pot to senility.

Group a number of examples or facts together and you get *statistics*. Statistics are numerical representations of groups of examples or facts that have been condensed to a single number. It is easiest to use statistics and easiest to remember them if you use round numbers. One student cited the fact that alcohol was the most abused and most dangerous drug available and supported the point with three statistics: 1) more than 50 percent of all crimes in America are alcohol-related; 2) more than 50 percent of all highway accidents are alcohol-related; 3) more than 100 million Americans drink. An example takes on more meaning with reinforcement from statistics. Knowing the facts makes what you say more meaningful and increases your credibility and reliability as a communicator.

Illustrations are extended examples. They are stories of facts or events used by the communicator to shed light on an idea. They are especially powerful because they can kindle interest by revealing real persons in real situations. A good conversationalist will likely have a collection of stories that can be recalled on the spur of the moment to add interest to the message.

When we use the *opinions* of others to support our ideas, we are asking our listener to accept our idea because someone with whom they have some association, knowledge, or identification also has accepted the idea. When we use another person's opinions, then, we must be certain that the listener knows who the person is. If the listener does not have this information, we can do one of two things: eliminate the opinion from our communication or provide him with information that would enable him to judge the competence of the source on this topic. We must be sure that the person we use has a good reputation and can be considered reliable. Very often, *why* a person says something can be as important as what is said. This means that we not only have to know something about our listener but also about the personal interests, prejudices, training, and experience of the person we are going to quote or cite. In addition, in quoting or citing another person, we must strive to preserve the intent of the person being quoted or cited. Off-handed, inaccurate quotations bear on the credibility of the person being quoted as well as on our own. In using the opinions of others, make them specific and make sure they support and develop your ideas accurately.

When you select forms of support to develop your message, seek a variety of types. Variety adds interest to your message. It provides a natural change of pace and, thus, holds attention. If you are going to use a personal experience, for example, cite a statistic and perhaps an opinion to reinforce your experience. Never feel confined to one type of support. You support an idea for the benefit of your listener, so his or her interest and attention should be a paramount consideration.

Your speech will also require *transitions* from one point to another to tell your audience where you have been and where you are going. Transitions are a means of getting from one point to another smoothly. For example, if you are going from one point on the effects of pot to the point on your state laws about pot, you might say, "As you can see, smoking pot is a very pleasant experience for most people. But before you all run out to get some, I should warn you what could happen if you were caught." Now you are set up to speak about the state laws.

The *conclusion* of a speech says that the speech is over, the communication is complete. Have you ever talked on the telephone and had the other person hang up without saying good-bye? You know that this can be an unsettling experience. The same is true of a speech without a conclusion. You will find it useful to have a pretty exact idea of your conclusion before you begin speaking. There is no worse feeling than shuffling from one foot to the other, thinking to yourself, "How am I going to get out of here?" A conclusion, prepared beforehand, will avoid this problem.

Many speakers conclude with "Thank you" or "Are there any questions?" If the speech is a good one, the audience will thank the speaker. If there are questions in the minds of the audience, they will likely ask them; usually this is determined by the format that is established beforehand. Thanking the audience or asking for questions does not take the place of a conclusion. As a beginning speaker, you should avoid this type of ending.

The minimal expectation for a conclusion is that it summarizes the major ideas in the body of the speech and gives a clear restatement of the major thesis. The conclusion will vary according to the type of speech. In an informative speech, it is often useful to summarize your main points. In a persuasive speech, you can also use a summary, but your main closing device will be to ask for commitment or action. No audience member who has been listening should leave wondering what the main idea was. Thus, a good conclusion lets the audience know that the speech is over. Any of

the ten kinds of material suggested for the introduction is also appropriate for the conclusion. Besides summarizing the major ideas and restating the major thesis, you want to end on a positive, impressive note. This can often be accomplished by using a:

1. *direct reference to your audience*
2. *personal, factual example*
3. *quotation from an expert*
4. *challenge or charge to the audience*
5. *slogan or catchy phrase that will stick in the mind*

For certain speeches, some instructors require a bibliography. A bibliography lists all the sources of information that you have used in your speech. It is usually given at the end of the speech outline. In the pages that follow, there is an outline and bibliography to guide you in preparing your own speeches. One side of the page gives an explanation of the outline process, and the other side demonstrates the process through a sample speech. You will notice that the speech we have used is a persuasive one and that it has a problem-solution order. The problem is explained and developed in the first two main points, and the solution is given and developed in the third main point. If you are preparing a speech based on experience or an informative speech, you will structure your material in the same way, including all the parts of the outline as shown in the left-hand column.

TITLE	Becoming Assertive
STATEMENT OF PURPOSE	My purpose is to persuade the members of the audience that they sacrifice many of their rights by not being assertive and that they should change their behavior.
INTRODUCTION	I plan to hold up a shoddy piece of merchandise that I bought but that I did not take back. Then I plan to tell them something that I felt and should have said when I bottled up my feelings instead. I will then tell them of a position I hold in an organization that I would rather not hold. Finally, I will let them know how many of us tend to be *yes* people—tending to do the work while others sit by and watch.

Transition from Introduction to Body	I want to first explain what I mean by *being assertive*. Secondly, I want to describe some of our basic rights, and, finally, I want to make suggestions for becoming assertive.

BODY OF SPEECH
Main Points

I. Being assertive means thinking, speaking, and acting on the fact that we exist and we want certain things.

Supporting
Material

A. In their book, *Stand Up, Speak Out, Talk Back!*, Alberti and Emmons explain assertive, non-assertive, and aggressive behavior.

B. Let me give you some examples of non-assertive, aggressive, and finally, assertive behavior:

1. Sharon would stay in the back of groups, allow others to make decisions, pass by potential friendships.

2. Bob would interrupt others, always make the decisions, use and abuse friendships.

3. Pat's style was self-enhancing because she would allow others to complete their thoughts, make her own decisions based on what she thought was right, and look to friendships as opportunities to learn more about herself and ideas.

C. We often get manipulated into doing things we don't want to do.

Transition from
point I to point II

But knowing what *being assertive* means is not enough. We also have to know our basic rights, because these are what we have to protect.

II. Our human rights are based on the fact that we are all created equal and that, in a moral sense, we should treat one another as equals.

A. I will show and explain a poster entitled "A Bill of Assertive Rights" from Manuel J. Smith, *When I Say No, I Feel Guilty*, pp. 24–71.

B. We have a moral right to renegotiate arrangements we feel are unfair or inequitable according to Bower and Bower in *Asserting Yourself*. Let me cite some of their examples of this renegotiation.

C. Why should we want to protect our rights?

   1. to get control of ourselves and to be more expressive

   2. to influence the way others behave towards us

Transition from point II to point III

Now that we know what we have to protect —our basic rights—we should examine some of the ways we have for changing our behavior to become more assertive.

III. If we are to become assertive, we must make a pledge to change our behavior—to do something about it. We should:

A. Take responsibility for ourselves.

B. Avoid over-apologizing.

C. Try not to rearrange someone else's life.

D. Be free to change our minds.

E. Feel free to make mistakes.

F. Learn to recognize unanswerable questions and feel free to say "I don't know."

G. Be careful not to depend on the goodwill of others.

H. Feel free to be emotional, as well as logical.

I. Say "I don't understand," or "I don't care," when we are confused or disinterested.

Transition from Body of Speech to Conclusion

By following some of these suggestions, we no longer have to be at the mercy of others; we can begin to take charge of our own life.

CONCLUSION

As we move toward greater assertiveness, we need to recognize the difference between assertive, non-assertive, and aggressive behavior. We also need to know what rights we have to protect. Most importantly, we must all answer the crucial question for ourselves: "Am I happy with my present behavior and with my self?" We must be free to make this judgment about whether or not we want to make a change. (Now I plan to end positively and energetically!) Becoming assertive will help you be direct and honest with others. You will gain goodwill and self-confidence, and will be able to pinpoint your real feelings—it will enrich the quality of your life. Most of all, being assertive will make you get more satisfaction out of the life you lead.

BIBLIOGRAPHY

Alberti, Robert E., and Emmons, Michael L. *Stand Up, Speak Out, Talk Back!* New York: Pocket Books, 1975.

Bower, Sharon Anthony, and Gordon H. Bower. *Asserting Yourself: A Practical Guide for Positive Change.* Reading, Mass.: Addison-Wesley Publishing Company, 1976.

Shostrom, Everett L. *Man, the Manipulator: The Inner Journey from Manipulation to*

Actualization. New York: Bantam, 1967.
Smith, Manuel J. *When I Say No, I Feel Guilty.* New York: Bantam, 1975.
Weaver, Richard L., II. *Understanding Interpersonal Communication.* Glenview, Ill.: Scott, Foresman and Company, 1978, pp. 219–239.

CHOOSING VISUAL MATERIAL

Visual materials serve three functions in a speech: they help to hold the attention of the audience; they provide information in the visual channel; and they aid audience retention. A study of visual materials showed that if an audience were merely given verbal information, after three days they would remember only 10 percent of what they had been told. If they were shown material without verbal communication, they would remember 35 percent. However, if both verbal and visual information were provided, they would remember 65 percent after three days.[1] Just because you have an aid does not mean that you are automatically assured attention, however. You may remember sleeping through all the films your teacher showed you in elementary school. An audience can sleep through visual materials as easily as it can sleep through a speech.

Your visual material should be chosen to help make your topic lively and interesting to your audience. There are several types to choose from. Architects and city planners often use models, either a larger or smaller replica of an actual object. A first-aid instructor or a nurse might use a live model to demonstrate mouth-to-mouth resuscitation or techniques in bandaging wounds. Some people are able to use the actual object under discussion. One student who was interested in car mechanics brought a carburetor to class as a visual aid. A wide variety of posters can be made or bought. Posters are often most useful when you are going to use graphs or talk about statistical material. Advertising agencies often use flip-boards, a series of posters held together by rings at the top, to give presentations to potential advertisers. For simple diagrams and drawings, the blackboard may be the best choice.

The first question you should ask about visual material is whether your speech is better because you are using this particular visual aid. Don't use it just for the sake of using it. If it does not really enhance your speech, get rid of it and use something else. If the material is complicated, prepare it beforehand. Make sure that it can be seen by everyone in the room and that there is a way to display it.

When you present your visual material, take care to talk to your audience—not to your material. Many people have a tendency to turn their backs on the audience, especially when they are using a poster or a blackboard drawing. It is also important to display your material at the proper psychological moment. An aid can be distracting, so take it out when you are ready to use it and put it away when you have finished with it.

Good visual material can make a speech lively and interesting, but it requires as much thought as the speech itself. Think about all your speeches, not just the ones where visual aids are required. Is there material that you can bring in to help reinforce and highlight those other speeches? If there is material, then use it. Your visual material might just provide that little extra touch that makes a good speech a great speech.

SUMMARY

Public speaking is an important means of communication in a democratic society. in public speaking, the source has most of the responsibility for the message. Whether or not the audience decides to accept the message depends on how well the source plans the messagi and how he or she is perceived by the audience.

In preparing a speech, the speaker first analyzes the audience. He or she attempts to find common ground with the audience in attitudes, values, beliefs, and goals, If the speaker's attitudes are different from the audience's, he or she attempts to minimize the differences.

Speech preparation involves choosing a topic that is of interest both to the speaker and to the audience. After the topic is chosen, the speaker gathers information from personal experience, from the community, and from the library.

Most speeches are informative or persuasive. Informative speeches present the audience with information about a subject and lets it draw its own conclusions. Persuasive speeches try to move the audience to commitment or action. Both types of speeches should be organized with a statement of purpose, an introduction, a body, and a conclusion.

Both types of speeches, too, should include a variety of different forms of support. Audience members tire from hearing a long string of statistics or a series of historical instances. Statistical and historical material should be combined with personal experience, opinion, and illustrations.

Visual material helps both speaker and audience. It provides variety in the speaker's overall presentation. It helps to hold the audience's attention, provides information, and aids retention of the material.

In a public speech one factor is seldom responsible for making the speech memorable. Rather, a combination of elements makes it effective. The successful public speaker will pay close attention to all the aspects of content in the preparation of his or her speech.

FURTHER READING

I Have Spoken: American History Through the Voices of Indians, compiled by Virgina Irving Armstrong. Chicago: The Swallow Press, 1971.
This anthology includes speeches and fragments of speeches made by Indians on problems of concern to them. Some of the speeches go back to the seventeenth century.

Ken Macrorie, *Uptaught.* New York: Hayden Book Company Inc., 1970.
Content is often a problem for students—trying to avoid obvious ideas, shopworn clichés, and trivial thinking. The challenge to find something worthwhile to express is clearly presented by Macrorie. This search is the key to finding the path toward mutual respect and instructive dialogue. although Macrorie's book is concerned with writing, the same problems face us in finding content for speeches.

Arthur Smith, *Language, Communication, and Rhetoric in Black America.* New York: Harper and Row, 1972.
This collection of articles by various writers about the communication experiences of black Americans ranges from discussion about dialect to rhetorical case studies.

Leonard A. Stevens, *The Ill-Spoken Word.* New York: McGraw-Hill, 1966.
This interesting and readable book discusses the spoken word. The writer looks at the history of speaking and asks some provocative questions about the role of speech in contemporary life.

NOTES

[1]Conwell Carson, "Best Memory by Eye and Ear," The Kansas City *Times,* April 19, 1967, p. 13A.

chapter 7

Public Speaking: Delivery

When a team of market researchers asked three thousand Americans, "What are you most afraid of?" the single, greatest fear reported was speaking before a group.[1] It is a natural fear for most of us. Veteran performers, teachers, and some of those we least expect to experience fear are subject to this emotion. Since it is a common apprehension and one with which most of us have to cope at some time or other, it is a good idea to find methods and procedures for dealing with it successfully. Also, understanding this type of fear is the first step toward channeling our energy more effectively. In this way, we allow our energy to work for us rather than against us when we speak in public. Once we are able to face the fear of speaking before a group rationally and thoughtfully, we are well on our way to coping successfully with the delivery aspect of public speaking.

RELATING CONTENT AND DELIVERY

In adopting a rational approach toward effective public speaking, we must first consider the relationship of content and delivery. Content is the beginning point and delivery is the end. If one does not have a strong content, the delivery is likely to be negatively affected. Just as important, however, is that despite an effective content, a weak or hesitant delivery can hinder, damage, or destroy it. The point is, we need both effective content *and* delivery to have a successful speech.

Both the content and the delivery of most public speakers can be improved. What is required is a thorough understanding of the various components and strategies, as well as their appropriate application and practice. But it should not end there. The effective public speaker always engages in some evaluation of his or her effort. Ask not only, "How did I do?" but also, "How could I do better?" Improvement should be a goal of every communicator. Seldom is anyone so good that there is no room for increased effectiveness.

In this chapter, we will discuss how to manage anxiety, or the natural fear that often accompanies the thought of speaking in public. We will also talk about what being effective means. Other aspects of delivery we will consider will be looking our best, moving our body, using our voice, presenting our selves, adapting to our audience, practicing delivery, and evaluating and trying again. In addition we will examine our role as listener and what we, as a listener, should listen for. Much initial fear can be eliminated if we establish a solid awareness and understanding of the various components that go into a speech—that is, taking the process apart and examining each factor. Self-confidence can be increased simply by knowing what we are dealing with. There is no mystery behind successful communication, and no one need have an edge on this market. Success is within everyone's reach if there is a willingness to go after it.

MANAGING ANXIETY

Why is it that we are so afraid of speaking before others? Perhaps the most important reason can be summed up in the phrase "fear of the unknown." We just do not know what the future holds. Although we want the approval of others, want to feel important, and want to be sucessful, we are afraid that these achievements may elude us. Yet how well we do—whether we achieve these goals or not—is in *our* hands. We hesitate, our heart pounds, our hands become cold and clammy just at the thought of not having chosen a good topic, of not being liked, of offending someone, of forgetting everything, stumbling and falling, or ruining the whole effort.

We dwell on the negative rather than the positive. We are not confident of the possiblity that we will receive rewards or that happiness may result. We limit the power of our imagination. Yet if we believe that we *are* going to succeed, that our speech *is* going to be effective, and that we *are* going to be liked by our audience, our performance will reflect these assumptions. This is an example of the self-fulfilling prophecy. If we predict disaster, the prediction will cause fear, the fear will inhibit us and lead to ineffective communication, and the prediction will come true.

Intensity of fear varies. For some it is powerful and overwhelming. For others, it is subtle and low-level. In most cases, however, we can function despite its presence. But to function more effectively we need to recognize that repeated worry can be harmful, that it is often exaggerated beyond what is reasonable, and that intense reactions need to be properly channeled. Recognition is an important step in moving toward a solution.

Fear is normal, even appropriate.iIn light of the tension and excitement associated with public-speaking, it is to be expected. If there were no fear at all, it would be unusual, even detrimental. Thus, fear can be a powerful motivating force that adds strength, energy, and conviction to otherwise lifeless ideas. Without some fear, ideas may not be conveyed with sufficient intensity to make them memorable.

What is needed? Courage. Courage, in this context, means the ability to see fear in a realistic perspective. We must be able to face it squarely, define it, consider possible alternatives, and function in spite of it. Remember, however, that our goal is not total confidence, that is, to eliminate fear altogether. This is both impossible and unrealistic. Even the most experienced and effective public speakers feel apprehensions and misgivings before facing audiences. There is much more to it than that. Communication is a skill that needs to be learned. We must be thoroughly prepared; we must know how to act under the circumstances; and we must have practice. Much of our fear will disappear once we have identified the requirements and learned the skill.

One of the best methods devised for getting over fear is desensitization. This is a personalized method involving a planned program for decreasing the fear connected with any particular event or situation. The procedure entails a slow approach to the fear-producing event with a variety of other similar circumstances. for example, if you know well in advance that you will have to give a speech to your class, sit down immediately and decide on the topic. With the topic in mind, plan a step-by-step sequence of events (somewhere between ten and twenty steps) leading up to that speech. Your sequence for a topic like "The Need for Writing Projects in all Classes" might look like this:

1. *Ask to your friends about writing projects in their classes.*
2. *Talk to your classmates about their views on writing projects in all classes.*

3.　*At a party, bring up the need for additional writing projects in all classes.*

4.　*Think about approaching some of your teachers to obtain their ideas about increasing the emphasis on writing.*

5.　*Talk to several of your teachers.*

6.　*Call on an academic dean to learn the procedure for requesting change.*

7.　*Collect signatures of students who support your suggestions for additional writing projects.*

9.　*Rehearse the speech alone.*

10.　*Go to the classroom, if possible, and give the speech as you would if everyone were there.*

11.　*Practice the speech before your closest friends or before your roommate.*

12.　*Give the speech to the class.*

The purpose of this sequence is to move from one step to another without a significant increase in the challenge involved. After moving through such a series of goals, you should find yourself speaking to your class with a minimum of apprehension.

You may want to choose different steps or arrange this plan in a different order. The important thing in creating a desensitization sequence is to make it personal—suited just to you—and to keep the distance between each step minimal. Make certain, for example, that each new step generates only a slight amount of increased anxiety.

Just before completing the final step—your goal—in the sequence, it might be helpful to practice some last-minute relaxing exercises. One last-minute check in the mirror will help guarantee that you look your best; in this way you will not be distracted by concern over your appearance. Because tension often occurs in the abdominal region, it is wise not to have a big meal just before the event. Checking the notes you plan to use to make certain they are in order is another important step in your preparations. On the way to the front of the class, take several deep breaths and release the air slowly. Take a moment to relax before you begin speaking; pause before saying your first word. If you have prepared thoroughly, followed your desensitization sequence, practiced some last-minute relaxing exercises, and developed a positive mental attitude, you should be ready to give your best performance and be as effective as possible.

BEING EFFECTIVE

We have talked about "effective" communication, but we really haven't stopped to define it. We could say that effective communication involves our ability to accurately and efficiently stimulate a sense of recognition in others, but this definition does not suggest the best method for being effective—the best way to stimulate this recognition. Instead, it provides the goal.

This goal can be achieved by demonstrating several different characteristics. However, one—the desire to communicate—provides the key to all the others. The desire to communicate provides the spark that makes all the other aspects of being an effective speaker easier to achieve. It results from:

1. *Having confidence in your choice of subject*
2. *Knowing that what you have to say is significant, relevant, and interesting*
3. *Feeling that what you say will be effective*

These characteristics can create the feeling that you are in command of your information, confident in yourself, and in control of the situation. They can generate the proper motivating impulse: "I want to convey this information to my audience." With a strong desire to communicate, your posture, movement, gestures, eye contact, and facial expressions will be affected. Your audience will respond to your presence because of the authority expressed in your body, voice, and language.

The desire to communicate will also affect the amount of energy we convey during our speech. An active and energetic speaker holds attention better than an inactive one. If our entire verbal and nonverbal message reveals complete involvement in our effort—suggesting that we are totally wrapped up in what we are saying—a sense of dynamism will be conveyed to our audience.

Being committed means looking directly into the eyes of the audience. An effective speaker does not talk to the floor, ceiling, or window. Neither does he or she look over the heads of the listeners. Direct eye contact reveals strength in our speech. It is the most effective way we have of making each member of the audience feel that he or she has been singled out for direct communication.

Another aspect of effectiveness is spontaneity. Nobody likes being read to. Nobody likes to listen to speakers who sound as if they had memorized their speeches either. Extemporaneous speaking—often referred to as the conversational approach—is the most impressive style. Although the ideas are determined beforehand, the words are determined at the moment of utterance. Spontaneity involves finding words that are appropriate for a specific situation, words that arise naturally from current feelings and attitudes.

Finally, being effective means revealing a positive attitude. We enjoy listening to a speaker who is confident, takes his or her speech seriously, and shows us that he or she is really concerned. Being dynamic, in other words, means being intellectually and emotionally powerful. If we *think* positive, our imagination will help guide our effort.

LOOKING OUR BEST

Being effective also includes looking our best. This is not to say, however, that we should put more emphasis on how we look than on what we have to say. The best guide is to both dress and act appropriately, so that our appearance and our actions will in no way detract from our message.

Clothes can have a negative effect if they are loud, conspicuous, revealing, or constricting. Comfortable clothes that conform to moderate styles are appropriate for most speech occasions. They minimize our concern for our attire, and they do not focus the audience's attention on our clothes.

What we often forget when it comes to clothes is that people are quick to judge our attitudes, feelings, or even position in life on the basis of the way we dress. If we dress sloppily, someone might think we do not care about what we are doing. If we are disheveled, the audience may think we are not very organized. A person in a business suit looks like a business person and may even appear conservative. What is important is not necessarily the accuracy of the generalization based upon what a person wears, but the fact that generalizations *are* made. We must be ready to accept the consequences of these generalizations based on how we dress and act. We do have some control if we are aware of their importance.

Our facial expressions can be just as important as the clothes we wear. If, when it is our turn to speak, we reveal a momentary frown or shake our head and throw our eyes up to the heavens (it's too late for help from up there) when we finish speaking, we can convey a negative overtone in our presentation.

Our face is our primary means of conveying sincerity. Our commitment and our concern are revealed in our faces. Empathy is the concept involved here; the audience responds to what it sees. If, in our speech, we feel hate, love, anger, or joy, an expressive face should reveal these feelings to our audience.

MOVING OUR BODY

The face does not exist apart from the body. Thus, an emotion conveyed by the face can be reinforced with the body. The body can convey meaning effectively and command attention. All bodily action, however, should be sincerely motivated, used appropriately, and not be overdone. It should enhance the verbal message and not detract from it. When an audience is distracted by body movements, it does not listen as attentively to what is being said.

Movements can be mesmerizing. For example, blinking lights—such as hazard lights on automobiles—attract more attention than those that are on all the time. We prefer motion pictures to still pictures. The most interesting commercials show products working; even still advertisements often depict action. With these examples in mind, we should use appropriate bodily action to sustain our listeners' interest.

Appropriate bodily action should be compatible with our speech and in harmony with the audience and occasion—action with which we feel comfortable. It should not be forced or unnatural.

The best advice is to move when it feels natural to do so. Too often, however, a speaker's feelings are affected by the anxiety of the moment, and he or she finds it difficult to know when it feels best. "Best" times are usually transitions between ideas or when an idea needs more emphasis. Often, a transition (such as the comment "The next idea we should consider is . . .") can be indicated if the speaker moves to the left or right. When an idea needs reinforcement or emphasis (such as the comment "Do you *know* what that means?"), the speaker can move in closer to the audience.

It should be remembered that no movement at all is better than distracting movement. When the movement looks rehearsed, it detracts from the speech. Also, when a speaker plays with his or her fingernails, rolls a pencil between the palms, taps a pen on the desk, or fidgets with his or her clothes, it makes listening difficult. Distracting mannerisms should be eliminated because of their strong negative influence. But it isn't easy.

The major benefit of movement is that it can provide relief for the speaker. Active and meaningful movement, whether bodily action or gestures, can not only punctuate a speech, but it also provides an outlet for the release of nervous tension.

Gestures

The use of our hands and arms is another outlet for nervous tension. In addition, gestures reinforce content and heighten attention. Most of us tend to be somewhat stiff when speaking in public and could benefit by using more gestures. For some of us, this may require practice. Sometimes, others can help us by pointing out where gestures could be effective. The best advice we can give is to stand in a position in which the hands and arms will be free to move if the urge to move them occurs.

USING OUR VOICE

The voice does more than simply convey words. The way in which the words are spoken gives us a great deal of information about the message. Imagine receiving the message "Come over here." Is it a command? Or is it an invitation? Is it to share in the mystery of a situation? We know not only by the situation but *how* the words are uttered. Our voice reveals things about us that may be far more important than the verbal message itself. Analyzing the way we speak helps to eliminate distractions and to increase our communication effectiveness. How loud or fast we speak, how high or low the utterance, how clear and distinct the message serve as part of the punctuation of speech. Without the symbols of written language—italics, punctuation marks, indentations, or varied type faces—the voice must provide its own variation, distinctions, and clarity in oral communication. We do this through our use of volume, pace, pitch, quality, and articulation.

Volume

Volume means the loudness or softness a person uses in speech. Perhaps you have had a teacher who talks very loudly; when the class period is over, you feel shouted at, almost bruised. When there is no change in volume—no variety—loudness loses its effectiveness, and we become more concerned about the discomfort we experience than with the meaning of the words.

Changes in volume can be effective as a means of emphasis. Such variations not only call attention to word meaning, but enhance it and thus help sustain attention. In altering intensity, lowering the voice to a lesser volume is especially effective.

Pace

Next to volume, *pace* is the easiest voice component to vary. Pace refers to the meter of our speech, how fast or how slowly we speak. If we speak too quickly, intelligibility may suffer. It may also be affected if we speak too slowly. If the rate of our speaking doesn't vary at all, we may lose the attention of our audience.

It is difficult to suggest an ideal speed or rate of utterance because it should vary according to the size of a room, its acoustics, the size and seating arrangement of the audience, the reactions of the audience, the nature of the occasion, the material of the speech, and our own needs or ability. Generally, 125 to 150 words per minute constitutes an adequate pace. If you are normally a fast speaker, you should pay attention to the pace at which you speak; you may be missing opportunities for emphasis or mood changes.

One of the most significant punctuation marks we have in oral discourse is the pause. Using the pause effectively will affect our rate of speaking. But we should be careful how we use it. Too often we want to fill voids in our communication with "uh," "you know," "like," or "okay"—vocalized pauses. These speech hesitancies can weaken our dynamism. The way to avoid vocalized pauses requires three steps:

1. *An awareness that we are using them*
2. *A desire to change*
3. *An effort to substitute a simple pause—no sound—in their place*

Pitch

Pitch is the range of tones we use in speaking. This modulation enhances attention and imparts meaning. The person who uses *no* changes in pitch can be accused of speaking in a monotone. A monotone not only denies the rich and subtle meanings of words but also causes decreased listener attention. Most of us use a variety of tones when we speak. Sometimes we use high tones, sometimes low ones.

Pitch, then, makes use of our natural voice range. Whether our range is classified as bass, tenor, or soprano, we still have much flexibility within that range. We can produce highs and lows that give our voice an interesting, expressive quality. When a speaker is really involved in a topic, cares about the audience, and delights in sharing his or her information with others, it is often revealed in the range of the voice. It is interesting to listen to.

Quality

Two extremes of *quality* may perhaps best demonstrate the contribution it makes to communication effectiveness. When we are angry, our voice reveals that anger through its harshness. When we are expressing words of affection or love, our voice is mellow or breathy. Although we do not have as much control over our voice quality as over our pace of speech, pitch, or volume, it can be used to reflect our emotional attitude. Vocal quality is a person's natural tone or the tone used to communicate a special feeling or attitude.

In speaking situations, it is likely that our listeners will be looking for signs of emotional commitment to our topic. If we feel hate or anger, the voice quality we use should reveal it. In this way we reveal complete involvement in the topic.

Articulation

Articulation is the speaker's skill in producing the sounds of the language. The aim of articulation is to be understood. Although there can be physical causes for poor articulation such as a hearing loss or badly aligned teeth, most articulation problems go back to our language models. If our parents, teachers, or peers had poor articulation, then we probably do, too, unless we have made a conscious effort to recognize and change these patterns.

Three common causes of articulation problems are sound substitution, omission of sounds, and slurring. Sound substitution is very common. Many people say "der," "dem," and "dose" for "there," "them," and "those." In this case a *d* has been substituted for the more difficult *th* sound. Americans are often dismayed to find they cannot get water in a foreign country. They would be more successful if they asked for "water" rather than "wader." In fact, the substitution of a *d* for a *t* in the middle of a word is widespread in American English. If you need any proof, try pronouncing these words as you usually do: "thirty," "Betty," "bottle." Unless you have unusually good articulation, you probably said "thirdy," "Beddy," and "boddle."

We also commonly omit sounds. For example, we sometimes say "libary for "library," dropping out the first *r* sound. We frequently omit sounds that occur at the ends of words such as "goin" for "going" and "doin" for "doing."

Slurring is caused by running words together. We frequently use phrases such as "yawanna go?" and "I'll meecha there." Slurring, as with other articulation problems, is usually a matter of bad speech habits, and it can be overcome with some effort and practice. Many people believe that they have a speech defect and are therefore unable to make certain sounds. This can be easily checked. For example, if you always say "der" for "there," make a special effort to make the *th* sound. If you are able to make it, you have a bad habit, not a speech defect.

Once you are aware of a particular articulation habit, then you can try to change it. Changing a habit is not easy, since it has probably been a part of you for a good fifteen or twenty years. Sometimes it helps to drill, using lists of words that give you trouble. Other times it helps to have a friend who has a good ear for detection remind you when you fall back into an old habit. Once you have accustomed yourself to looking for the problem, you will catch yourself more and more often. If you have several articulation problems, do not try to solve them all at one time. Work on one sound at a time, and when you can handle that sound, then attempt another one.

PRESENTING OUR SELVES

The ability to bring our total, real selves to a speech situation is labeled *presentness*. When we appear before a group of listeners, we should strive to reveal all that is unique about us: our personal attitudes, values, motives, and interests. When we hear and see someone speak, we want to hear not only their words but feel their emotions. We want to be impressed by their presence.

Several factors can hinder us in presenting ourselves fully:

1. *If we read our speech or recite it from memory, the words we utter will not sound like our own.*

2. *If we project a negative view of ourselves, it will communicate itself to our listeners.*

3. *If we apologize or give the impression that what we have to say is unimportant, we may convince our audience that what we have to say is not worth listening to.*

Our goal should be to free ourselves from these restrictions—to involve our total personality in our speech. Why is this important? Because listeners respect those who accept themselves. They are responsive to those who can open up and release their thoughts and feelings. The more of our complete selves we offer to others, the more we are likely to be respected, listened to, and believed.

ADAPTING TO OUR AUDIENCE

Throughout this discussion, we have said that our delivery should be appropriate for the occasion, message, and audience—as well as appropriate for ourselves. When we say "appropriate for our audience," we mean that it should be directly related to their needs, wants, and interests—not just in content, but in presentation. We must remember that a message that does not hold attention may not be heard or listened to.

Thus, if delivery is not adapted to the audience, there may be little point in talking.

The main factor that will improve our adaptation to our audience can be summarized in one word: *feedback*. Feedback, in public speaking, is our ability to know, by looking at our audience and listening to its members, whether or not they have heard, seen, or understood our message. Feedback also includes our use of that information to improve our message so that the meaning we intend is the meaning received by our audience.

Effective feedback has several advantages:

1. *It makes each speech situation unique because the reactions of the audience directly affect the nature of the message.*
2. *It adds liveliness, immediacy, and excitement to the speech event, since an element of unpredictability is involved.*
3. *It reveals that the speaker cares about the audience and the message, since his or her comments are directly related to the influence of one or the other.*
4. *It involves the members of the audience in the communication. They become part of the content. Thus, the message is more likely to hold their attention and more likely to be meaningful for them.*

When we are choosing our subject, thinking about content, preparing our supporting materials, organizing our ideas, and considering the language we plan to use, we must think about ways of relating what we are doing to our audience—the *specific* audience we will speak to. We must allow for this, too, as we practice our delivery.

PRACTICING DELIVERY

How can we practice delivery to the extent that we feel comfortable with the content and language and yet are not so locked into it that it sounds memorized or mechanical? Fortunately, there is a way that has proven very successful for most public speakers. The process for practicing delivery that has worked best for us follows these rules:

1. *Prepare the content thoroughly.*
2. *Organize the content into a full-sentence outline.*
3. *From the full-sentence outline, extract a key-word or short-phrase outline to use in rehearsal.*
4. *Place the word or short-phrase outline on one side of a 3 by 5 card. Hold the card in your hand as you rehearse the speech.*

5. *Find new, fresh language for each idea every time you rehearse the speech. Do not use the same words every time.*
6. *If the speech is short, strive to get rid of the 3 by 5 card as quickly as you can, or, perhaps, leave it on the table and refer to it only if absolutely needed.*

Using the above method, you will be less likely to find your language becoming frozen. When actually giving the speech you will have several alternative ways for putting your ideas into language—not just one. When you forget, you will not be looking for just one word, rather, you will be able to fill the gap with any of a number of alternative words. You will have flexibility.

In following the above approach, you will be using the most common mode of delivery: the extemporaneous method. Your ideas will be thoroughly prepared beforehand, but your words will be determined at the time of utterance. The words will be inspired not only by the ideas, but by the audience, the situation, and your own feelings at the time.

Some comments on the practice sessions may also be of help. Try to make them as similar to the real situation as possible. It will help decrease your anxiety if you can imagine your audience present at each rehearsal. Also for practicing:

1. *Stand up. Face your hypothetical audience squarely.*
2. *Look over your outline before beginning. If it is a short speech, put it away; if it is long, depend on it as little as possible.*
3. *Check the time before and after the speech to determine the length of the speech.*
4. *Deliver the speech all the way through without stopping.*
5. *Check the outline to see what you have omitted.*
6. *Go through the practice again.*
7. *Put the speech away for awhile to put some distance between practice sessions. A practice session just before going to bed will allow the subconscious to work on it while you are sleeping.*

Notes can become a crutch. They can be depended upon or referred to so often that they become a barrier between the speaker and the audience. If used, they should be used openly and freely (not hidden), and should be referred to in a comfortable and natural way.

EVALUATING AND TRYING AGAIN

Many speakers feel their work is completed after they utter the final words of their conclusion. However, some of the most valuable speech work begins after a speech is over. That is the time to ask if you reached your goal and discover what effect you had on your audience.

These questions can be answered by the feedback you receive during and after your speech. If you were looking at your audience while giving the speech, how did they respond? Did they look interested or did they look bored? Did you have their attention at the begining of the speech and lose it later? If so, why? You may be able to answer some of these questions while the speech is going on, but you can probably best discover the answers after the speech is over.

Some of our most useful feedback comes in terms of questions and discussion following a speech. Questions often indicate whether the audience followed the speech and understood what we were saying. Lively discussion often tells us that we have stimulated thinking among audience members. Our most negative feedback may be no feedback at all. The audience is apathetic; they have no questions and no comments. If directly asked what they thought of the speech, they might reply, "It was a nice speech. I liked it"—a comment that is so general that it has little value.

Often it is necessary to interpret feedback. For instance, let's say that your object in speaking is to have an audience sign a petition. After the speech is over, several audience members shake your hand and say "great speech" and go off without signing the petition. Now your problem is to evaluate their feedback. If it was such a great speech, why did they not sign the petition?

The classroom situation provides an unusual opportunity for speech analysis. During the first speeches, your instructor (and perhaps your classmates) will probably spend a lot of time discussing your speech—especially with regard to your delivery. We would all like to think that we have delivered a perfect speech, but that hardly ever happens the first time or even the second. You will be receiving some criticism that will be useful to you. Sometimes this criticism may seem very threatening since most of us dislike being criticized in public. It may be useful for you to remember that this criticism refers only to the speech content and to the way you delivered it. If you accept it in this sense, you will be able to change bad habits and to become aware of and overcome some communication difficulties you may not know you have. Once you are aware of your problems, you are ready to try again. By the time you give your last speech, you may be very close to giving a perfect speech.

LISTENING

Although speaking is important, we spend far more time listening than speaking. As a matter of fact, we devote more time to listening than speaking, reading, and writing combined! Despite this fact, however, listening is our least proficient skill. Why? There are several reasons:

1. *We are lazy.*
2. *We don't want to listen.*
3. *We don't know how to listen.*
4. *We listen for the wrong things.*
5. *We equate hearing with listening.*

Let's look at that last point first. Hearing is done with the ears alone. Listening not only involves the ears but goes further; it also involves our intellect and our emotions—that is, we must make sense out of what we hear. We cannot just sit by and hear at random and expect listening to occur. Listening is an active process.

Therefore, we must apply ourselves if we are going to listen. Research has shown that immediately after listening we remember only about 25-50 percent of the subject matter To remember more than 50 percent we must direct our attention *actively* to the process. In addition, the fact that we listen to ideas does not necessarily mean we fully comprehend all the implications of those ideas. Full comprehension may require even greater concentration and application.

The problems of laziness, lack of desire, inadequate knowledge, or listening for the wrong things *can* be overcome, however. The solution involves much the same procedure we use to overcome negative attitudes and poor habits: practice, practice, practice. Fortunately, we can perfect our listening skills by listening to public speeches, and these skills, once perfected, can help us in our academic classes and all areas of life.

There are several suggestions that will help develop better listening skill:

1. *Prepare for listening. We must mentally prepare ourselves for the event by ridding our minds of other distracting thoughts and finding a reason to listen.*
2. *Concentrate on listening. Try not to let our minds wander by thinking about what we are doing, asking ourselves questions about the event at hand, listening to the ideas presented, and avoiding being distracted by the delivery.*
3. *Keep active in listening. Reveal alertness and interest; give the speaker appropriate feedback through facial cues and eye contact, and keep from being impatient.*
4. *Suspend judgment. Search for the speaker's essential message. Do not get sidetracked by trivial facts or points. Hear the speaker out; don't jump to conclusions.*

Sometimes it will help to know what to listen for. Reviewing Chapter 6 will be very helpful in this area. In addition, the following is a brief summary of points to consider in listening critically to public speeches. Ask yourself, has the speaker:

1. *Considered the audience?*
2. *Adapted to the situation?*
3. *Chosen a significant, relevant, and interesting topic?*
4. *Provided adequate sources to support the topic?*
5. *Organized the speech efficiently and effectively?*
6. *Selected strong ideas backed by sufficient supporting materials?*
7. *Stated ideas in language that is appropriate and lively?*
8. *Revealed energy and enthusiasm in delivering the ideas?*
9. *Offered an experience that you will very likely remember?*

When you are listening, check yourself. Are you falling back into your old habits? Are you letting your attitudes affect your listening? If you want to learn more about effective communication, discover more interesting ideas, and improve your ability to concentrate, analyze, evaluate, and strive to improve your listening skills.

SUMMARY

Effective delivery *and* content are necessary to make a successful speech. Neither is more important than the other, since each directly affects the other. The effective speaker must strive for quality in both areas.

It is often difficult for us to think rationally and calmly about the public-speaking event because of the fear we have of it. Trying to overcome this fear little by little is one of the best ways to manage this anxiety.

Effective communication is our goal. It is best achieved if we acquire the desire to communicate. This desire will affect our enthusiasm, our directness with our audience, our spontaneity, and our overall attitude.

We also have to look our best. Not only should we wear appropriate clothes but be aware of our posture and our facial expressions. The audience tends to feel what it sees. Thus, we must try to make sure that what they feel is what we want them to feel.

Moving our body also adds to our effectiveness. Our movement should be appropriate for our subject, purpose, audience, and for the occasion. We must remember, however, that no movement at all is better than movement that distracts the audience. But bodily action that reinforces meaning, commands attention, and channels nervous energy can benefit public speaking.

We can also use our voices in effective ways. Variation in volume, pace, pitch, quality, and articulation will add extra dimensions to a speech. Vocal dynamism projects both intellectual and emotional power.

To use the public-speaking situation as an opportunity to present ourselves to an audience is a realistic and important objective. We should strive to eliminate factors that cause ourselves to be obscured or hindered in order to let our total selves emerge in delivering our speech.

Our delivery should be closely adapted to a particular audience. Effective use of feedback makes each speech situation unique, adds liveliness, reveals concern, and involves the audience.

The way we practice our delivery can also allow for audience adaptation; it can make us flexible and comfortable in front of our listeners. Above all, practice can help us to develop naturalness before an audience. A relaxed delivery will free us to enhance our ideas with all our potential.

Finally, we should make an effort to improve our listening skills. We must prepare ourselves for listening, concentrate on it, keep active in it, and suspend our judgment. In addition to listening for the speaker's adaptation to audience and situation, we must examine the content and delivery of the presentation. We cannot underestimate the importance of our listening skills, for we are listeners more often than we are speakers, and without a good recipient, any message will be lost.

FURTHER READING

Herbert Fensterheim and Jean Baer, *Don't Say Yes When You Want to Say No.* New York: Dell, 1975.
> The authors treat fears under the categories of impersonal and interpersonal phobias. They provide useful suggestions for controlling anxiety including relaxation exercises, systematic desensitization, and *in vivo* (in life) desensitization. A "Full Relaxation Exercise" dialogue, which could be converted to an audio-tape recording, is presented in the appendix.

Royal L. Garff, *You Can Learn to Speak.* Salt Lake City: Wheelwright Press, 1966.
> A popular book that you can probably find in your local library, this guide covers many aspects of public speaking that are useful to beginning speakers.

John T. Wood, *What Are You Afraid Of?* Englewood Cliffs, N.J.: Prentice-Hall, 1976.

Wood's personal style and his excellent examples make this a readable and valuable book. He convinces us that we can grow if we are willing to both accept and face our fears. Through relaxation and desensitization, Wood shows that we can cope with our fears rather than run from them.

Harold P. Zelko and Marjorie E. Zelko, *How to Make Speeches for All Occasions.* Garden City, N.Y.: Doubleday, 1971.
A practical and easily read book on how to plan and organize a speech. This work will serve as a good reference.

NOTES

[1]David Wallechinsky, Irving Wallace, and Amy Wallace, *The Book of Lists* (New York: William Morrow, 1977), p. 469.

chapter 8

Persuasive Communication

Each of us is influenced throughout life by two opposing forces: the urge to change and the urge to remain the same. Part of us likes the old ways, the familiar, the friends we have now, the book that confirms what we already believe. Another part of us searches for the new, the better way, an experience we have never had before, a television program that gives us a whole new perspective. Trying something new, whether it is a new job or a new relationship or a new course, has an element of excitement—but change also carries the threat that we will not be able to handle the new experience or that we will end up worse off than we were in the old, familiar situation. It is clear that change is not necessarily positive; it is equally clear that progress—in a person, in a nation, in the life of humanity as a whole—is possible only if some things change.

One of the chief characteristics of communication is its power to effect change. Talking to your father about your values may result in a change in relationship, in greater understanding and trust between you. Reading about a new field of study may cause you to change your major. Working with others in a small group may produce a new traffic light on the corner of your block. Delegates from many nations sit around a table and agree to stop a war. The power of communication to alter people's lives is fundamental and all-pervasive.

This chapter is about that power; it deals with *persuasion*, communication that is designed to effect changes in attitudes or behavior. Persuasion involves the use of verbal symbols and nonverbal behavior by the "source" with the intention of producing a change in the "receiver." Almost every time you say anything to anyone else, you are persuading. When you ask your parents for money, when you tell an Internal Revenue Service agent that your tax report was accurate, when you indicate to the instructor that the hour is over, when you tell the sales clerk you need time to think about the purchase—you are involved in the act of persuasion. Persuasion is common in all communication situations; it occurs in interpersonal relationships, in the more formal public-speaking situation and in small groups. Thus, every chapter of this book concerns itself with persuasion.

The persuasive speaker touches our lives from the moment we rise in the morning with "It's time to get up!" to the time we turn off the television after hearing an author promoting his or her latest book on the late-night talk show. It is as important in our society as it is necessary. Understanding some of the components of the persuasion process will enable you to better evaluate and analyze the persuasion techniques of others, to improve your own ability to persuade, and to become a better contributor in decision-making processes involving change.

The communicator who intends to produce changes in others but fails is still involved in the persuasive process because of his or her intent. Persuasion may result because of the characteristics of a particular person who has the ability to produce changes in others. Persuasion may result from the message itself, since certain elements in discourse are intended to alter behavior. But even though the intention of a persuasive message is to change the receiver, the communicator is not really the persuader. The communicator simply provides stimuli that encourage the receiver to persuade himself or herself. Thus, the receiver is the true persuader. You may be persuaded to vote for a political candidate, for example, because you are satisfied that he or she is more honest or more concerned than the opponents. On the basis of the information you receive, you persuade yourself that your vote may provide you with "cleaner" government. The candidate only provides the stimuli to convince you.

Because persuasion really occurs within the listener, one primary function of the communicator should be to get and hold attention. If a listener's sensory receptors—eyes and ears especially—are not attracted to the stimulus—the idea or message—no persuasion can occur, even though forceful symbols may be used by the communicator. The source's intent to persuade or the use of persuasive elements of discourse do not in themselves guarantee that change will take place. As in other forms of communication, success is measured by what happens at the receiving end, in the listener. The communicator who uses symbols and ideas that are familiar, have variety, reveal more intensity than competing stimuli, are repeated, and show novelty or unusualness will gain attention and hold it better than a communicator whose message does not demonstrate these characteristics. The next time you try to persuade someone to do something, test this idea by changing your voice, your language, your meaning, your gestures, or your bodily action to see if such a change has higher attention-getting value. In persuading others, however, it is important that the technique not become so obvious that it attracts attention to itself. Also, persuasive techniques are usually used in conjunction with each other—seldom in isolation. The importance and value of the concept of attention should be kept in mind as the other components of the persuasive process are discussed.

Because major portions of the material that could be treated in a chapter on persuasion have been treated elsewhere in this book, we will focus here on seven major areas that directly concern persuasion: 1) the speaker's image; 2) the means of persuasion; 3) suggestion as a form of persuasion; 4) attitude change; 5) the effects of persuasion; 6) resisting persuasion; and 7) ethical considerations and propaganda in persuasion. The nuts and bolts of putting a persuasive speech together have been discussed in Chapter 6, Public Speaking: Content. The way to deliver an effective, persuasive speech has been considered in Chapter 7, Public Speaking: Delivery. The persuasive proposition is treated in Chapter 5, Small-Group Communication.

THE SPEAKER'S IMAGE

The effectiveness of any public speaker depends on how he or she is seen by the audience. Audience perception of the speaker is determined by *ethos*—the speaker's personal characteristics that make him or her more or less believable and trustworthy in the minds of the audience.

For a speaker to be effective, he or she must have favorable ethos. Research has pinpointed three variables that go into the creation of this quality: expertness, trustworthiness, and dynamism. A speaker is seen as expert when he or she is competent in a subject; as trustworthy when he or she presents honest, acceptable arguments; and as dynamic when active, bold, and aggressive. For the greatest possible message acceptance, all these variables should be present. For example, if a used-car salesman is judged to be competent but not trustworthy, his effectiveness in selling cars will be greatly hampered. A teacher may be perceived by students as both competent and trustworthy, but if her teaching is dull, passive, and tired, her effectiveness is reduced.

Speaker ethos affects an audience before the speech begins, throughout the speech, and after the speech is over. Prior ethos is based on the knowledge the audience has of the speaker before he or she begins to speak. This knowledge may be based on personal experience if members of the audience know the speaker personally, or it may be based on the vicarious experience of audience members who know the speaker through agencies such as the mass media. The audience may also have impressions of the speaker based on the groups to which he or she belongs. For example, if the members of the audience know that the speaker is a Black Panther or a member of the American Medical Association, they may have an opinion of the speaker based on their impression of that group. Sponsorship may be another basis for prior knowledge. If the Ku Klux Klan sponsors a rally, we know that the speakers at that rally have certain attitudes—that is why they have been chosen to speak. Finally, prior knowledge may be based on mere physical appearance. The audience looks at the speaker seated on the platform and makes certain judgments: he is well dressed; she looks kind-hearted.

All this prior knowledge may either hurt or help a speaker. Billy Graham's prior image as an emotional evangelist has worked against him in an intellectual university setting. He has often begun a speech by asking if all the members of the speech and psychology departments were present. This question let the audience know that Graham was aware that some people came to watch him "perform"—not to hear his message. One aid in establishing prior ethos is to have someone introduce the speaker. Introductions are especially useful in establishing the speaker's competence and trustworthiness.

Ethos is also created while the communication is going on. It can be created by the speaker's choice of topic, by his or her approach to the topic, by the extent to which the audience identifies with the speaker's ideas, and by the types of appeal the speaker uses. Dynamism is largely determined by the speaker's style of delivery. All these factors help develop ethos during speech.

The ethos that occurs after the speech is mostly a continuation of the ethos that has been created before and during the speech. This ethos is no longer controlled by the speaker—it largely depends on whether he or she has lived up to, has been less than, or has gone beyond the audience's expectations.

Ethos in public speaking is a quality of the speech occasion, the speech itself, and, of course, the audience. All of these factors interact. A speaker may have great ethos with one audience and hardly any at all with another audience. Skillful preparations, including careful audience analysis, will help most speakers improve their own speaker ethos.

Ethos—the image of the communicator in the eyes of the receiver—has been singled out for special treatment because it is of major importance in persuasion. It may indeed wield a stronger influence than other means of persuasion—such as argument, evidence, appeals to motives, or appeals to emotion—although it is important to remember that the total effect is what counts. In many cases, it is difficult to know which factor in the persuasive effort has the most influence.

MEANS OF PERSUASION

If you have ever been asked to make a case to the faculty or administration for abolishing a requirement at your school, or if you have ever planned an argument against pollution to present to a group of industrialists, or if you have ever been motivated to persuade someone else to join a cause or organization to which you belong, you have probably been faced with decisions that concern *means*—how to influence a receiver or group of receivers most effectively.

There are, basically, three means of persuasion: 1) *logos*—using sound reasoning and dependable evidence, 2) *pathos*—relating the desired change to the attitudes and emotions of the listeners, and as we have just seen, 3) *ethos*—demonstrating the good will, wisdom, and character of the communicator.

These three elements are not mutually exclusive, nor should a persuasive communication be designed to contain only one of them; different situations require varying degrees of logos, pathos, and ethos. A balance is the ideal in most situations. Making a case before the faculty or administration would probably require more evidence—cold facts—than the other two situations. Faculty members or administrators tend to value logos and to make judgments only after serious consideration and study of the matter. An emotional plea would probably detract from the credibility of the communicator, since a student would, very likely, be seen as immature if he or she pleaded the case with passion. The more evidence the student could amass, the more likely he or she could make the desired change in the listeners.

Arguing against pollution is a different situation. It is unlikely that the facts and other data you could gather would have significance to an industrialist. In many cases, they already know the facts, or think they do. Although your credibility may be low, you might have a chance to persuade them by making an impassioned plea for the salvation of our earth and the preservation of something inhabitable for future generations. Another use of pathos might be even more effective: presenting the possiblity of a boycott of the products produced by this particular industry. This would have an emotional impact, since industry's primary goal is making money.

Finally, convincing someone to join a cause or an organization might require some logic, some emotion, and a good deal of ethos. Your ability to persuade the other person in this case would probably depend, to a great extent, on what he or she thought of your own wisdom regarding this choice and your other choices as well—those to which the other person may have been exposed in the past. How important your character is to the other person, whether he or she wants to be associated with you, even your good will in approaching the other person may affect your success in convincing him or her to join. People sometimes forget that the establishment of high credibility—effective ethos—is not a function of a specific situation. It begins when your association with another person begins and develops throughout your relationship.

There is no formula for choosing the best means of persuasion. Sometimes you need to use more logic—a clear purpose, strong evidence, a unified structure, and cogent reasoning—as opposed to appeals to the audience's feelings or to the straightforward establishment of your credibility in the other person's eyes. Choosing the best means requires audience analysis; you need to know who the audience is, how old its members are, their sex, how they feel about your ideas or topic, and what they know of you as a communicator. Such analysis may be made of one person, of a group of people, or of the public at large.

If your analysis of your listener(s) indicates that the audience's attitude seems to favor your idea, you can heighten this feeling by giving an emotional plea. The addresses given before conventions of political parties are examples of this kind of persuasion. In conversation with another person, you can give a personal example or anecdote to indicate that your feelings about this idea are the same as your listener's. In a small group, facts and additional evidence are often provided to heighten the unanimity of feeling.

When listeners are neutral or apathetic, which is the common state of most listeners, some evidence along with some emotion and a strong case for the speaker's credibility may cause them to change their behavior. Listeners are so consistent in their neutral reaction to most ideas that we have coined another definition: "Persuasion is the art of moving apathy in your direction."

With a hostile audience, the evidence should be powerful. To provide support for strong evidence, one's credibility should also be strong. The person bent on the persuasion of a hostile listener should be warned that this is a difficult situation; there is little hope for success in changing the behavior of someone who is truly hostile. An informative approach—establishing the idea as an important one through the presentation of facts and opinion with no emotional pleas whatsoever—may be an effective tactic. With sufficient information, and time to think over the ideas and to contact others regarding them, the listener may at least become more open to your message.

It is probable that anything you do before, during, or after a persuasive communication will bear in some way on your logos, pathos, or ethos. The more concerned you are with influencing, the more care you should take in controlling the means you use to persuade. Think about these factors next time you are in the listener's position. What does the communicator have to do to make you say, "I'm sold—you convinced me!" to a salesperson, "Wow—that was an impressive speech" to a public speaker, or "That was a compelling advertisement" to your television set? Logos, pathos, and ethos should all blend to form the means of persuasion in such a way that they are neither distracting nor obvious. It is not the technique, after all, to which the listener responds—it is the idea or the message. Generally speaking, and with regard to the use of these means in an honorable fashion, it is not as important to note *how* one is convinced (whether it was logos, pathos, or ethos) as to note that one *is* convinced —that someone's behavior has actually changed as a result of a stimulus you produced through means of persuasion.

Occasionally, you will see a persuasive message that has been designed without careful audience analysis or a message that is clearly designed for an audience that does not include you. The effect of such a message can be to arouse laughter or anger instead of the change desired by the source. A billboard showing a bathing beauty in a bikini to advertise a new car, for example, may arouse contempt in a viewer who is sophisticated enough to recognize and resent the obvious suggestion that having the car will also get one the woman. Sometimes errors in audience analysis can cause the message to have an effect that is the opposite of the one intended. A speech intended to be powerful enough to generate fear in the audience may appear funny, laughable, or ludicrous because the speaker goes too far. It is better to err on the side of caution and moderation than to openioneself to ridicule or loss of credibility because of exaggeration or unnecessary hyperbole.

SUGGESTION: THE STILL, SMALL VOICE

Advertising often plants the name of the product in the listener's consciousness through a creative jingle, a catchy phrase, or a memorable tune. The listener is stimulated to remember the name of the product without ever having responded to the product in a critical way at all. He or she may even find that the tune will constantly recur and be whistled or hummed in idle moments. this process, through which persons respond more or less uncritically to persuasive stimuli, is known as *suggestion*. The degree to which a persuader is aware of suggestion and controls it may determine his or her effectiveness.

Suggestion works in a variety of different ways. Like many of the other components of communication, each suggestion technique can be adapted to a specific situation. We will discuss the use of ethos as it relates to suggestion. We will also note how the presence of other people contributes to suggestion. Creating an appropriate atmosphere can be important. Finally, we will mention a variety of other techniques that the persuader can use to suggest a change to the listener. Variety and flexibility should be considered in the use of any or all the techniques mentioned.

Advertising gimmicks represent a significant portion of the persuasive stimuli that affect us in our daily lives. Advertisers, of course, spend millions of dollars to get the "right" saying or the "right" music for their product. With the tremendous amount of money expended on creating this kind of suggestion, it is little wonder that we are almost constantly bombarded. Most advertisers are satisfied if their product gains the attention of the listener. They believe that this recognition alone will cause the listener to buy the product, since he or she will have been subconsciously influenced to purchase it by the suggestion of the advertisement.

A technique commonly used by advertisers is *ethos* (previously discussed on page 207.) Used in this context, ethos refers to the persuasive power that operates through suggestion by association. Many writers refer to this technique as "prestige suggestion." Advertisers make use of this device when they pay prestigious figures to endorse their products. Since these famous people have a previously established favorable ethos, the advertisers who hire them hope that the viewer will be persuaded to react positively to the product as well. You have undoubtedly believed something or acted in a particular way simply because a source you considered important suggested it. Popular sports figures and film stars are often used in this manner—partly because they are accustomed to eliciting the attention of audiences. It is interesting to see Bill Cosby, O. J. Simpson, or Catherine Deneuve perform in an advertisement.

The influence of prestigious figures is not limited to advertising. One of the authors of this text, for example, once went out and bought an expensive long-playing record of the sounds of earthquakes, ionospheric swishes, whistlers, tweeks, and the dawn chorus just because a high school science teacher spoke so highly of it. It was a once-in-a-lifetime opportunity to have these sounds on record—and the record was listened to only once. This, too, was uncritical acceptance. Ethos is often at work when someone says, "I'd believe (or do) it, if I were you." Your action is then dependent on the prestige value of the source. Even if we rationalize the behavior with a phrase like, "Oh, I was going to do it anyway," the prestigious figure may have been the final stimulus that tipped the scales and caused you to act. This kind of suggestion is unlikely to do much more than simply tip the scales, but in many cases this is all that is desired.

Another source of suggestion is a crowd of other people. Have you ever noticed how your behavior changes when you are with a large group? James A. Winans, an early writer on communication, noted that men's minds are "overcome by mass suggestion" when in a "psychological crowd." We are less critical and discriminating—more emotional and responsive. "A crowd of men, usually polite," according to Winans, "will hoot at strangers, women, or authorities. Men usually reserved will slap each other on the back, shake hands with strangers, parade in lockstep, laugh, shout, sing with abandon."[1] An effective public speaker capitalizes on this tendency when he encourages his audience to sit close together directly in front of where he or she is speaking. People who are seated close together are more susceptible to *social facilitation*—each person's responses will be increased by the mere presence of others. The speaker's jokes will be funnier, a sorrowful message will be more grievous, and inspirational sentiments will be more uplifting. In a sense, other people around us give us implicit suggestions on how to act. We may laugh at another's joke because those around us laugh, even if we then have to ask a friend to repeat the punch line. We may applaud a performance because those around us applaud, even if we dislike it. When we are with others, we also feel less inhibited, and their reactions and responses are more readily communicated to us.

There are also certain sounds and body movements that tend to affect the audience psychologically when they are performed in rhythm by the group. The use of rhythm can help to create an atmosphere for uncritical acceptance. Rituals, chants, songs, hand-clapping, cheering, and the like heighten suggestibility by lowering our critical abilities in a particular setting and reducing our will to evaluate critically. Some church services rely heavily on these techniques in their worship. You may recall rhythmical performances occurring at political conventions, pep rallies, and rock concerts as well.

Suggestion also occurs when an appropriate atmosphere is created. Often, a great deal of time and effort are expended to produce a conducive climate. When a public speaker delivers his message in an assembly hall, tabernacle, or synagogue, the speech seems important and grand. A location can affect suggestiblilty. When President Jimmy Carter gave his first informal address to the public, sometimes referred to as his "fireside chat," he appeared on television sitting in a comfortable chair wearing a cardigan sweater—conveying a relaxed, down-to-earth image through the surroundings and his attire. When a person wants to suggest making love, the persuasive communication can be heightened by soft music, dim lights, and wine.

We tend to think of the analysis of crowd behavior as being a fairly recent study, dating perhaps from the mass rallies in Germany in the 1930s, but mass behavior had been studied in depth even before that time. H. L. Hollingworth, writing in *The Psychology of the Audience* in 1935, noted several ways through which suggestion can operate. Suggestion is more likely to have an impact if the persuader attempts to convey the suggestion in such a way that it seems to originate with the listener. It is likely to be more effective if it is presented with force and vividness, if it is made positively rather than negatively (the persuader argues in favor of his own ideas rather than against an opposing view), and if it is presented more than once (that is, if it is repeated). The power of suggestion will be increased as well if the persuader increases his own prestige, aligns his suggestions with the dynamic motives and beliefs of the listener, and refrains from suggesting opposing or rival courses of action.[2]

Each of the following techniques can also increase the possibility that suggestion will occur: the persuader asks questions to which the listener can answer "yes"; creates an appropriate emotional tone or mood for the message; assumes that the listener will agree with him or her; achieves common ground with the listener by appealing to his or her beliefs, wants, needs, and desires; identifies himself or herself with the listener's causes; and phrases his or her ideas to utilize the energy of the listener's motives.

Suggestions and associations are generated in the minds of listeners with or without the specific intention of the source whenever communication occurs. The persuader who attempts to channel those suggestions to his or her own ideas, beliefs, or actions is simply capitalizing on a present and unavoidable force. The persuader who successfully controls the force is using suggestion positively—in his or her be-half—rather than being controlled by it or allowing the suggestion to occur in random fashion.

Persuasion by suggestion is one of the most subtle forms of exerting control through communication. Becoming aware of the power of others' suggestions, whether they are intentional or unintentional, begins when you ask yourself why you do what you do and believe what you believe. Your behavior and your values come, in part, from the influence of others, and much of that influence is in the form of suggestion. It is one of the main communication techniques, for example, through which parents train their children to behave in ways that are acceptable to the parents and to society at large.

USING PERSUASION TO CHANGE ATTITUDES

A person's attitudes, like his or her behavior and beliefs, are learned. Your attitudes are the result of your experiences, the influence of individuals and groups in our society, and your personal values. Who a person is at any one time depends in part upon his or her past. Exposed to a stimulus to change—such as a persuasive message—you may resist be-cause the change represents an alteration of past behavior and involves some feeling of risk. This is true even if the stimulus to change comes from within yourself. Thus, change is likely to occur slowly and over a long period of time. The realistic persuader will limit his or her expectations and not be disappointed when changes take time to happen.

The rate and degree of change that is possible in any situation depends upon the attitudes of the sources and the receiver toward that change. Changes in behavior begin with changes in attitudes. An *attitude* is a positive or negative feeling that we associate with an object, an event, another person, a situation, and so on. It is the mental position that we take for or against something. A shift in your attitude about something will often eventually result in a change in your behavior. If someone convinces you to dislike a course you are taking and attending regularly, you may begin to attend it less regularly—a behavioral response corresponding to your shift in attitude.

The speaker in a persuasive communication is likely to have a consi-stent and predictable attitude toward the message. Since he or she is advocating the change, the speaker will have a favorable attitude toward the message, usually one that is quite definite and compelling. The listener, on the other hand, may have almost any attitude toward the message. He or she could be favorably disposed—showing moderate interest or even great enthusiasm. The listener could be negatively

disposed toward the message—showing strong antagonism or rejection. He or she may also have a neutral attitude—showing apathy, ambivalence, indifference, or ignorance about the topic.

In addition to the listener's attitude toward the speaker's particular message, the persuader should note a general attitude toward change that many people exhibit. Generally, it is safe to assume that people believe what they want to believe. Most of us are ego-centered, with a strong commitment to our own interest. When presented with a persuasive message, people will select, organize, and interpret stimuli in accordance with their own motives—that is, they will modify their behavior in keeping with what is important or gratifying to them. Because most people act and think this way, you should do more than simply tell another person what you wish him or her to accept or believe. Although explaining your point of view to the listener clearly and distinctly is important, you also have to show how his or her acceptance of your message will be personally gratifying.

You have to be concerned with the needs that motivate individuals to action or belief. If you wish to change your listener, you must first influence his or her attitudes, and individual feelings are almost always tied up with some kind of self-interest. This is not necessarily ruthless or selfish, since people associate their own self-interest with many positive values, both for themselves and for others. You might be able to change an attitude, for example, if you showed a person that your idea would guarantee his or her physical well-being—an appeal to the desire for good health, which we all agree is a worthwhile attitude. You could appeal to the need for pleasurable feelings—sex, adventure, or fun. You could appeal to the listener's interest in acquiring money or material things, in gaining the good will or attention of others, in achieving personal success or social status or esteem, or in enjoying freedom or realizing individual desires and ends. These are all desirable goals for which most people in our society strive.

We also have feelings of duty, and to those who are duty-conscious, you could appeal to their obligations to family, state, nation, business, religion, and so on. Most of us have positive attitudes toward telling the truth, keeping promises, and otherwise maintaining the mores and rules of our culture. An effective persuasive message might indicate that the change proposed will satisfy one of these needs. Finally, we could appeal to the listener's desires to maintain his or her self-image and to engage in commendable behavior: be kind and fair; exhibit courage, honesty, tolerance, persistence, or sincerity, for example. When listeners feel that your idea will satisfy their needs, they will be disposed to change their attitudes.

You are not likely to arouse an emotion simply by describing it or by telling the listener he or she ought to feel it. The appeal should be vividly presented with illustrations that show real people in real situations. In this way, the listener can be led to sympathize and empathize. The listener will become part of the persuasion process if the right mood is present and if the persuader has succeeded in getting on *common ground* with him or her—offering ideas with which the listener can identify.

As a persuader, you can create attitude change through three processes identified by Herbert C. Kelman, a writer on opinion change.[3] Kelman says that attitudes can be changed by compliance, identification, or internalization. If you provide the listener with either rewards or punishments for adopting behaviors and attitudes, you are using *compliance.* The listener is likely to alter his or her behavior and attitudes for the moment but not to change basic attitudes or the fundamental reasons for holding those attitudes or acting the way he or she does. The mother who rewards children with candy for good behavior while she is grocery shopping may alter their mischievous behavior for the moment, but such behavior is likely to recur again or as soon as the children are outside the supermarket.

A persuader who seeks to influence the listener(s) to be more like the persuader or some other person is using *identification.* The listener may be encouraged to adopt attitudes similar to those of the speaker or of others. When a persuader uses himself or herself as the "model," he or she is using *ethos* to promote the cause. If others are used, they are established as "idols" for emulation. It might be possible, for instance, for you to encourage a son to be more like his father, a young woman to be more like her teacher, a parishioner to be more like his or her minister, or a citizen to be more like a politician he or she admires. Often, this change, too, is temporary, for it is based on identification rather than intellectual agreement. If the new attitude or behavior is not reinforced by others or if the listener and the "idol" are separated for a period of time, the attitude or behavior is likely to revert to the way it was originally.

If the persuader can convince the listener that the change in behavior or attitude is in agreement with the listener's basic values, then the message is likely to be internalized and integrated with the listener's own values. This process—*internalization*—encourages the listener's to be influenced at a deep level and to adopt the recommended course of action because he or she is truly convinced of it intellectually. A salesman might use this technique to convince a person to buy a product because of the utilitarian value of the product—that is, the person could see himself or herself using the product a great deal.

We cannot control other people's behavior all the time. Thus, we try to persuade them to change their attitudes in an attempt to eventually alter their behavior. The effect or outcome of our attempts will be different with different situations, different participants, and different messages, but in every case, lasting changes in behavior will result only if attitudes are changed.

WILL THE CHANGE LAST?

If you are able to influence another person to change his or her attitudes and, thus, his or her behavior, how enduring can you expect these changes to be? A receiver may experience an immediate change in attitude, but this is no guarantee that the change will be long-lasting. Time will decrease the effect of the stimulus to change. Regression to original attitudes will also be caused by contrary information that reaffirms the original feeling. The credibility of the source or the stimulus for change and how often a receiver is reminded of the fact of and reason for the change will also determine how long that change will be sustained.

The type of communication from which one received the persuasive stimulus may also determine the effects that can be expected. In all cases, attitude change takes time, but the permanence of the change is likely to vary with the type of communication used. In the interpersonal arena, for example, changes often require the support of continued interaction, since interpersonal influence is vitally important in securing even small amounts of attitude change in a receiver. Although it is unlikely that one interpersonal encounter will alter your life, continuing encounters do affect both your attitudes and behavior.

Attitude and behavior change often result when we join groups, as well, because in groups we engage in numerous transactions with others. Some change in attitudes will occur just by the sheer number of encounters alone. It is within interpersonal and small-group communication situations that the largest shifts of attitudes occur. To test this possibility, observe group members' attitudes when you become part of a new group and see if they become more alike as the group develops together. Remember what happened to your own attitudes when you started college; the changes that occurred then will be affected by further changes after you leave college and join different groups.

Both interpersonal and small-group communication have a direct influence on the type of communication involved in both public speeches and the media because in our intimate or friendly conversation with others, we discuss what happens publicly. There are few, if any, research findings on the long-range effects of public speaking. Long-range effects are difficult to determine because important speeches are often criticized and evaluated immediately. In addition, the role of interpersonal and small-group communication on the effects of the public speech has not been studied. Remember the last time you heard an important presidential address—one that covered issues that touched your life and that of your friends? It probably became the topic of conversation the day after it was given. For most people, conversations about the address are more important in changing or freezing attitudes than the address itself. This fact reaffirms the importance of interpersonal and small-group communication in changing our attitudes. Seldom do we make independent judgments based on a single public speech that are not influenced in this manner.

Even the media, surprisingly enough, play a small role in affecting attitudes and bringing about behavior change. They influence how we generally view events, but this occurs over a period of time. Advertisers, who are perhaps the heaviest users of the media for persuasion, have to persuade only a small percentage of their audience to achieve success. The increase in sales that results from effective advertising is due to the size of the mass media audience rather than the powerful effects of the media. Much of the successful persuasion that occurs in advertising affects relatively unimportant matters in our lives, such as which brand of toothpaste to buy. In more vital matters, the media are likely to reaffirm and stabilize our attitudes rather than to change them. It is probable that the programs you watch reaffirm your life style: a college education is useful, parents are respected, athletes are admired, nice cars are esteemed, bright teeth are socially desirable. Seldom do the media challenge these habitual life-style attitudes and, thus, the media play a major role in reinforcement rather than in creating new attitudes or altered behavior.

Another reason for the media's lack of influence on viewers' attitudes is simply the viewers' own awareness. Listeners are harder to persuade because just as the techniques of mass persuasion have become more sophisticated, so have the listeners. They know the intent of advertisers, of politicians, and of some editorial comments. Because of their sophistication, their resistance is increased.

RESISTING PERSUASION

As a persuader, you need to know methods of bringing about change; as a listener you need to know how to resist persuasive attempts. Understanding the possible techniques—the skills a persuader might seek to use—is one means of resisting or, at least, listening intelligently. When someone attempts to appeal to altruistic motives, to keep your mind filled with a desired action, to achieve identification, to create a favorable mood, to arouse an emotion, or to find a *key need*—something you desire greatly—you can respond with some knowledge of the intent.

The more committed the listener is to a certain point of view, the less likely it is that anyone will be able to change it. Often, attempts to change such a listener result in a greater, not lesser, commitment to the original attitude. A person whose approach to life results from his atheistic beliefs, for example, will not be very receptive to a person who promotes a fundamentalist religious viewpoint or a proreligious message of any type. Such a message will provide the atheist with more reasons for resistance and may even provoke him or her to anger. For this reason, members of some fundamentalist sects are instructed not to encourage friends or spouses to join (provided they are not already members) if their feelings or beliefs lie elsewhere. The likelihood of arousing an antagonistic response is too great.

Public commitment by a listener may cause him or her to become resistant to persuasive communication. A man who calls himself a "nondrinker" may consume alcoholic beverages at home but prefer not to do so in front of others. If he refuses a drink at a social gathering, saying, "I don't drink," he will probably feel that his future behavior must become consistent with this position. The "nondrinker" may become even more resistant to alcohol than previously because of this public commitment. Had this public position not been taken, he might have been willing to accept an occasional drink "just to be social." When a commitment is announced publicly, however, people become inflexible, for example, a doctor and a diagnosis, a lawyer and an opinion, a teacher and a grade, or a manager and a policy decision. In each of these situations, the person who has the power to make a decision—whether it is giving a grade or determining why a patient shows particular symptoms—will be much more resistant to making a change in that decision after he or she has become publicly committed to it.

Understanding the relationship between public commitment and resistance is useful for both persuaders and listeners. As a persuader, you should realize that trying to change someone else's public stand will be much more difficult than trying to alter a view that he or she has expressed privately to you. This is one of the reasons that negotiations between labor unions and management are held in private, often with a total blackout of information to the public. Each side realizes that the public announcement of a position makes it much more difficult to negotiate and change that position.

If you are a listener, and especially if you wish to remain open to the possibility that you will change your attitude about something, it will help to avoid public commitment to a particular attitude until you have weighed all the alternatives. Because a public statement of your attitudes tends to cause them to become frozen, the authors advocate a *suspension of judgment* until all the evidence is in. On the other hand, when you are confident that you wish to retain your attitudes and resist efforts to change them, you will find it helpful to announce your attitudes as widely as possible. This will reinforce your conviction that the attitudes are not easily changed.

Another means of resisting persuasion is active *refutation*—proving that a proposed change is undesirable by arguing against it. We build defense systems against encroachments on our basic values and needs, and most of us have been trained to resist by arguing. The listener is not a passive sort, prone to sit by and see his or her values and needs—especially those that reinforce a life pattern—dashed to the ground with no resistance. In most situations in which a listener tries to refute persuasion, the logic or sophistication of the listener's argument is not as important as the energy with which he or she tries to resist. Intense energy will lend support to the listener's resistance, just as it will lend power to a persuader's effort to effect change. In a sense, the listener persuades himself or herself that he or she wants to resist, perhaps in spite of a refutation that seems superficial, based on strong biases, or supported by weak evidence. Thus, the persuader has the job of breaking through the listener's energy as well as dealing with misunderstanding or lack of logic.

People are seldom converted overnight. Even the mass conversions at Billy Graham's rallies do not reflect an immediate change of belief or a change in their way of life by those willing to testify publicly. Many of those who go forward are already believers and are reaffirming their beliefs. Attitude change occurs slowly for most people, because they are personally committed to their current views, because they have made a public commitment, or because they actively argue against change.

ETHICAL CONSIDERATIONS

Persuasive communication can be critically evaluated and judged. When you say that a particular communication transaction is "good," you mean literally hundreds of different things. Some judgments of communication have nothing to do with morality, with rightness or wrongness of the message, or the motivation of the source. You may, for example, see a film that presents values completely different from yours; it is still possible for that film to be a "good" one in the sense that it uses skillful photography. Sometimes a "good" communication is simply one that turns out well for you. If you have a discussion with a friend in which you both express your affection for each other, you might come away feeling that it was a "good" conversation in the sense that it made you feel good.

Ethical judgments of communication are different from both these examples. *Ethics* deals with rules or standards of right conduct. When we refer to the ethics of a communication, we usually apply words like *good* and *bad, right* and *wrong* in their moral sense. We express our judgment that the source or the message is praiseworthly or blameworthy, that is, we evaluate the communication in the light of our own personal value system.

If you say that a communication transaction is unethical, you may be referring to the source's purposes or goals, to the means or methods used in the communication, or to the accuracy of the information in the message. It is generally thought, for example, that it is wrong to communicate with the intention of harming someone. It is usually considered wrong to use communication techniques to manipulate a receiver without his or her knowledge, which is done in subliminal communication or in other techniques affecting the unconscious mind. It is also considered wrong for a source to present a message as true that he or she knows is not true.

There are no strict ethical guidelines that can be neatly applied to every persuasive situation. However, there are some broad criteria that you can apply as a speaker and as a listener when you are trying to evaluate the ethics of persuasion. One of these is that the persuader should not place his or her own special ambitions above the welfare of the listener(s). A car salesman who convinces you, for example, that this is *not* the time of year to buy a car, who tells you that you would be better off keeping your present car, or who says that you should consider what is best for you goes a long way toward convincing you that his intentions are "good" because he seems to value your welfare more than making a sale. If, on the other hand, you try to talk your roommate into cutting a class because you need a ride to town and your roommate is the only person around with a car, you probably need to reevaluate the ethics of that persuasion.

Often, a persuasive speaker will recognize that it adds to his or her credibility to *appear* to be ethical, even though his or her real motives are unethical. Car salesmen continually have to fight the image of being untrustworthy, smooth operators who are out to make a fast, easy buck. Thus, the admirable values expressed in the salesman's comments about your keeping your present car would probably be weighed in relation to his later behavior. If the salesman follows his speech about using your own judgment with an offer to take you for a test drive "since you are here in the showroom," you would probably be wise to suspect his motivation and to question the ethics of his communication.

The central ethical principle in these examples involves satisfying oneself that the communication being tested does not show a source who is more concerned with his or her own welfare than with the welfare of others. This is not to say that it is unethical to be concerned about your own needs. It means that you may not ethically satisfy your needs at the expense of someone else.

Another broad guideline useful in judging the ethics of a persuasive communication is that the ends do not justify the means. It is clearly wrong, by this criteria, to lie to your roommate in order to convince him or her to cut a class to take you into town. If you say that you have urgent personal business when you actually just feel like going shopping, you have violated this ethical principle. Sometimes, of course, the situation is not that clear cut. You may be convinced that it would be good for your best friend, who has been working hard on a term paper all week, to get out on a Friday night. One way to persuade your friend to take a break would be to say that *you* need to get out and that you do not want to go alone. In this case, the end (getting your friend to take a break) involves another's welfare rather than your own, but the means (lying about your own motivation) is still considered wrong.

Public speakers, like communicators in any type of communication situation, should observe another ethical standard, the demand that information be made available to all. This standard of fairness is reflected in our constitutional protection of the freedoms of speech, press, and assembly. It places a burden on the communicator, for often he or she has had some special opportunity to explore and analyze the idea or subject matter and, thus, holds an advantage over the listener. Aware of this possible advantage, the ethical communicator will, in addition to expressing ideas clearly and frankly, show the listener fully and fairly why he or she holds them. This implies, too, that the communicator needs to be informed—possessing enough information on an idea or topic so that he or she can respond intelligently to another person's question.

Deliberate suppression of information is considered unethical, as are the distortion of information and the doctoring of quoted materials and statistics. Reporting with accuracy should be the goal of every communicator. Through deliberation and good judgment, the rational activity known as persuasion can result in mutual understanding, but only if the communicator is careful to make all possible information available to the listener.

People who give advice to others, either in a professional capacity or in interpersonal relationships, also have special ethical obligations. We all need the support of someone else's perspective occasionally when we try to make decisions about our own lives. We can get this support from family members, friends, and professional counselors such as social workers or psychologists. It is unethical, however, for the advice-giver to impose his or her values on the person whom he or she is helping. This means that a therapist, for example, must be careful not to simply tell the client what to do about problems. This kind of advice makes the client dependent on the therapist instead of better able to solve his or her own difficulties. In interpersonal relationships you should be careful to respect your friend's right to make up his or her own mind. The temptation to persuade someone that you understand the problem and know what is best for him or her can be great, and people who are in trouble often ask for this kind of persuasive "support." In the long run, however, such advice is probably not helpful. Often, the best support you can give a troubled friend is to listen and to respond to what your friend says about the problem. This kind of understanding response is better than trying to impose your solution on other people's problems.

Propaganda

The term *propaganda* is generally associated with schemes devised to spread ideas that might not otherwise be heard, that is, the artificial and cultivated dissemination of particular ideas. It is the belief of those who spread propaganda—whether it be nations, governments, organizations, or individuals—that others would not learn about these ideas without their intervention.

At the present time, the word *propaganda* has negative connotations. People believe that propaganda is a sinister process, involving lying, and that it is based on the deliberate attempt to manipulate by concealed and underhanded means. These feelings date from the First World War when propaganda was employed in an attempt to influence the final outcome of the war. More recently, Watergate and the attempts by the government to regulate public attitude by selectively controlling information to favor their viewpoint and doctoring information to create a particular impression enhance the general negative feeling associated with the word.

Propaganda can be used in a positive sense. As it is used today, it is related to persuasion because it has become associated with the practice of influencing the emotional attitudes of others. It is also related to suggestion because suggestion is the "fundamental mechanism employed by all forms of propaganda."[4] Through propaganda the disseminator catches the audience's attention and attempts to propagate his or her unfamiliar doctrine. Often, it requires a considerable period of time to build a receptive frame of mind in others.

A chapter on persuasion is incomplete without some mention of propaganda for it *is* possible to take persuasion too far. Whatever the specific means employed—whether they be the use of stereotypes, selecting only those facts that are suitable to a particular theme, repetition, assertion, appeals to authority, or downright lying[5]—to be forewarned is to be forearmed. We should not underestimate the power of the determined propagandist. When one media presentation is able to reach millions of people; when we know that man can be an irrational animal; when we know that political and religious propagandists, as well as advertisers, spend a great deal of effort, time, and money to appeal to our emotions—we can begin to realize the potential impact of propaganda.

In some instances—as in political discourse—we can accept half-truths because we also know that politicians are not philosopher-kings. "Culture," however, "cannot long withstand perversions of truth. When culture becomes politics, revolutionary politics in particular, there can be no criterion for truth and its inseparable companion, rationality...."[6] It is our responsibility as citizens to recognize propaganda for what it is and to beware of its effects. Not enough can be said about the essential importance of truth-telling in maintaining both personal and national sanity.

SUMMARY

The purpose of persuasive discourse is to change existing attitudes or behavior in another person. Changing another's attitudes is difficult because attitudes are imbedded deeply in one's patterns of behavior and belief. A communicator does not really persuade a listener to change an attitude or a behavior; the listener persuades himself or herself. Persuasion, to be successful, must wear away attitudes as water wears away stone. No matter what means are used—whether it be logos, pathos, or ethos—extreme patience and skill are required before change can be expected. The effect of persuasion is likely to be short range unless continuous reinforcement is provided. The less a listener has to "give," the more likely he or she will be to change an attitude or a behavior.

Suggestion is the most subtle form of persuasion. Common techniques in suggestion include persuasion by association, by encouraging social facilitation in a crowd, and by creating an appropriate atmosphere. The communicator who uses suggestion will be most effective if he or she attempts to make the suggestion seem to originate with the listener and presents the persuasive message with vividness, force, and a positive approach.

Although it is difficult to change attitudes, there are several methods the persuader can use: he or she can associate the desired change with the self-interest of the listener, present the message in such a vivid manner that the listener's emotions are engaged, use punishment or reward to encourage the change, attempt to identify the changed behavior with a model or an idol, or convince the listener that the change is congruent with his or her basic values. The most lasting changes in behavior require a change in fundamental attitudes.

The permanence of a change in attitude or behavior depends upon the type of communication used to effect the change. Interpersonal and small-group situations are the most effective settings for bringing about permanent change because they permit the communicator to engage in many persuasive transactions with the listener. The persuasive effect of a public speech depends upon the degree to which that speech is discussed in interpersonal and small-group situations. Messages that we receive through the mass media are more likely to confirm our existing attitudes than they are to change them.

To understand persuasion is to understand how we resist persuasion ourselves and to understand why others resist it. Resistance is a natural posture. Our fundamental pattern of beliefs, or living, for that matter, guides us, and when we are in doubt, we stick to this pattern or fall back on it rather than change. We are indifferent to most issues, but about those that affect us, our minds are already made up. That is what makes persuasion difficult and what makes our understanding of it important.

Ethical judgments about persuasion refer to the communicator's moral responsibility. One may question the ethics of a source's purposes, goals, means, or methods, as well as the accuracy of his or her message. It is generally considered unethical to manipulate the listener, to communicate with the intention of harming someone, or to distort the truth in a communication. Another ethical requirement is that the persuader should not place his or her own welfare above the welfare of the listener. Those who give advice to others should be careful to avoid imposing their values on the listener. It is possible to take persuasion too far, and we need to be aware of the influence of propagandists.

Persuasion is a powerful communication strategem that can be used effectively and ethically to alter the attitudes and behavior of the listener. Understanding persuasion is important for both the source and the receiver: the source can develop effective persuasive messages through this understanding; the listener can comprehend the intention of the persuasive source and, if appropriate, resist these messages.

FURTHER READING

Robert E. Alberti and Michael L. Emmons, *Stand Up, Speak Out, Talk Back.* New York: Pocket Books, 1975.
>This book is designed to help people overcome their personal powerlessness. It is a practical, well-written book on assertiveness and should help guide the reader toward a pattern of behavior that will aid in enhancing both self-confidence and self-respect.

Sharon Anthony Bower and Gordon H. Bower, *Asserting Yourself: A Practical Guide for Positive Change.* Reading, Mass.: Addison-Wesley Publishing Company, 1976.
>Are you seriously looking for some positive change in your life? Are you unable to speak up for your legitimate rights? This book provides a *complete* step-by-step program for the serious student. It presents a thorough and comprehensive approach.

J. A. C. Brown, *Techniques of Persuasion: From Propaganda to Brainwashing.* baltimore: Penguin Books, 1963.
>This is an absorbing book which questions the notion that man is a rational animal. The author demonstrates, through the use of numerous examples, how man falls easy prey to advertisers and political propagandists. He discusses everything from propaganda in advertising and the media to attitude formation, religious conversion, indoctrination, and brainwashing.

Jerry Bruno and Jeff Greenfeld, *The Advance Man.* New York: William Morrow, 1971.
>This book tells what goes on behind the scene in the planning of a political campaign. It is invaluable for anyone interested in politics or in understanding the political process.

Napoleon Hill and E. Harold Keown, *Succeed and Grow Rich Through Persuasion.* Greenwich, Conn.: Fawcett Publications, Inc. (A Fawcett Crest Book), 1970.
>This is an excellent collection of articles on the relationships between ethics and persuasion by some outstanding writers. It provides a broad perspective covering the democratic premise, some philosophical perspectives, and mass persuasion. The articles in this paperback book provide stimulating and challenging reading and require no background, prior introduction, or special vocabulary for understanding.

Irving J. Rein, *Rudy's Red Wagon: Communication Strategies in Contemporary Society.* Glenview, Ill.: Scott, Foresman, 1972.
>This is a book about manipulators. The author uses cartoons, ads, newspaper colums, and menus to illustrate his points. His chapter on

the rhetoric of the used-car salesman is particularly interesting are useful.

Carl P. Wrighter, *I Can Sell You Anything.* New York: Ballantine Books, 1972.
Here is a paperback book about the persuasion of advertising. It is a straightforward look at how advertising works told by a Madison Avenue adman who minces no words, hits you between the eyes by naming products and practices, and enjoys letting you in on the details. The excitement reflected in the writing—like a good ad—makes you part of the product. The author describes how admen do it, how they get away with it, and how you can see through it.

NOTES

[1]James A. Winans, *Public Speaking: Principles and Practice* (Ithaca, N.Y.: The Sewell Publishing Company, 1915), p. 287.

[2]H. L. Hollingworth, *The Psychology of the Audience* (New York: The American Book Company, 1935), pp. 142-144.

[3]Herbert C. Kelman, "Processes of Opinion Change," *Public Opinion Quarterly*, 25 (1961): 57-78.

[4]J. A. A. Brown, *Techniques of Persuasion: From Propaganda to Brainwashing* (Baltimore: Penguin Books, 1963), p. 25

[5]*Ibid.*, pp. 26-28.

[6]Arnold Beichman, "Six Big Lies About America," *New York Times Magazine*, June 6, 1971, pp. 32-33.

Index

Who's Who in America, 168
Why Am I Afraid to Tell You Who I Am? (Insights on Self-Awareness, Personal Growth and Interpersonal Communication), 52
Will the change last? See Persuasive communication, will the change last?
Winans, James A., 214
Winning Through Intimidation, 40
Wood, John T., 202
World Almanac, The, 169

Wright, Richard, 28
Wrighter, Carl P., 231
Writing versus speaking. *See* Verbal communication, speaking and writing

You Can Learn to Speak, 202

Zelko, Harold P., 203
Zelko, Marjorie E., 203